THE
PERTHSHIRE
BOOK

Books edited and written by Donald Omand

The Caithness Book, Inverness 1972

The Moray Book, Edinburgh 1976

Red Deer Management, Edinburgh 1981

The Sutherland Book, Golspie 1982

The Ross & Cromarty Book, Golspie 1984

A Kaitness Kist (with JP Campbell), Thurso 1984

The Grampian Book, Golspie 1987

The New Caithness Book, Wick 1989

A Northern Outlook: 100 Essays on Northern Scotland, Wick 1991

Caithness Crack, Wick 1991

The Borders Book, Edinburgh 1995

Caithness: Lore & Legend, Wick 1995

The Perthshire Book, Edinburgh 1998

The Argyll Book (forthcoming)

The Hebrides Book (forthcoming)

The Fife Book (forthcoming)

Monograph

The Caithness Flagstone Industry, University of Aberdeen 1981

THE
PERTHSHIRE
BOOK

Edited by

Donald Omand

Birlinn

First published in Great Britain, 1999
by Birlinn Limited
Unit 8
Canongate Venture
5 New Street
Edinburgh, EH8 8BH
Internet www.birlinn.co.uk.
info@birlinn.co.uk.

British Library Cataloguing-in-Publication Data
A Catalogue record for this book is available
from the British Library.

ISBN 1 874744 84 X (hardback)

ISBN 1 874744 75 0 (paperback)

Printed and bound in Finland by W.S.O.Y.

CONTENTS

ACKNOWLEDGEMENTS xi

INTRODUCTION
Donald Omand, Continuing Education Organiser
Centre for Continuing Education, University of Aberdeen............xiii

SECTION ONE

1 GEOLOGY AND LANDSCAPE
Dr R Duck...3

2 PREHISTORY
Dr J Stevenson 19

3 THE ROMANS
G Maxwell...35

4 THE DARK AGES
A Small 47

5 THE MIDDLE AGES
D Hall 59

6 EARLY MODERN TIMES
Dr J Eagles 75

7 MODERN TIMES
J Duncan 89

SECTION TWO

8 THE RURAL ECONOMY
Dr P Duncan...105

9 STRATHEARN
J Foster..115

10 THE RIVER TAY
Dr P Duncan 125

11 THE TROSSACHS
L Stott 139

12 THE CITY OF PERTH
Professor J Caird...151

13 CASTLES AND MANSION HOUSES
Dr B Walker and C McGregor 165

14 VERNACULAR BUILDINGS
Dr B Walker and C McGregor 177

15 INDUSTRY AND COMMERCE
T Cooke...187

16 PLACE NAMES
I Fraser 199

17 THE TRAVELLING PEOPLE
Dr S Douglas 211

18 PERTHSHIRE SCOTS
Dr S Douglas 219

19 TALES AND LEGENDS
Dr S Douglas...227

BIBLIOGRAPHY 237

INDEX 249

LIST OF PLATES

Plate 1   Loch Tay from the north-east

Plate 2   Pitcur

Plate 3   North Mains, henge and barrow

Plate 4   Drumturn Burn, hut circles and field systems

Plate 5   Pitkellony, Muthill. Two massive bronze armlets

Plate 6   Fourteenth century stave-built bucket

Plate 7   Remains of medieval wattle and daub building. Perth
           High Street excavations 1975–77

Plate 8   Strageath Roman Fort

Plate 9   Ardoch Roman Fort

Plate 10   Chronicle of Perth

Plate 11   Palace of Scone

Plate 12   Perth Bridge and North Inch from Bridgend, *c.* 1840

Plate 13   Blairgowrie Raspberry Pickers

Plate 14   Muthill War Memorial, 1919

Plate 15   Perth Station, *c.* 1900

Plate 16   Dewars Distillery, *c.* 1914

Plate 17   The Dunning Thorn Tree

Plate 18   Aberfeldy, Wade bridge over the Tay

Plate 19   Blair Atholl, Blair Castle

Plate 20 Loch Turret

Plate 21 Loch Ard, the Queen's View

Plate 22 Ben Venue

Plate 23 Aerial view of Perth in flood

Plate 24 Ruthven Castle from the south-west

Plate 25 Drummond Castle, north side

Plate 26 Elcho Castle, north-east

Plate 27 Mausoleum, Methven churchyard

Plate 28 Cottown

Plate 29 Flatfield

Plate 30 Elcho farmhouse and steading

Plate 31 Jock Lundie, *b*. 1906

Plate 32 Belle Stewart, *b*. 1906

LIST OF FIGURES

Figure 1   Pre-1975 Counties of Scotland   xv

Figure 2   Local Government in Scotland: The New Councils   xvi

Figure 3   Simplified map of the solid geology of Perthshire   6

Figure 4   Geological cross-section of Perthshire   13

Figure 5   Distribution of Pictish Symbol Stones   48

Figure 6   Distribution of Souterrains   51

Figure 7   Possible sites of early Christian activity   55

Figure 8   Distribution of '*Pit*' place-names   56

Figure 9   Distribution of '*Bal*' place-names   57

Figure 10   Location of place-names   62

Figure 11   Tayside Region: Forest and agricultural land   109

Figure 12   River Tay: Source to Perth   126

Figure 13   Location of Ports and crossing points on the Tay Estuary   132

Figure 14   Perth 1774   156

Figure 15   Perth: Stages and growth   161

Figure 16   Economic and employment status 1991   189

Figure 17   Economically active population 1961 and 1991   190

Figure 18   Travellers' sites in Perthshire and Kinross   214

Acknowledgements

We wish to acknowledge help and suggestions received from Miss Rhoda Fothergill, Mrs Lorna Mitchell and Mrs Wendy Duncan as well as information obtained from a variety of private sources and companies especially Hydro-Electric PLC and Edradour Distillery.

We wish to thank the following for their assistance: Campbell Distillers Ltd., General Accident, Stagecoach Holdings PLC and United Distillers. We would also thank Hildegarde Berwick of Perth Museum for information on Perth Glass.

Mrs Joyce Brown, Thurso, Highland Council Libraries Service, gave valuable assistance with the Bibliography.

Plates 2, 3, 4, 6 and 7 are Crown copyright; Royal Commission on the Ancient and Historical Monuments of Scotland. They are reproduced with permission.

INTRODUCTION

Primarily Perthshire is the catchment area of the River Tay. Through its land from Helensburgh to Stonehaven runs the Highland Boundary Fault, a geological zone that separates the Highlands from the Lowlands. In its most literal sense Perth is the gateway to the Highlands.

Many people have declared Perthshire to be Scotland's Fairest County. Sir Walter Scott in his book *The Fair Maid of Perth* claimed that 'amid all the provinces in Scotland if an intelligent stranger were asked to describe the most varied and the most beautiful it is probable he would name the county of Perth'. Scott added that 'Perthshire forms the fairest portion of the Northern Kingdom'. Few people would disagree with this eulogy including Queen Victoria who was enraptured with the area.

Perthshire has superb hill and mountain scenery, woodlands and parks with contrasting glens, straths, lochs and moors. Its fertile countryside is legion: for beef, sheep, fruit and timber. Tourism and distilling are other important industries. Lying at the very heart of Scotland Perthshire has a rich diversity of scenery, wildlife, prehistory and history which is reflected in its stone monuments, Roman remains, Pictish stones, medieval and modern castles. This centrality is still reflected in its growth and importance as a focal point for communications.

The city of Perth, a compact town embraced by hills, is one of Scotland's most historic burghs. Within the past two decades archaeological excavations have greatly added to our knowledge of the evolution of the burgh. A wide scatter of towns and villages throughout Perthshire have their own character and charm lying as they do in hinterlands of agricultural wealth and unspoilt scenery.

From at least the time of Kenneth Macalpine Scottish kings have been enthroned on the Stone of Destiny at the ancient ecclesiastical centre of Scone. Happily the Stone has been returned to Scotland, to Edinburgh and not Scone, its original home.

As we go to press there is discussion that three new towns could be created around Perth to help solve the problem of the influx of people into the area. The reason for this in-migration (many of them young professionals) is easy to understand: scenic and climatic attraction of the area, the proximity of Glasgow and Edinburgh and the high calibre of life within Perthshire.

Note

The areas of Strathearn and The Trossachs while not in Perthshire have such historic links with the county that it was felt appropriate to include them in this volume.

Conversion: Metric/Non Metric

1 metre	= 3.28 feet	1 foot	=	0.30 metres
1 kilometre	= 0.62 miles	1 mile	=	1.61 kilometres
1 hectare	= 2.47 acres	1 acre	=	0.40 hectares

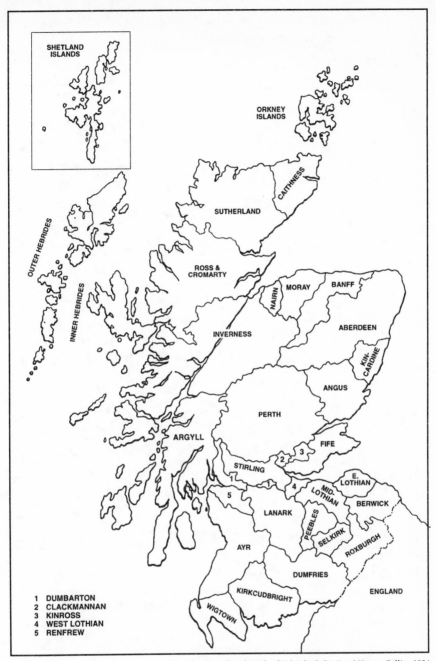

SHETLAND
ISLANDS

ORKNEY
ISLANDS

CAITHNESS

OUTER HEBRIDES

SUTHERLAND

INNER HEBRIDES

ROSS &
CROMARTY

NAIRN MORAY BANFF

ABERDEEN

INVERNESS

KIN-
CARDINE

ANGUS

ARGYLL

PERTH

FIFE

STIRLING

2 3

1

4

E.
LOTHIAN

MID-
LOTHIAN

BERWICK

5

LANARK

PEEBLES

SELKIRK

ROXBURGH

AYR

DUMFRIES

ENGLAND

KIRKCUDBRIGHT

WIGTOWN

1 DUMBARTON
2 CLACKMANNAN
3 KINROSS
4 WEST LOTHIAN
5 RENFREW

Collins Encyclopaedia of Scotland (Ed. John/Julia Keay) Harper Collins 1994

Figure 1

The Pre-1975 Counties of Scotland

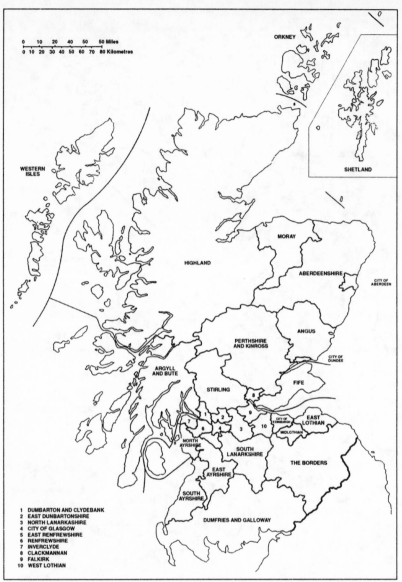

The New Councils: issued by the Scottish Office

Figure 2

Local Government in Scotland

SECTION ONE

ONE
GEOLOGY AND LANDSCAPE

INTRODUCTION

The aim of this chapter is to provide a concise account, for the non-specialist reader, of the relationships between the underlying geology and the magnificent scenery of Perthshire. For those who would like to delve deeper into the subject, it is suggested that reference should be made to the following works; Anderson (1984), Armstrong *et al.* (1985), Cameron and Stephenson (1985), Craig (1991), Price (1976, 1983), Sissons (1967), Stephenson and Gould (1995), Walker (1961,1963) and Whittow (1977).

PHYSICAL SITUATION

The journey northwards from Perth towards the northern frontier of Perthshire at Drumochter Pass, along either of the twin arteries, the A9 road or the Highland Railway, presents the traveller with a dramatic contrast in landscape. Whereas the southern part of the traverse is characterised by gently rolling, mainly agricultural lowland, the region from Dunkeld to the north is one of high rocky hills and mountains with steep, often wooded, slopes. The remarkable variation in scenery along this route is a reflection of the nature of the underlying rock types and their geological history. It provides a fine example of the control exerted by geology on scenery and land use. The very abrupt change in landscape is delimited by one of the three largest crustal fractures traversing Scotland, the Highland Boundary Fault. In broad terms, the rocks to the north of the Highland Boundary Fault comprise principally ancient, crystalline metamorphic types, of Precambrian to Lower Cambrian age (older than *c.* 590 Ma) and younger intrusive igneous complexes of Caledonian age. By contrast, the rocks to the south of the fault are mainly composed of relatively younger, sedimentary formations with associated extrusive igneous rock assemblages, largely dating to Lower Devonian times.

Differences in hardness of the various rock types and structural weaknesses, such as numerous faults, have been exploited by the ice masses that covered the region during the Pleistocene glaciation and which profoundly influenced not only the scenery of Perthshire but the whole of Scotland. The northern metamorphic rocks are generally hard and have therefore provided more resistance to the effects of ice, nature's most powerful eroding tool, than the relatively softer rocks to the south. In

3

consequence, high, rugged peaks remain as characteristic of the north, separated by incised glens often hosting deep, narrow, rock basin lochs. The less resistant rock types of the south have, however, been planed off by the repeated passage of ice masses over them and present a much more subdued and low lying topography, typically veneered by deposits laid down by melting ice.

Perthshire, forming the very heartland of Scotland, is an area of profound geological and geomorphological contrasts which lead to the equally fundamental scenic divisions characteristic of 'Highland' and 'Lowland' Perthshire. The former is a southern portion of the major physiographic province of Scotland known as the Grampian Highlands whilst the latter is situated in the northern part of the Midland Valley or Central Lowlands. A second major fault, defining the southern limit of the Midland Valley, is termed the Southern Upland Fault and trends from Dunbar in East Lothian to near Cairnryan, Wigtownshire. In simplified terms the Midland Valley was formerly considered as a central rift valley bounded by the Highland Boundary Fault to the north and the Southern Upland Fault to the south. In modern geological terms, however, the Midland Valley is described as a 'terrane', that is a block of the Earth's crust of fundamentally different geological affinities from those around it. Similarly, the Grampian Highlands, bounded to the north by the Great Glen Fault, extending from Inverness to Fort William and along which are developed Lochs Ness, Oich and Lochy, is also considered as a terrane. The structural incision through Perthshire, the Highland Boundary Fault, is thus defined as a terrane boundary separating the Grampian Highland Terrane from the Midland Valley Terrane. This fault is best thought of as a complex zone of fractures, or fracture system, rather than as one simple planar break, with a long geological history of development and movement. From Cowie, just to the north of Stonehaven, on the Kincardineshire coast, the fault zone trends south-westwards to meet the Clyde coast near Helensburgh. Thence it passes beneath the bed of the Clyde to cross the northern part of the Isle of Arran ultimately extending to Clare Island off the Atlantic coast of Ireland.

The plate tectonic mechanisms and processes by which these crustal segments became juxtaposed is a matter of both great debate and controversy amongst geologists, as is the timing of their 'docking'. The Highland Boundary Fault was active, though the movements along it did not all affect the total length, from Lower Ordovician (c. 500 Ma) to Tertiary times. In localized zones, especially close to the village of Comrie where Glen Artney has been developed by glacial erosion along it, the fault is still an 'active' dislocation, giving rise to frequent earth tremors. This has caused Comrie, whose parish is bisected by the fault, to be known as the

'Shakey Toun'. Its famous and recently renovated Earthquake House, equipped with seismographic instruments, was built at The Ross in 1869 to monitor earth movements.

HIGHLAND PERTHSHIRE

The metamorphic rocks of Highland Perthshire are divided into two Supergroups, the Moine and the Dalradian. Though the field relationships between these sequences are by no means clear in places, the Moine is generally held to be the older. At Gilbert's Bridge in Glen Tilt the passage from the Moine to overlying Dalradian rocks is clearly exposed in the river gorge with no apparent tectonic discordance between the two formations. Both are the product of the repeated regional metamorphism and multiple deformation (folding and faulting) of what were originally sedimentary rock sequences, principally of marine derivation, comprising shales, mudstones, sandstones, conglomerates and limestones. The Grampian Highlands are the deeply eroded and uplifted remnants, or roots, of a great mountain belt composed of deformed and metamorphosed rocks. Metamorphism, involving the growth of new minerals, recrystallisation of existing minerals and the development of new rock fabrics, took place under the elevated temperatures and pressure at great depth (10 to over 20 km) within the Earth's crust. Folding also occurred, whilst the rocks were in a semi-plastic state, on a variety of scales and styles, often with one set of folds being superimposed upon another in response to changing stress conditions. Faults represent brittle, as opposed to ductile, deformation of rock masses and were formed at higher levels in the crust as the rocks became uplifted and stripped of their overburden through time. These events principally took place in what has come to be known as the Caledonian Orogeny. This was a complex plate tectonic collision 'event' extending from Middle Ordovician to Middle Devonian times, with major activity between *c.* 520 and 400 Ma, which was also responsible for the creation of the Norwegian and Swedish mountains and the Appalachian Mountain chain of North America. Many major and minor bodies of igneous rocks were intruded into the metamorphic assemblages during this period, several of which are present in Perthshire. The Caledonian earth movements have resulted in a dominant alignment of fold axes and fault planes in a south-west to north-east direction, the so-called Caledonian trend, exemplified by the Highland Boundary Fault, the Loch Tay Fault and other major structures traversing the Grampian Highlands.

Moine

In the Grampian Highlands the Moine is broadly comparable with that of its type locality of the Northern Highlands of Sutherland. Rocks of the Moine assemblage crop out in a broad tract of the far north of Perthshire (Figure 3). The dominant rock type is psammitic granulite, grey in colour; a granular quartz, muscovite mica and feldspar bearing regional metamorphic rock, often containing pyroxene and garnet, which began life as shallow marine sands. The term 'Central Highland Granulite' was at one time applied to describe the Moine rocks of Highland Perthshire. These rocks characteristically have a 'flaggy' appearance due to their tendency to split along the original sedimentary bedding surfaces, which have survived metamorphism. This is particularly so in the area around the village of Struan where the local formation name of the Struan Flags was aptly applied. Excellent sections of the Moine can be seen along the A9 in cuttings at several lay-by locations to the north of Blair Atholl (Thomas, 1988).

The age of Moine sedimentation is not known with certainty but it is believed that these sequences represent, at least in part, an offshore facies of the terrestrial, alluvial Torridonian rocks of the North-West Highlands and may therefore be of equivalent age. At least two phases of deformation,

Figure 3

Simplified map of the solid geology of Perthshire and Kinross-shire showing principal localities and features referred to in the text

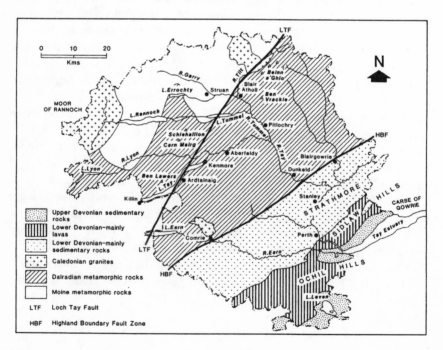

resulting in the formation of complicated fold structures and planar fabrics, have affected the Moine rocks. In the first of these, the original shallow marine deposits were metamorphosed and deformed during the pre-Caledonian, so-called Grenvillian Orogeny of *c.* 1000 Ma. Subsequent metamorphism and deformation took place during the Caledonian Orogeny. Despite their long and complex metamorphic and deformational history, Moine rocks in many areas preserve remarkably clear indications of their original sedimentary parentage in the form of sedimentary structures. For example, at the base of the gorge of the beautiful 'Salmon Leap' section of the River Garry, downstream of the road and railway bridges at Struan, exposure of water-worn psammitic rocks display good examples of cross bedding, which help to determine that the sequence is isoclinally folded (folded so tightly that the fold limbs are parallel). Washout channels and load injection structures, or sedimentary dykes, may also be seen.

Dalradian

The Dalradian rocks are, for the most part, metamorphosed and highly deformed marine sediments, deposited from turbidity currents, of late Precambrian and Lower Cambrian age. The latter age has been determined by the discovery of fossils of trilobites in rocks of the Upper Dalradian near Callander. The Dalradian crops out to the south of the Moine in a broad belt to the north of the Highland Boundary Fault (Figure 3). In Highland Perthshire it is much more varied in both lithology and bed thickness than the Moine. This has resulted in a greater degree of differential erosion by ice yielding more rapidly varying topographic detail in the areas underlain by the Dalradian than those of the Moine assemblages. The Dalradian rock types reflect the regional metamorphism of a suite of parent rock types more diverse than the precursors to the Moine. Mudstone and shale formations have been altered to, *inter alia*, slate, chlorite phyllite, quartz schist, mica schist and garnet mica schist, quartz sandstone to quartzite and limestone to marble. Indeed various types of schistose, mud-derived (pelitic) rocks, often friable in character, dominate the Dalradian succession, in contrast to the sand-derived (psammitic), relatively hard and flaggy rocks, that typify the Moine.

Dalradian sedimentation, which post-dates the Grenvillian Orogeny responsible for the early phase of metamorphism and deformation of the Moine, probably commenced with a transgression of a late Precambrian sea across a basement complex composed of Torridonian, Moine and older rock assemblages. Complex, multi-phase folding and the development of many faults took place during the Caledonian Orogeny. Of particular note in Perthshire is the Loch Tay Fault. Along much of its development, from Glen Tilt to its junction with the Highland Boundary Fault in the

Trossachs, this zone of fractured rocks has been exploited by ice and scoured to form a negative relief feature. In the north-east it underlies the upper, 'straight', part of Glen Tilt and in the south-west of Perthshire it controls the trend of the central, and deepest, sector of the characteristic 'S' shape of Loch Tay. Remarkable and violent agitations of the waters of Loch Tay near Kenmore, which were observed on 12 September 1784 (Fleming 1788), have been attributed to movements along this fault plane.

The two highest peaks in Perthshire, Ben Lawers (1214 m) to the north of Loch Tay and Schiehallion (1083 m) to the south-east of Loch Rannoch, have both been sculpted out of Dalradian rocks. The former is especially noted for its rare Arctic-Alpine plants which thrive on the calcium-rich soils of the peak. These soils are formed by the weathering of calcareous schists, known as the Ben Lawers Schists, which characterise this mountain. Schiehallion is capped by a tough formation of quartzite, the Schiehallion quartzite, which has served to protect softer schists beneath from denudation. The southerly inclination of the quartzite is, in part, responsible for the familiar conical shape of the mountain. In a similar way, the same formation crops out to form the summit of Carn Mairg (1042 m) farther to the south and, interbedded with various types of schist, underlies much of the tract of land forming Scotland's longest glen, Glen Lyon. The three peaks of the Beinn a'Ghlo range (rising to a maximum of 1121 m) to the north-east of Blair Atholl are also dominated by quartzite, whereas the lower slopes are underlain by extensive beds of marble. The latter, quarried for roadstone on the southern flank of Glen Garry overlooking Blair Atholl, support belts of noticeably greener vegetation amid the generally heather-clad moors of the Highlands. To the north and west of Loch Tay, similar vegetation contrasts help to define the so-called Loch Tay Limestone which is in reality a marble similar to that of Blair Atholl. Schists intercalated with sheets of metamorphosed basic igneous rocks, known as epidiorites, form the mountain of Ben Vrackie (841 m) north of Pitlochry, a fine vantage point from which to pick out, by vegetation differences, the areas underlain by marble in Glen Garry beneath to the lower slopes of Bienn a'Ghlo. For the less adventurous, fine, easily accessible exposures of the Dalradian mica schists are to be seen forming the rapids of the Falls of Dochart at Killin in the south-western corner of Perthshire.

The oldest Perthshire Dalradian rock sequences also preserve a record of an ancient period of glaciation which took place about 650 Ma in Precambrian times. This takes the form of a tillite (a lithified till or glacial deposit) formation known as the Schiehallion Boulder Bed, which is well exposed on the northern and north-western lower slopes of the mountain. This unit contains erratic cobbles of rock types exotic to the Grampian

Highlands which may well have been transported by, and deposited to the sea floor from floating icebergs. Similar glaciomarine deposits crop out on the island of Islay, where they are known as the Port Askaig Tillite and in Norway and it is believed that they may be part of the same sequence as the Schiehallion Boulder Bed.

An economically important zone of strata-bound barium, zinc and lead mineralisation was found in 1975 to the south of Loch Tummel in the Ben Eagach Schist, a graphite schist formation, of the Dalradian. In a belt some 7 km in length and 100 m in thickness, arguably the most significant economic mineral of those discovered was barium sulphate (barytes, $BaSO_4$) which has uses in the manufacture of white paint and wallpaper, the medical industry and, importantly, as a component of oilfield drilling muds. The stratiform nature of the deposit and the presence of fine interbanding with the original sediments, suggests that the metals (Ba, Zn and Pb) were introduced at the time of sedimentation, pre-dating the metamorphism and deformation. The probable source of mineralisation was from hydrothermal fluids, perhaps emanating from a concealed igneous source, escaping into the Dalradian sea. Currently, barytes is worked at the Foss Mine north of Aberfeldy and heated debate continues as to whether workings should be permitted to open elsewhere in this area of outstanding scenic beauty.

Evidence of the early extraction of economic minerals is to be found on the south side of Loch Tay at Tomnadashan near Ardtalnaig. Here cavernous excavations in the hillside mark the sites where various ores, mainly those of copper including malachite and bornite, were mined in the 19th century (Bainbridge, 1980). The workings were in veins, emplaced in the Dalradian schists and believed to be the product of hydrothermal activity related to a Caledonian igneous intrusion at depth.

Caledonian Igneous Rocks

As mentioned above, the Caledonian tectonic events were associated with the emplacement of major igneous bodies. These are principally, though not exclusively, of granite composition. In Perthshire, of particular note are the Moor of Rannoch, Comrie and Glen Tilt granite plutons (Figure 3). The former, the largest in the area, underlies the western confines of Perthshire and extends westwards from Loch Rannoch to form the bedrock beneath much of Rannoch Moor. Distinctive erratic blocks eroded from this igneous body and transported by Pleistocene ice have proved especially useful in the reconstruction of ice transport pathways away from the Rannoch Moor area. The Moor of Rannoch and Comrie bodies belong to a large group of granitoid intrusions in the Grampian Highlands and

Southern Uplands of Scotland known as the Caledonian Newer Granites. These were emplaced in late Ordovician to Silurian-Devonian times, towards the end of the Caledonian deformation events, the two Perthshire masses in particular yielding dates of around 400 Ma.

By contrast, the granite of Glen Tilt, along with smaller bodies in the Pitlochry area forming Ben Vurich, Meall Gruaim and Dunfallandy Hill, cut across early tectonic structures but have themselves been subject to later regional deformation and metamorphism. These granites were thus intruded at earlier times than the Newer Granites and belong to a group known as the Caledonian Older Granites, emplaced between 500 and 600 Ma. The contact between the Glen Tilt granite and the surrounding Moine rocks is of special note because it was first described by James Hutton (1726–97), the famous Edinburgh geologist, often held to be the 'Father of Geology', who originated many of the fundamental principles of the science. In Glen Tilt, Hutton demonstrated veins of granite ramifying from the pluton into the surrounding rocks. This observation was held to demonstrate the igneous origin of granite and also that granite was not the original part of the Earth, as had hitherto been believed, since it was intruded into older rocks.

LOWLAND PERTHSHIRE

That part of Perthshire in the northern part of the Midland Valley, to the south of the Highland Boundary Fault, is underlain almost entirely by sedimentary and contemporaneous igneous rocks of Lower Devonian age. Younger sedimentary formations of Upper Devonian age characterise Kinross-shire around and beneath the Loch Leven basin (Figure 3).

Lower Devonian

Towards the termination of the deformation processes of the Caledonian Orogeny, the Moine and Dalradian rocks had become elevated into a mountainous belt, greater in both altitude and area than the present-day Scottish Highlands. In consequence, vigorous erosion of the rocks by large rivers flowing swiftly down the steep slopes of these high mountains, periodically took place. Since land plants had yet to evolve, this process was exacerbated by the lack of vegetation to bind weathered rock debris and protect it from denudation. During Lower Devonian times (c. 408–387 Ma), when the climate was warm and arid, major rivers were thus responsible for the removal of vast quantities of sediment (from the Caledonian Mountains) which were transported principally to the south, into the then subsiding belt of low ground known today as the Midland

Valley. The resulting sequences of sedimentary rocks are often collectively referred to as the Lower Old Red Sandstone, even though rock types other than sandstones are interbedded.

The environment of deposition was one in which coarse sediments, comprising boulders, cobbles and gravels, were laid down in the form of extensive and often coalescing fans at the foot of the steep mountain slopes, extending out over the flat plains of the valley. The resulting coarse-grained rocks, known as conglomerates, crop out virtually continuously along the Highland Border from Stonehaven to Arran as, for example, immediately to the north of Blairgowrie. Finer particles of sand were transported to greater distances away from the mountain front and were deposited on extensive alluvial plains by braided river systems, flowing to the south and south-west. These were to become the extensive sequences of red sandstones, formerly used for building purposes, which dominate the Lower Devonian. In the periods between high discharge events, as flood waters receded, shallow, ephemeral lakes became established among the accumulations of fluvial sediments. It was in these depressions, hosting quiescent bodies of water, that the very finest particles of silt and clay grade were deposited from suspension. On lithification, these were to form mudstones. The term 'molasse', which originated in Switzerland, is often applied to the Lower Devonian rocks of the Midland Valley. This term is used to describe such post-tectonic sediments, derived by the erosion of a mountain range (in this case the Caledonian Mountains) after the cessation of orogenic activity.

During the period of accumulation of the Lower Devonian sediments, volcanic activity was prevalent in the Midland Valley giving rise to thick piles of lavas and localised zones of ashes and agglomerates, intercalated with the sedimentary formations. The lavas, principally of andesite and basalt, form much of the uplands of the Sidlaw Hills to the north of the Tay Estuary and the Ochil and North Fife Hills to the south-west and south. This provides yet another example of the effects of differential erosion, ice having planed the relatively soft sediments underlying Strathmore to low levels, leaving the more resistant igneous rocks as ranges of hills. Of particular note are Kinnoull Hill (222 m) and Moncrieffe Hill (221 m), respectively to the north and south of the Tay, near Perth. The layering clearly shown by the south-facing crags of the former is the product of many extensive lava flows and reflects the episodic nature of volcanism. The spectacular rock cuttings of the M90 Friarton intersections to the south of Perth were excavated in these lavas.

Cavities, known as vesicles, remaining in lavas as gases escape often become sites of precipitation of secondary minerals, notably silica in its banded form of agate. Agates are to be found in the andesites of the Ochils but the best localities are further to the east in north Fife, on the slopes of Norman's Law and along the Balmerino-Wormit coast.

Middle and Upper Devonian

Marking the end of the Lower Devonian sedimentation and volcanism, new earth movements took place in Middle Devonian times (387–374 Ma) effectively ending sedimentation. The northern part of the Midland Valley became characterised by compressive stresses leading to the development of large scale folds with a north-east to south-west trend, parallel with the Highland Boundary Fault. Beneath the flat and fertile land of Strathmore, with its distinctive red soils, lies the Strathmore Syncline, a 'downfold' causing rocks of the northern limb to be inclined to the south-east and those of the southern limb to dip to the north-west. Adjoining this is the Sidlaw-Ochil anticline, an 'upfold' of north-westerly inclined rocks of the Sidlaws forming the northern limb and south-easterly dipping rocks of the Ochils forming the southern. At that time, long before the formation of the Tay Estuary, the lavas of what are now these hill ranges were continuous across the area. The axes about which folding occurred were not horizontal but inclined, or plunging, to the south-west. Whereas folding about horizontal axes leads to parallel outcrop patterns in layered rocks, so-called plunging folds give rise to broadly U-shaped outcrop patterns. This is picked out by the open U-shaped configuration of the Sidlaw and Ochil lavas which 'join' to the south-west of Perth (Figure 3).

Thus uplifted, the Lower Devonian rocks became an area of strong erosion during Middle Devonian times. No rocks of this age are found in Perthshire. During the Upper Devonian (374–360 Ma), however, conglomerates and sandstones, laid down by eastward draining rivers, accumulated in near-horizontally inclined beds resting with marked unconformity upon the irregular land surface eroded into the folded Lower Devonian rocks. The angular discordance between the Lower and Upper Devonian strata, and 'gap' of Middle Devonian rocks in the geological record, is superbly exposed at Whiting Ness, Arbroath, Angus. In Kinross-shire, which is essentially underlain by sandstone of the Upper Devonian, also known as the Upper Old Red Sandstone, the contact with older rocks is not obvious.

Post-Devonian

After the deposition of the Upper Devonian a period of faulting occurred during which the subsidence of the Tay Graben (rift valley), took place between the North Tay and South Tay faults, trending almost parallel with the axis of the Sidlaw-Ochil anticline. This permitted the lowering of undeformed Upper Devonian rocks to occupy the central rift beneath the Carse of Gowrie, the best example of a true rift valley in Scotland, between the folded Lower Devonian rocks (Figure 4). Today the Friarton Bridge recreates a link between the lavas to north and south of the rift, as seen to good effect from Kinnoull Hill.

During late Carboniferous to Permian times (*c.* 290 Ma) numerous vertical dykes of dolerite, with similar trends to the North and South Tay faults, were emplaced in the Devonian rocks. One such body creates Campsie Linn, near Stanley, where it crosses the River Tay. The subsequent geological history of Perthshire in Mesozoic and Tertiary times (*c.* 250–2 Ma) is virtually unknown but it is likely that the main physical features as seen today may have existed by the end of the Tertiary. The onset of glacial conditions during the Pleistocene was to have a profound effect on the eventual scenery of the region and to mark an important part of the geological story.

Figure 4

Sketch geological cross-section, north to south from the southern edge of the Perthshire Grampian Highlands to Kinross-shire

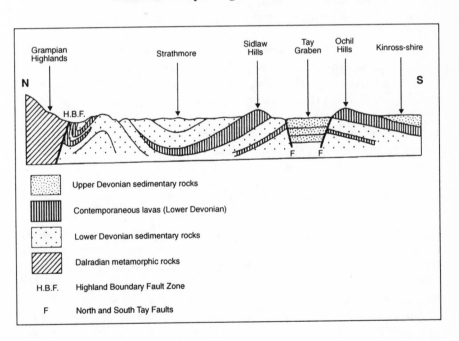

QUATERNARY

Reference has repeatedly been made above to the impact that glaciation has had on the form of the ground. Along with the whole country, Perthshire experienced several glaciations during the Pleistocene (2 Ma–10,000 years) and what is seen today may be considered as the net effect of these, each event tending to obfuscate the products of its predecessor. The glacial landforms within the area are principally due to the last major glaciation, known as the Devensian. This event took place between about 27,000 and 14,000 years ago and reached its maximum development about 18,000 years ago. Striations on rock surfaces and the distribution of erratics indicate that ice advanced across Perthshire from a major centre of ice accumulation and dispersal occupying the basin of the Moor of Rannoch. In general, the ice advanced in an easterly direction across the area, broadening, scouring and deepening pre-existing valleys and depositing extensive blankets of till, thickening towards the valley floors. The lower Tay valley was deepened and the estuary developed (McManus, 1971). As ice receded, the mountains and uplands became progressively ice-free until eventually active glaciers occupied the major valleys including, from north to south, those of Rannoch-Tummel, Glen Lyon, Strathtay and Strathearn. The exposed hills were then subject to intense frost shattering leading to widespread scree formation, a process which still continues though less severely.

Geologically speaking, lochs are but temporary features on the surface of the Earth, destined to become infilled with the sediments brought down by influent rivers. Nevertheless, the long narrow, ice-gouged rock-basin lochs of the Scottish Highlands are collectively one of the most significant scenic legacies of the Pleistocene glacial events. In Perthshire the major water bodies include Lochs Earn, Tay, Rannoch and Tummel, their long narrow forms reflecting the shape of the former ice masses which occupied their basins. The maximum depth of Loch Tay is 161 m (Duck and McManus, 1985), recorded in the central part of the loch where it is scoured along the plane of the Loch Tay Fault. Perhaps more remarkable is that the bottom is 55 m below sea level, a testimony to the tremendous erosive powers of ice. The deepest part of Loch Earn (87.2 m) is located towards its western end, also coincident with the Loch Tay Fault which crosses the loch beneath Glen Beich and Glen Ample. This loch was formed where two ice masses, advancing from Glen Ogle and the Balquhidder area, coalesced, thus concentrating their erosive powers.

The large water body of Loch Leven, which dominates Kinross-shire, had a different mode of origin. It occupies the central part of a natural bedrock depression underlain by Upper Old Red Sandstone, less resistant to erosion than the igneous rocks which surround it. It was formed at the end of the last glaciation from kettle holes left in the glacial deposits by retreating ice and is the largest body of water in Scotland created by such means. The two major deeps in the loch represent dead ice hollows, where the last blocks of ice melted. Numerous small lochs in Perthshire have a kettle hole origin, notably the chain of water bodies between Dunkeld and Blairgowrie, the Lochs of Craiglush, Lowes, Butterstone, Clunie and Drumellie, which occupy shallow hollows in deposits laid down by rivers draining from melting ice.

The weight of ice resting on the crust had caused it to become depressed during the Pleistocene. As melting and recession took place a rise in sea level occurred in response to the lowered land level. Thus, the sea advanced westwards over lower Strathtay and Strathearn, inundating the Carse of Gowrie. Subsequent rebound of the land in response to the removal of its load has resulted in the emergence of these lowland agricultural areas, now mantled with glaciomarine clays overlain by marine deposits.

The last area to lose its ice at the end of the Pleistocene was probably Rannoch Moor, the original centre of accumulation and dispersal. By about 10,000 years ago Perthshire was ice-free. The rivers in the glens created by glaciation and, latterly, the activities of man were thus to assume prominence as the principal geological agents.

As an example of the latter, the advent of hydro-electric power generation saw major changes to the lochs and natural drainage systems of Highland Perthshire. Loch Tummel, for instance, was more than doubled in length and its natural level raised by over 5 m when the River Tummel was impounded by the Clunie Dam in 1950. Thus, the famous Queen's View westwards towards Schiehallion is now very different from that observed on Queen Victoria's visit of 1844. Similarly, the levels of Lochs Garry and Lyon have been raised, whilst Loch an Daimh off Glen Lyon is formed from two lochs joined together by damming. Lochs such as Faskally, on the River Tummel north of Pitlochry, and Errochty, near Trinafour, are entirely artificial.

It should not be forgotten that geology is a science of the present and future as well as the past. Geological processes are always in operation, though often they act imperceptibly. Lochs are gradually infilling by river-borne sediments and uplands are steadily being worn away by the insidious processes of weathering and erosion. More obvious though are sudden or catastrophic events such as landslides on the Perthshire mountains or dramatic floods on the River Tay. The Tay is the foremost British river in terms of discharge, delivering on average 180 cubic metres of water per second (cumecs) into the Tay Estuary. In the notorious Perth flood of January 1993 a peak discharge of 2269 cumecs was recorded on the seventeenth of the month and the corresponding daily mean flow of 1965 cumecs represents a UK record (Black and Anderson, 1994). It is therefore hardly surprising that the Tay transports in excess of one million tonnes of land-derived sediment particles into its estuary per annum. So, although Perthshire is no longer experiencing many of the forces which have fashioned it in the geological past, contemporary geological processes are ever and everywhere at work, and will keep on shaping and modifying the form of the land.

Glossary

agglomerate Coarse-grained, blocky, fragmental rock created by explosive volcanic activity.

alluvium (adj. alluvial) General term for the sedimentary deposits laid down by a river along its course.

andesite A fine-grained, grey-brown, volcanic or **extrusive igneous rock**.

anticline Fold which is arched upwards, such that the layers of rock dip away from the **axis**, with older rocks in the core.

ash Fine-grained fragmental rock created by explosive volcanic activity.

axis (fold) A line drawn along the points of maximum curvature of a **fold**.

basalt A fine-grained, black, volcanic or **extrusive igneous rock**.

braided A river course which is divided into many channels by bars of sand and gravel.

calcareous Containing calcium carbonate.

chlorite Soft, green, platy silicate (containing silicon and oxygen) mineral found in low grade **metamorphic rocks**.

conglomerate Coarse-grained **sedimentary rock** composed of pebbles, cobbles and boulders derived from older rocks and cemented together.

cross bedding Small scale layering in **sedimentary rocks** in which the individual layers are at an angle to the main bedding planes. Produced by the migration of the slip faces of ripples or dunes.

dolerite Dark coloured, medium grained, **intrusive igneous rock**.

dyke Vertical or near-vertical, cross-cutting igneous intrusion with a sheet-like form. See also **sedimentary dyke**.

erratic A rock or boulder carried from its source by a glacier or an iceberg and deposited when the ice melts.

extrusive Volcanic **igneous rock** formed from molten material erupted onto a land surface – lava.

fault A planar fracture, or zone of fractures, in a rock mass along which relative displacement of adjacent blocks has occurred.

feldspar Important group of silicate (containing silicon and oxygen) minerals common in **igneous** and **metamorphic rocks**. Varieties include orthoclase (potassium rich, pink in colour) and plagioclase (sodium and calcium rich, white-grey in colour).

fold A bend in bedded rocks or any planar rock mass, formed by compression during **orogeny**.

garnet A group of silicate (containing silicon and oxygen) minerals, often deep reddish-brown in colour, that lack cleavage and whose crystals are usually well formed and equidimensional. Common in some **metamorphic rocks**.

granite A course-grained **plutonic igneous rock** composed mainly of **feldspar, quartz** and **mica**.

hydrothermal Associated with the action of hot fluids derived from bodies of **igneous rocks**, especially **plutons**.

igneous rocks Rocks that have crystallised or solidified from the molten state, may be **extrusive** or **intrusive**.

intrusive Igneous rock formed from molten material emplaced at depth in the Earth's crust and exposed by subsequent erosion.

kettle hole Depression in glacial deposits, often containing a small loch, left by the melting of a block of ice detached from a glacier.

limb (of fold) One of the two sides of a **fold**.

limestone A **sedimentary rock** composed mainly of calcium carbonate usually derived from accumulations of shells or marine organisms or by precipitation from seawater.

lithification The processes of compaction and cementation which result in a sediment becoming a **sedimentary rock**.

lithology The physical features of a rock.

marble A **metamorphic rock** formed by the alteration of a **limestone**.

metamorphic rocks Rocks that have formed at depth by the alteration and recrystallisation of pre-existing rocks as a result of elevated temperatures and pressures.

mica A group of complex silicate minerals (containing silicon and oxygen), varying from colourless to brown/black, highly reflective and characterised by a strongly platy habit.

mudstone A **sedimentary rock** similar to a **shale** but without distinct laminations.

muscovite Colourless or transparent variety of mica.

orogeny The process of mountain building by the compression, deformation and uplift of rock sequences.

pelite (adj. pelitic) A general term for a metamorphic rock formed by the alteration of a **mudstone**.

phyllite A fine grained **metamorphic rock**, coarser than **slate** but finer than **schist**, characterised by the parallel alignment of fine flakes of **mica**.

pluton (adj. plutonic) A very large **igneous** intrusion, e.g. a body of **granite**.

psammite (adj. psammitic) A general term for a **metamorphic rock** formed by the alteration of a **sandstone**.

pyroxene Group of dark green to black silicate (containing silicon and oxygen) minerals rich in iron, calcium and magnesium.

regional metamorphism Formation of **metamorphic rocks** on a very large scale during **orogeny**.

rift valley Down-faulted area between two parallel **faults**.

sandstone A **sedimentary rock** consisting of sand-sized grains of **quartz** and possibly other minerals, cemented together.

schist (adj. schistose) A medium-grained **metamorphic rock** with a strong platy fabric due to the parallel alignment of flakes of **mica**.

scree Loose, angular blocks of rock accumulated on the slopes and slope foot areas of mountains; formed by frost weathering.

sedimentary dyke Near-vertical sheet of mud (now **mudstone**) which has been squeezed upwards into overlying sands (now **sandstone**) by the weight of over burden.

sedimentary rocks Rocks, characteristically layered or bedded, formed by the accumulation of layers of clay, silt, sand, gravel or boulders, and organic material or precipitated salts.

shale A dark-coloured, fine-grained, laminated **sedimentary rock**, which splits easily along the laminations, composed largely of clay, **mica** and very fine **quartz**.

slate A fine-graned **metamorphic rock**, which cleaves easily, formed by the alteration of **shale** and **mudstone.**

striations Parallel ribs and grooves scratched by a moving glacier on the rock surfaces over which it passed.

syncline Fold which is bent downwards, such that the layers of rock dip towards the **axis**, with younger rocks in the core.

tectonic Relating to deformation of rocks (**fold**ing and **fault**ing) during **orogeny**.

trilobites Extinct group of arthropods.

turbidity current A fast flowing current transporting a high sediment load, commonly triggered by the disturbance of soft sediments on a slope.

unconformity Surface of contact between two rock formations arising from the folding and erosion of the lower formation, often during **orogeny**, before the deposition of the upper formation.

quartz SiO_2, a very common mineral, usually transparent or white in colour. Occurs in many **igneous** and **metamorphic rocks** and is the main constituent of **sandstones.**

quartzite A very hard metamorphic rock formed by the recrystallisation of a pure, **quartz sandstone.**

Simplified Geological Timescale

Era	Period	Years B.P. (before present)
Cenozoic	Quaternary (Holocene and Pleistocene)	0–2 Ma
	Tertiary	2–65 Ma
Mesozoic	Cretaceous	65–144 Ma
	Jurassic	144–213 Ma
	Triassic	213–250 Ma
Palaeozoic	Permian	250–286 Ma
	Carboniferous	286–360 Ma
	Devonian (Old Red Sandstone)	360–408 Ma
	Silurian	408–438 Ma
	Ordovician	438–505 Ma
	Cambrian	505–590 Ma
	Precambrian (Dalradian and Moine)	>590 Ma
Origin of Earth		4600 Ma

Ma = million years

Two
PREHISTORY

INTRODUCTION

The subject of this essay covers a wide canvas, embracing some seven and a half millennia from the arrival of the first post-glacial settlers to the historically attested Picts. In that period man in conjunction with the forces of nature transformed the natural environment, leaving all but the highest peaks affected by his activities. In addition, the direct traces of man's presence, in the form of archaeological sites and monuments, were imposed on and moulded the landscape. Many of the monuments have been destroyed over the succeeding centuries; some survive in much altered states, while others outwardly appear much as they did soon after their construction. Whilst we can never know how these sites were perceived by their builders, we can now, with the aid of archaeological and environmental evidence, begin to piece together a story describing the main threads of the development of settlement in Perthshire, a county blessed with a great richness of archaeological sites, monuments and artefacts.

THE NATURE OF THE EVIDENCE

The prehistoric archaeological record of the county has been profoundly influenced, either directly or indirectly, by the underlying geology and topography. These factors not only affected which areas were suitable for settlement, what materials were available to build houses and what type of agricultural regime would be effective, but they have also contributed to the later history of the archaeological sites themselves, determining which sites have survived to the present day as upstanding monuments, and which have subsequently been destroyed by ploughing or remain visible only as cropmarks in fields of ripening cereals.

Upland Perthshire, largely that part of the county lying to the north of the Highland Boundary Fault and consisting of highly folded, erosion-resistant Dalradian rocks, is a zone of relatively good preservation of monuments. These have survived not only because the destructive effects of later agriculture have been less severe there than in the lowlands, but also because large areas of once densely settled ground have been lost to agriculture since a deterioration in the climate during the early first millennium BC. In contrast to highland Perth, the lowlands cannot boast a large number of upstanding monuments. This does not mean that these areas were less densely settled than the uplands. On the contrary, the lowlands were the major areas for settlement, and much of what is rich agricultural land today has been farmed since the neolithic period, resulting in the wholesale levelling of monuments as upstanding structures. Many of the sites, however, have not been totally destroyed by ploughing and, over the last twenty years, the prehistoric archaeology of the lowlands – particularly Strathmore, the Carse of Gowrie and Strathearn – has been transformed as the result of the discovery of large numbers of cropmark sites. This has revealed a density of sites comparable with the best-preserved upland relict landscapes, and has also led to the identification of a range of site types not found as upstanding monuments anywhere in Perthshire. Much work now requires to be done in the interpretation of these hundreds of new sites, and it will be many years before the full impact of their discovery can be absorbed into the prehistory of the county.

THE FIRST SETTLERS (7000 BC TO 4000 BC)

Once the glaciers had retreated at the end of the last Ice Age and the temperature warmed sufficiently to allow the return of plants and animals to the Scottish landmass, it was possible for small groups of hunter-gatherers to reoccupy the country. Moving northwards, these hunting bands gradually expanded into new territories, and probably advanced fairly rapidly into the Forth-Tay area. Precisely when the first groups arrived in Perthshire is not known, but radiocarbon dates obtained from early mesolithic sites elsewhere in Scotland indicate that, in some areas, at least, settlement was under way by 7000 BC and, although no mesolithic sites of this date have been found in Perthshire, there is every reason to believe that occupation would have been established by the 7th millennium BC.

The coastal topography of Perthshire in the millennia following the end of the Ice Age was very different from that of today. In the wake of the retreat of the ice, sea level rose as a result of the release of melt water from the glaciers and around Doune sea level has been shown to have been as much as 49 m above present levels. However, the glacial meltwaters not only caused an immediate rise in sea level, but also set in motion a much slower process of isostatic uplift of the land, resulting from the release of the weight of the ice from the landmass. In the following millennia that part of central Scotland which includes Perthshire rose relative to the sea, so that by the 8th millennium BC sea level may have been some 36 m below its present level, producing a coast-line very different from that of the present day. By the 7th millennium, the probable period of mesolithic colonisation, sea level was once again rising, flooding the coastal zone and inundating the Firths of Tay and Forth, with tidal waters eventually extending well beyond the modern shoreline, before falling once again to roughly the present level during the later prehistoric period. This marine transgression not only resulted in the flooding of much of what had been dry land in coastal and estuarine Perthshire during the early mesolithic period but also led to the deposition of marine (Carse) clays over earlier land-surfaces in the lower reaches of the Tay and Forth river systems, thus masking the remains of any low-lying mesolithic settlement sites and rendering their discovery by normal archaeological means most unlikely.

The evidence for mesolithic settlement throughout Perthshire is disappointingly slight, given the range of coastal and inland habitats available but, on analogy with areas to the north and east, it is possible to build up a picture of this period. What evidence there is comes from stray finds of stone or bone tools and environmental samples and, together, they suggest that Perthshire was settled by small bands of hunter-gatherers who occupied relatively large territories, which included within them a range of habitats that could be used at different times of the year in order to exploit particular seasonal resources. There would have been no permanent settlement sites but a series of camps established in each of the different habitats. In the past, it was thought that mesolithic settlement was largely restricted to the coastal fringes, but recent research and the evidence of chance finds of stone tools has shown that mesolithic territories extended from the coast to deep into the hinterland and there is every reason to believe that these communities penetrated far up the valley systems of the Forth, Earn and Tay, leaving only the highest and remotest areas unexplored by the end of the period.

Although none of the mesolithic camp sites, similar to that at Morton, Fife, have been found or excavated in Perthshire, a number of stray finds of tools and artefacts bear witness to the way of life of these hunters and gatherers. In the Forth valley the remains of whales have been found in association with the Carse Clays (see above) and at Blair Drummond, alongside the bones of one such whale there were mattocs made from red deer antlers, which had been used by mesolithic man to strip the blubber and meat from the stranded animal, while a log boat hollowed out from a tree-trunk of Scots pine and reported to have been found in deep deposits by the River Tay and Friarton on the outskirts of Perth, may be the earliest craft of this type to have been discovered in Scotland. These discoveries emphasise the part water played as a source of food, as well as a means of moving around the extensive territories that supported the complex mesolithic communities.

THE EARLIEST MONUMENT BUILDERS (4000 BC TO 2500 BC)

By the end of the 5th millennium BC most of the ground that was to be permanently settled in Perthshire over the next millennia had already been explored and was probably well known to groups of mesolithic hunters. Indeed by that time patterns of use must have been long established and the population may have grown to the extent that it was close to the maximum carrying capacity of the ground. At about this time there are signs of widespread change evident in the archaeological record; changes which in the past have been described as the agricultural or neolithic revolution and accounted for by the arrival of new settlers from the south who introduced the characteristic traits associated with the neolithic period, namely the construction of burial and ritual monuments, the adoption of agriculture, and the use of polished stone axes and pottery. Also associated with the beginning of the neolithic period are a number of vegetational and environmental changes, the evidence for which comes from soil and pollen samples. These changes include a decrease in some types of tree pollen and a corresponding rise in plants characteristic of open conditions (both changes suggesting clearance of the forest cover), the appearance of cereal pollen and other plants found in association with soils that are being cultivated and an increase in the amount of soil particles being washed into water courses, which, like the pollen evidence, suggests the clearance of the forest for agricultural purposes. It may not be necessary to ascribe these changes solely to the arrival of new peoples from England via south-west or south-east Scotland, as has been proposed in the past. Rather, an expanding indigenous mesolithic population may have adopted a range of new ideas (the immediate origins of which undoubtedly did lie to the south), as an adaptation to pressures from their own changing circumstances.

Whatever the explanation for these changes in the archaeological record, the period from the beginning of the 5th millennium BC witnessed a rapid expansion in the evidence for human occupation over large parts of Perthshire. This probably reflects a major growth in the population during the course of the next millennium and a half, which is likely to have occurred as a result of the development of pastoralism alongside the introduction of arable crops, notably cereals. However, with a small number of possible exceptions, neolithic settlement sites or field-systems are largely absent from the archaeological record in Perthshire. One of the exceptions is what may be a sub-rectangular timber house revealed as a cropmark on gently-rolling ground at Clash, to the south-east of Callander. It closely resembles a building excavated at Balbridie on the bank of the Dee in Aberdeenshire, which has been dated to the neolithic period. The failure to find the remains of any neolithic houses amongst the extensive remains of later prehistoric settlements on the moorlands of north-east Perthshire, as well as their almost total absence from the cropmark record in Strathearn and Strathmore, suggests not that we have yet to find them, but that they may not be there to be found. This calls into question the nature of neolithic settlement, in particular the traditional picture of settled communities surrounded by arable plots and raises the possibility of neolithic society owing more to the nomadic way of life of the preceding mesolithic groups.

Although little may be known of the economic foundation of these neolithic communities, they have left us with a wealth of burial and cere-monial sites, constructed in either stone, earth or timber. These survive either as upstanding monuments in the upland areas or have been revealed as cropmarks in the arable lands. Our knowledge of the monuments of the neolithic period in Perthshire has been greatly broadened and deepened in the past decade, partly as a result of field-survey and excavation, but also because of the discovery by aerial survey of a plethora of new sites and new types of site. The impact of aerial photography in Strathearn and Strath-more on the picture of neolithic monuments, particularly those built of timber, is only beginning to be assessed as, until the advent of this technique, only a limited range of stone-built neolithic monuments were known in these areas.

The variety of neolithic monuments ranges from those associated with burial (chambered, long and round cairns and ring-cairns), to a group which are thought to be ceremonial in function. The latter include the well-known stone circles and standing stones, as well as the rapidly growing list of larger enclosures and linear monuments, such as henges, pit-defined enclosures and cursuses. To this list can also now be added the cup-and-ring markings, which are found either on their own or carved on stone monuments, and have recently been demonstrated to be predomi-nantly of neolithic, rather than Bronze Age, date.

Although the distribution of neolithic polished stone axes is relatively even throughout those parts of Perthshire where they might be expected to be found, the same cannot be said about the disposition of the monuments. Setting aside, for the time being, the problems of site destruction and dis-covery, the distribution of the various types and categories of monument is uneven and patchy. The chambered and long cairns, for instance, show a markedly south-western bias, with particular concentrations on the more marginal ground around the middle Earn valley and on the hills between Braco and Callander; whereas none are to be found on the relatively high ground in lower Strathearn, Strathmore and the Carse of Gowrie, nor in Strathardle or Glenshee. Similar concentrations and apparent absences can be seen in the distribution pattern of stone circles and cupmarkings, as well as in other monument types. There is, as yet, no generally agreed explanation for the disposition of the neolithic monuments; it has been suggested that Perthshire might have belonged to two different cultural regions – one looking to the south and west, the other to the north and east – each with its own distinctive sets of funerary and ceremonial practices but also having a wide range of shared characteristics. Alternatively, and bearing in mind the probable common mesolithic ancestry of the peoples and the way in which they exploited wide-ranging territories, it is possible that the neolithic peoples used particular parts of the country for different activities, and this included the construction of specific monument types in what was deemed to be the appropriate part of the group's territory.

Amongst the neolithic monuments, the chambered tombs and long cairns are likely to be the earliest to have been built, starting as early as the opening of the 4th millennium BC and perhaps continuing in use for more than a thousand years. The cairns show considerable variation in form, ranging from trapezoidal to oval chambered tombs, some with end-chambers, while others have chambers placed laterally along the length of the mound. At Cultoquhey, outside Gilmerton, there was no artificial cairn, the chamber had simply been set into the side of a natural mound, whereas at Auchenlaich, Callander, Scotland's longest cairn, the man-made mound was some 320 m in length.

Perthshire is particularly rich in the remains of neolithic stone settings, which range from stone circles, 'four-poster' stone settings (so named after their resemblance to the uprights of a four-poster bed), stone alignments of up to four stones, and the Perthshire speciality the 'two-poster' stone setting. These monuments, which appear to be relatively simple and straightforward when viewed in the field, can turn out on excavation to be complex monuments with long histories; for example, the well-known stone circle at Croftmoraig, Strathtay was shown to have been remodelled on more than one occasion, and the stone monument which survives today was preceded by a circle of timber uprights. Similarly, at Moncrieffe House stone circle, the stone phase was secondary to a timber circle sitting within a penannular ditched enclosure which has been classed as a small henge.

The timber settings beneath Croftmoraig and Moncrieffe serve as an introduction to the discovery in recent years of a large number of crop-marks of neolithic timber and ditch enclosed structures in the ploughlands of Perthshire. These monuments are primarily ritual or ceremonial in nature, but amongst them are large timber buildings, possibly the remains of houses. The ceremonial sites range from relatively small structures, such as timber circles and even a timber 'four-poster', through medium sized enclosures, which include a number of henges, the best known being the excavated example at North Mains, Strathallan and, lastly, to large ditched enclosures (Plate 2). Included within the latter group are the roughly circular enclosures at Leadketty, Dunning and at least two long, rectilinear enclosures, known as cursuses (Blairhall and Milton of Rattray).

Perhaps related to the cursus monuments is the Cleaven Dyke, the most remarkable neolithic earthwork to survive in Perthshire. It runs for some 3.2 km across the level ground between the Rivers Tay and Isla, and comprises a turf-revetted gravel bank accompanied by two flanking ditches. Until recently the Cleaven Dyke was thought to be a Roman military earthwork associated with the nearby legionary fortress at Inchtuthil, but excavation has now shown that it is of neolithic date, though its form is without direct parallel elsewhere in Scotland. The scale of the earthwork is witness to the huge physical effort necessary to construct the larger neolithic monuments, while its survival as an upstanding site for much of its course is remarkable and a reminder of how much of the non-stone, neolithic monument landscape may have been lost to sight as a result of later ploughing.

In addition to the stone and timber monuments, there is one further group of remains, cup-and-ring markings, which form a notable characteristic of the neolithic period in Perthshire. These enigmatic markings are widely, though not evenly, distributed throughout the county. Markings occur singly or in clusters on rock outcrops, as well as incised onto stones incorporated into monuments, particularly stone circles and other types of stone setting. There is a tendency for marks on rock outcrops or boulders to be grouped into localised clusters and these clusters themselves may be found in distinct groups. One such grouping lies in Strathtay, between Balnagard and the eastern third of Loch Tay. Here there are numerous examples of localised clusters with a range of simple and more complex arrangements of cups and cup-and-ring markings. The meaning of these markings is lost to us, but recent research has shown that they are not randomly disposed in the landscape and may relate in some as yet undefined way to ancient patterns of land use, such as upland pasture or routeways. Although cupmarkings are likely to have been carved in the neolithic period, the use of the decorated stones continued into the late 3rd and early 2nd millennia BC (the Early Bronze Age), as they are occasionally found incorporated in later monuments, for example as a cover-stone in a cist found on top of a large cairn at North Mains, Strathallan. Whilst the original meaning of the stone at North Mains may still have been understood when it was placed on the cist, the three cupmarked slabs built into the structure of the Later Iron Age souterrain at Pitcur must surely have been collected as curios belonging to a remote and long-forgotten past (Plate 4).

All the monuments mentioned so far were deliberately built for either ceremonial or domestic use. However, one further important site, the stone-axe factory at Craig na Caillach, which falls outwith both of these categories, must be considered in this discussion of the neolithic in Perthshire. The factory (in reality a quarry and associated processing areas), which lies high above the valley floor to the east of Killin, is one of the few examples of this type of site so far identified in Scotland and has recently been partially excavated. The excavations showed that the quarried material was first prepared as rough-out axes on site, then polished to produce the distinctive neolithic axe forms. Products from the Killin factory have been found widely distributed throughout Scotland and beyond and it is clear that polished stone axes, as well as other types of stone object, were regarded as more than simple tools. They are beautiful objects in their own right and played an important part in the complex world of social contacts where the axes may have been passed as high status gifts from one group to another, perhaps at seasonal gatherings at the great ceremonial enclosures.

Until recently, the study of the neolithic period in Perthshire was stuck in the doldrums – the sites and artefacts were relatively well-known, largely confined to the upland areas and little excavated. The last fifteen years has seen the picture change dramatically. Aerial photography has filled the lowlands with the cropmarks of new neolithic sites, most of which are of classes of monument not found in the uplands, while excavation has begun to reveal the complexities of these sites which were built and re-used over long periods and, at the same time, is unearthing a mass of artefacts and environmental data which add so much to our understanding of the neolithic.

THE AGE OF ROUND CAIRNS AND CISTS (2500 BC TO 1500 BC)

There is no clear-cut break between the neolithic period and the Bronze Age but, from the middle of the 3rd millennium BC, a number of changes in the archaeological record become apparent. The nature of the field remains is little altered, with the emphasis still on burial and ceremonial monuments and an apparent dearth of settlement sites. The pollen record suggests that substantial inroads had been made into the forest cover and that arable farming had become more widespread, both of which probably indicate the development of a sedentary way of life. Metal-working technology – first copper, then bronze – was gradually introduced, although the wholesale use of bronze for tools became common long after the introduction of metal. The most obvious changes appear in the burial record, clearly indicating significant developments in beliefs and also suggesting a growing complexity in social organisation with the appearance of greater social stratification than in earlier periods.

Chambered and long cairns ceased to be built or at least used in the traditional ways by the middle of the 3rd millennium BC and the multiple burial-site of the neolithic was replaced by single inhumation or ceremonial burial, with individual graves sometimes grouped into clusters and, in some cases, covered by cairns. Round cairns are not exclusive to the Bronze Age but the majority are assumed to belong to this period, with many of the larger ones measuring over 30 m in diameter and up to 3 m in height, remaining as prominent features in the landscape for the next 4000 years. Some were carefully positioned so that they could be seen from great distances. One such, on Pole Hill to the east of the Coupar Angus road just north of New Scone, is clearly visible on the horizon, but what is now not so obvious is that the two ridges to the south-west, Arnbathie and Murrayshall Hill, are also crowned by hill-top cairns. Not all cairns were situated in such elevated positions. There is, for example, a group of three on the haughland of the River Tay to the south of Dull and it is worth considering that these too would have been prominent landscape features had the rich land in the flood plain of the Tay been cleared of forest by the date of the construction of the cairns.

Surprisingly few cairns have been excavated in Perthshire but, on analogy with those in neighbouring counties, it is clear that construction of the mound was normally only one of many phases of activity associated with burial and veneration of the dead at these sites. At Beechmount, Coupar Angus, a relatively small cairn has recently been examined in advance of redevelopment, revealing a long and complex history of activity on the site which began in the late neolithic period and continued in the Bronze Age with the construction of a cairn, which was redesigned on more than one occasion and eventually covered a number of individual graves.

During the Bronze Age, burials were not restricted to cairns and a large number of so-called flat cemeteries have been discovered, particularly in the agricultural areas where ploughing often revealed the sites. The cemeteries range from a single stone-built cist, containing a crouched inhumation or cremation, to groups of cists which are sometimes found together with uncisted cremations covered by, or contained in an earthenware pot. The latter are also frequently discovered set into gravel or sand mounds reminiscent of man-made cairns. Like the cairns which contain successive burials, the flat cemeteries appear to have been used over long periods and must, despite their name, have been marked in some way, possibly by a timber post. Burials were also made in, or close to, monuments of earlier periods: a standing stone, at Balnagard, by Aberfeldy, which was presumably erected in the neolithic period, was found to have a cist close to its base, while at Sandy Road, Scone, an urn burial had been inserted into the middle of a stone circle.

The rituals and ceremonies associated with burials found in cairns or flat cemeteries may have differed, but there is no distinction between the grave goods that accompanied the dead to the netherworld from either type of site. These range from pottery vessels specially made for burials – Beakers, Food Vessels and Cinerary Urns, to more everyday articles such as flint knives, scrapers and strike-a-lights. Occasionally, more exotic items were included, such as a small number of bronze implements, as well as items of jewellery, the most elaborate being jet necklaces of the type found accompanying a cremation in a cist at Easter Essendy.

THE AGE OF SETTLEMENTS (1500 BC TO AD 500)

In the centuries after 1500 BC there is a profound change in the archaeological record. The pattern of life established in the neolithic period, which continued to develop during the first half of the Bronze Age, is replaced by a new order. For the first time settlement sites become common, dominating the archaeological record, whereas ceremonial and burial sites which had held sway for the previous three millenia, hardly feature in the new catalogue of sites. The elaborate pottery styles of the early Bronze Age also disappear, to be replaced by undistinguished vessels; on the other hand, bronze tools and weapons become more plentiful, occasionally being found in hoards, which may have been the stock-in-trade of peripatetic bronze-smiths or deposited as ritual offerings to the gods.

Of all the Scottish counties, Perthshire can perhaps boast the greatest variety of settlement types – hut-circles, ring-ditch hut-circles, ring-ditch timber round-houses, souterrain settlements, crannogs, homesteads, ring-forts, duns, brochs, defended settlements, and forts – but, because so little excavation has been carried out, our understanding of individual site types, let alone the relationships between the various forms of settlement, is rudimentary. Their construction and use is spread over a period of some two millennia and, although the dating of some of the types is well known, the lack of modern excavation severely hinders an understanding of the chronology of the various site types. Many of the upland settlements, particularly the stone-walled forts, have been recognised since the 18th century, and earlier studies have concentrated on these well-preserved high status sites. This has had the effect of focusing attention on the upland fringes, where most of the forts have been preserved and it is only with the advent of aerial photography of the lowland cropmark sites that a more balanced picture of the late Bronze Age and Iron Age settlement patterns has emerged.

Although a new picture of the settlement pattern has been revealed in the past fifteen years, the full impact of these discoveries has yet to be

assessed and it is sometimes difficult to break away from traditional inter-
pretations and approaches. During the course of this period, permanent
settlement extended further than at any previous or subsequent time. This
was at least partly due to a more favourable climate in the earlier part of
the period which favoured the upward expansion of settlement, particularly
in the highland glens in the north-east of the county where hut-circles
have been found at heights of up to 500 m above sea-level. Not only did
permanent farms reach into remote corners of the county during this
period, but settlement densities in the richer lowlands appear to have been
on a par with those seen in the 18th century. The phase of expansion was
reversed as a result of climatic deterioration in the second half of the
period, with what appears to have been disastrous consequences for the
more elevated areas.

The picture that has emerged of late Bronze Age and Iron Age settlements is complex, and the situation at the later end of the period has
been further complicated by the question of the origin of the Picts (the
archaeological evidence indicates that the peoples described by classical
authors as the Picts were the descendants of the earlier Iron Age tribes). By
the last quarter of the 2nd millennium BC, much of the county was
occupied by dispersed farms comprising round timber houses (hut-circles)
surrounded by their fields and this basic pattern continued, with some
modifications, right through to the early Pictish period in the first half of
the 1st millennium BC. Some of the best examples of these farms have been
preserved in remarkable numbers in north-east Perth on the high-level
terraces and side valleys flanking the Rivers Ardle and Shee and along the
Highland edge to the north of Blairgowrie and Alyth (Plate 3). More than
800 individual hut-circles, including Dalrulzion-type double-walled
houses – a Perthshire peculiarity, have been recorded in this area alone,
giving some indication of the level of the population in the early 1st millennium BC. The reasons for the density of hut-circles is not immediately
apparent, but their survival as upstanding monuments may in part be due
to the deterioration in the climate at this time which resulted in cooler and
wetter conditions. The area never fully recovered from this climatic
reversal and, unlike the lower-lying ground in Strathmore, the Carse of
Gowrie and Strathearn, medieval and later agriculture has failed to retake
this land, thus preserving some of the finest prehistoric farming landscapes
to survive in Britain.

Pressure on the land brought about as a result of climatic deterioration
at the beginning of the 1st millennium BC may have been a contributory
factor in the development of a wide variety of defended settlements which
characterise much, if not all, of the next 1000 years. These range from
small-scale sites such as crannogs (timber-built island dwellings on lochs)

and palisaded homesteads to multi-ramparted earthwork and massive stone-walled forts. Aerial photography has shown that the forts are not confined to the upland fringe but are also common in the lowland straths, where they are intermingled with groups of timber round-houses. Few of these sites have been excavated, consequently the social and chronological relationships of the open hut-circles and round-houses with the defended settlements and forts can, as yet, only be a matter of speculation. Although the forts are widely dispersed, with their density generally reflecting the quality of the surrounding farmland, there is a *lacuna* in the distribution in the valleys of the Rivers Ardle and Shee, which could be interpreted to suggest that the climatic deterioration had catastrophic consequences in these north-eastern glens, leading to the near total collapse of population numbers.

Lack of excavation makes it difficult to provide a tight framework of dating for the enclosed settlements, but it is likely that their construction and use is spread throughout the period from about 1000 BC to the third quarter of the 1st millennium AD, that is, from the Late Bronze Age to the Pictish period. The hill-top sites occupied by many of the forts may have been settled in earlier times, and it is clear from the existing lines of ramparts at forts, such as Dunsinane (of Shakespearian fame) and Barry Hill, that the defences were remodelled on many occasions. This is not to say that these sites were continuously occupied, and the various phases of use may have been separated by periods of abandonment. Incorporated in the refurbishment of the rampart of a small fort at Inchtuthil was dressed stone that could only have come from the nearby Roman legionary fortress. The re-use of Roman stonework indicates that the site was re-occupied after the garrison was withdrawn from the fortress and raises the question of how many of the defended sites were built or in re-use during the early Pictish period (AD 1–500) other strong candidates include the massive stone-walled fort which represents the final defence at Barry Hill and the innermost wall at Dunsinane, as well as the fort at Kingseat, Dunkeld (the name Dunkeld, which was perhaps originally applied to the fort, has been translated as the 'Fort of the Caledonians', the *Caledonii* being the name attributed by classical authors to one of the local tribal groupings). Falling right at the end of the prehistoric tradition of fort-building, and technically outwith the chronological scope of this paper, comes the fort at Dundurn, St Fillans, which stands at the western end of the Pictish province of Strathearn.

During the course of the 1st millennium BC and extending into the 1st millennium AD, there is the appearance of a profusion of distinctive enclosed and open settlement types. Amongst the former there are small numbers of brochs and duns, which are found predominantly in the east of the county and are ultimately of northern or western origin, but are part of a thin scatter of such sites found in the south and east of Scotland. Why such exotic settlement types should be found so far outside their normal range is not known, but it may point to the arrival at about the beginning of the Common Era of small groups, possibly warrior bands, from the north or west bringing their distinctive settlement forms with them. Other enclosed settlement types are of purely local, or at least eastern Scottish origin. Amongst these are a group of round-houses enclosed within a concentric stony bank, which have only recently been identified in the hills to the east and south of Callander. This is probably a local variation on a theme common in eastern Scotland and examples of this type of settlement can also be seen amongst the cropmark sites, though in the lowlands the enclosure is formed by a timber palisade rather than a stony bank.

One of the more interesting of the enclosed settlement types is to be found in the valley of the middle Tay and its tributaries. The ring-forts of northern Perthshire (annotated as 'Homesteads' on the Ordnance Survey maps) form a distinctive, tight-knit group and, although included here amongst the enclosed settlements because of the substantial wall which surrounds them, they share many characteristics in common with hut-circles. Only a small number have been excavated and the dating evidence has been inconclusive but, like the brochs, they probably date to late in the Iron Age and may even belong to the Pictish period.

Falling between enclosed and open settlements are the crannogs, many examples of which have been located close to the shore of highland and lowland lochs. Their distribution is now weighted towards the Highland zone; originally they were probably equally common in lowlands but have been prone to destruction in the past two centuries as a result of the drainage of so many of the lowland wetlands. Unlike their medieval counterparts, the prehistoric sites were often built of timber and, for the most part, survive only as swellings on the floor of the lochs. Recent underwater surveys have shown that there is an unexpectedly large number of crannogs, often filling hitherto unexplained gaps in the Iron Age settlement pattern, and that the sites can easily be identified by the stumps of the timber uprights which still project through the bed of the lochs. Excavation of a site at Oakbank, on the northern shore of Loch Tay a short distance west of Kenmore (a full size replica is currently under construction on the opposite side of the loch), has shown that not only did the crannog act as a refuge for the human population but that it also provided shelter for a substantial flock of sheep (the evidence coming from a large deposit of sheep dung found amongst the timbers of the crannog). Unlike brochs, crannogs appear to have been used over a long period of time. Oakbank has been dated to the first half of the 1st millennium BC, while comparable sites elsewhere in Scotland were still in use as late as the middle of the 1st millennium AD.

There is a corresponding range of forms amongst the open, or non-defensive, settlements. One of the first types to be identified was the Dalrulzion double-walled hut-circle; dating to the middle of the 1st millennium BC, it is only found to the east of the Tay-Garry corridor and along the Highland edge as far as Kincardineshire. Perhaps better known is the souterrain, a particular variant of which has been found in large numbers in the lowlands of Perth, as well as in Fife and Angus. The souterrain is not a settlement type in its own right but was attached to a timber round-house and probably served as a store. The typical souterrain comprised a curving, stone-built, underground chamber or sometimes a group of interlinked chambers, roofed either with timbers or covered by stone lintels (Plate 5). Although many have been excavated, dating evidence is somewhat sparse as the chambers appear to have been kept remarkably clean, but the distinctive Perth types are generally considered to have been built and used for a relatively short period at about the beginning of the Common Era.

Although settlements account for the overwhelming majority of sites known from this period, small numbers of burials, predominantly from barrows or cairns, have also been recorded. Until the advent of aerial photographs, the only burials known were two round barrows covering extended inhumations at Inchtuthil, close to the post-Roman fort mentioned earlier, one of which was clearly also post-Roman in date as it had been constructed over the counterscarp bank of the Roman fortress. Aerial photography has revealed a number of barrow clusters or barrow cemeteries comprising both square and circular ditched burials which are presumed to be of Iron Age date, some possibly belonging to the early Pictish period. The square barrows are easy to identify from aerial photographs as the ditches that surround them are characteristically interrupted by causeways at the corners, while on occasion within both the round and square barrows the outline of the grave-pit can clearly be seen.

Lack of excavation, the prevalence of conditions non-conducive to the survival of metal finds and the use of materials which are unlikely to be preserved have together meant that artefactual remains from the Bronze Age and Iron Age are relatively uncommon. Such finds that do survive show that there was a high degree of craftsmanship in a wide range of materials, both for everyday objects and for high status goods. By the middle of the period iron had probably replaced bronze as the medium for most edge tools, but bronze continued to be used for sheet-metal vessels, such as a large feasting cauldron found in Blair Drummond Moss, or cast to make personal ornaments – simple pins, penannular brooches and more elaborate items, for example a pair of boldly massive armlets from Pitkellony, Muthill (Plate 5).

THE END OF THE PREHISTORIC PERIOD

Culturally there was no sharp break between the end of the early Pictish period and the early Middle Ages, but by the third quarter of the 1st millennium AD new forces were at work which heralded the end of the old order, bringing Perthshire into a wider, literate and Christian world. The Age of Settlements comes to an end with the demise of the fort-building tradition and the abandonment of the round-house settlements, leaving a *lacuna* in the settlement record which lasts until the end of the medieval period.

Note

A number of sites and monuments are mentioned in the text; most can be found on the latest edition of the relevant Ordnance Survey 1:50,000 map sheets. Further information about individual sites can be obtained from the volumes listed in the Bibliography, while detailed accounts and aerial photographs of many of the sites can be consulted at the offices of the Royal Commission on the Ancient and Historical Monuments of Scotland in Edinburgh. Archaeological material found in Perthshire is on display in Perth and Dundee museums and other items will soon be available in the new Museum of Scotland, Edinburgh.

THREE

THE ROMANS

INTRODUCTION: TOPOGRAPHY AND TRIBES

There is a charming antiquarian conceit that, on Rome's earliest invasion of Scotland, the legionary troops responded to their first sight of the River Tay by hailing it as a second Tiber. This dramatic image captures the essence of a response which lies at the heart of Roman military dispositions within the bounds of Perthshire. Whether reacting to the physical problems posed by natural obstacles or to the subtler stimuli of political geography, there is evidence that the Romans were aware of the complex issues raised by invasion and occupation of such an area and possessed a range of tactical and strategic options with which to address them.

Blocking or overlooking their path as they advanced north-eastwards into Caledonia lay the Ochil Hills with the outlying buttresses of Ben Vorlich, the Sidlaws and the foothills of the Grampians; across the most convenient line of march between these upland ramparts flowed the equally formidable barriers of the Tay and the Earn. Within this physical context secure bridging or fording points had to be found on the rivers and their tributaries, some to be guarded by a garrison of suitable strength, while at the necessary intermediate positions way-stations and watch-towers sprang up, ensuring that the eventual structure of occupation lacked neither muscle nor sinew. Before that stability could be attained, an assessment of the political situation was essential. Pockets of resistance had to be identified and neutralised, centres of philo-Roman tendency protected and nurtured. The whole area had to be blanketed by military operations in considerable strength. There was a call for far-ranging reconnaissance by land and sea, for the collection and synthesis of intelligence, for the movement and supply of vast numbers of men.

Before advancing into hostile territory the Roman army would have been well acquainted with not just the lie of the land, but also its political complexion; the extent of tribal territories, the position of centres of power, the relationships of a tribe with its neighbour and its likely attitude to Rome. Information of this kind relating to the native peoples of Perthshire was doubtless available to the commanders of the earliest invasion force, but of that dossier we can recognise only the slightest traces and to reconstruct it we depend on the partial evidence of the eventual deployment of garrisons. The testimony of the Alexandrian geographer Ptolemy is the only detailed statement on this topic that has come down to us from antiquity. Composing his world-map in the middle of the 2nd century AD, Ptolemy appears to have leant heavily upon his most eminent predecessor in this field, Marinus of Tyre, much of whose carto-graphic information for North Britain was probably collected during the initial conquest of that area. From this source we learn – apart from the Roman name for the Tay (*Tava*) – the identity of a number of native peoples likely to have occupied parts of Perthshire and the adjoining districts in the Roman period. Unfortunately, they are located by reference to the sites (probably Roman military sites) that lay within their territory, or by their spatial relationship to each other, which allows considerable scope for error. Used in conjunction with other evidence, especially that of place-names, the archaeology of later prehistoric settlement and the growing testimony of Early Historic studies, the information provided by Ptolemy is worthy of appraisal.

What must first be understood is the high degree of selectivity manifested throughout the Ptolemaic map. This is especially true of the named sites or *poleis* (Greek for 'cities'), only ten of which are indicated in each 'subsection' of the northern parts of Britain (N Scotland, S Scotland, N England and Ireland). The mapmaker seems to have been more concerned to provide uniform density of cover than strict accuracy and there is no evidence that the ten *poleis* selected are necessarily the most important. Secondly the allocation of certain sites to each tribe is conveyed by the phrase 'amongst whom are situated A,B,C . . .' which need not mean more than the *poleis* lie within the map-area covered by the letters of the tribal name; indeed, it is possible that the positioning of the tribal areas was governed by their relationship to the adjacent coastline, rather than to places in the interior.

With this in mind, it becomes easier to reject the Ptolemaic implication that the southern parts of Perthshire might have fallen within the territory of the *Damnonii*, whose *poleis* allegedly extended from Irvine (*Vindogara*) in the south-west as far as an unidentified site *Victoria*, some way to the north of *Alauna* (which is reasonably equated with a fort in Strathallan, probably Ardoch). The possibility of a single tribe, or even a tribal grouping, controlling lands in Ayrshire as well as Strathearn is remote and it would be more reasonable to assume that the *Damnonii* came no nearer Perthshire than the headwaters of the Forth, marching on the east with the *Votadini*, whose territory Ptolemy depicted as stretching far down into Lothian and beyond; in the Early Historic period, this bipartite control of the Forth-Clyde isthmus persisted as the northern provinces of the British kingdoms of Strathclyde and the Gododdin, reappearing a little later in the jurisdictions of Lennox and Stirlingshire.

The cartographic vacuum left by the removal of Damnonian claims now requires to be filled. Between the Forth and the Moray Firth four tribes are recorded by Ptolemy: the *Caledonii*, the *Taexali*, the *Vacomagi* and the *Venicones*. Of these, two are positioned by reference to physical features. The Caledonians' territories are said to extend from Loch Long to the Beauly Firth, by which we should perhaps understand not that they inhabited only the Great Glen or the wastes of the Grampian massif, but rather (as the historian Tacitus implies in the *Agricola*) that all the peoples north of the isthmus claimed a common Caledonian identity; nevertheless, the place-names Dunkeld (?Dunchailden), Schiehallion and Rohallion may indicate a heartland in the upper Tay. The *Taexali* giving their name to the promonotory of Kinnaird's Head, probably controlled the north-east from Buchan to the Dee. If Ptolemy's depiction of the Vacomagi as lying to the east of the Caledonians is to be trusted, then Strathmore and the Mearns must surely have been theirs, although the fact that two sites on or near the Moray Firth are also ascribed to them raises questions that must be addressed later. The remaining group, the *Venicones*, located to the south and east of the *Vacomagi*, would thus have covered much of southern Perthshire, embracing Strathearn (possibly together with Menteith), Kinross and much, though not necessarily all, of Fife.

The archaeological evidence which might directly support or disprove the foregoing hypothesis is not at present available and we must depend instead on the indirect testimony of aerial photographs, largely untested by excavation, which appear to show cropmark traces of later Iron Age settlements. Such records combine to provide a consistent picture throughout most of Perthshire, with a vast preponderance of settlements comprising unenclosed groups of round timber-built houses, often sunken-floored or associated with souterrains (underground passage-like features) and pits – a pattern which is totally unlike that to be seen south of the Forth. However, regional variations are beginning to be recognised within the area; the massive, interrupted ring-ditch type of round-house, with accompanying irregularly shaped souterrains, has yet to be identified south of the Tay, although its distribution extends north-eastwards to the limits of Angus. Similarly, the developed form of the 'Angus' souterrain, now known in its hundreds in Perthshire north of the Tay, cannot be traced far into Strathearn on the west or much beyond the boundary of Fife on the east. That Class II Symbol Stones of the Pictish period display a comparable pattern of dispersal suggests a continuation of long-established political or cultural divisions to which the evidence of Ptolemy allows us to put a tentative name.

MILITARY MONUMENTS AND THEIR MAKERS

Such an extended discussion of the geographical data is justified by the obvious importance which the Romans attached to the conquest and occupation of the Perthshire area. This importance is manifested in turn by the variety, scale and number of Roman military works constructed hereabouts, many of them surviving as outstandingly impressive field-monuments. One could hardly choose a better area of Scotland, or Britain as a whole, in which to display the wide range of structures employed by the Roman army in the enlargement of their Empire.

The Army Structure

For the initial phases of reconnaissance and campaigning the army operated in relatively large battle-groups, composed of roughly equal numbers of legionary and auxilary troops. During the Roman period in Scotland, legions consisted of approximately 6000 men, mainly infantry and recruited solely from those possessing Roman citizenship. In Britain at the beginning of the first sustained invasion of Scotland around AD 79, there were four legions, the Second *Augusta*, the Second *Adiutrix*, the Ninth *Hispana* and the Twentieth *Valeria Victrix*, whose base-fortresses were respectively Caerleon, Chester, York and Gloucester. Each legion was composed of ten cohorts, the first being nominally 1000 men strong, the others only 500. Legionary troops represented the cream of any province's military strength, their fighting capability, engineering skills and general level of organisation and training being on a far higher level than any hostile native warband might ever hope to attain. The *auxilia* were, for the most part, drawn from non-Roman peoples within or on the frontiers of the Empire and organised in regiments either 500 or 1000 strong, (a *cohors* if infantry, an *ala* if cavalry) and subdivided respectively into centuries and troops. For most of the time they operated as independent garrisons of forts and fortlets, deployed at convenient intervals across the frontier areas of a province, but during campaigns of conquest or defence they would be brigaded together in groups, to act alongside the legionaries, often bearing the brunt of attack in battle as being the more expendable arm.

Temporary Field Monuments

Of the temporary encampments which housed both types when operating together in the field there are more than twenty-five examples in Perthshire. Consisting originally of only a simple rampart thrown up from the spoil of an external ditch and designed perhaps for use during a single night's stopover on the march, such ephemeral enclosures would soon have tumbled into decay. That so many have been recorded within the area is therefore remarkable and it is almost miraculous that in three or four instances significant traces of these earthworks still survive above ground. Before the agricultural improvements in the later 18th century twice as many must have been readily recognisable and from the plans of William Roy we know that at Lintrose and Dalginross, almost the whole of the perimeter could be easily recognised. Nowadays we must rely on their cropmark traces being observed and photographed from the air.

The camps vary greatly in size and plan, although several discrete categories can be distinguished. The largest sites, at Ardoch, Innerpeffray and Grassy Walls, average about 50 ha in area and are mostly a regular parallelogram in plan with long sides half as long again as the short. Almost identical in plan but of half the capacity at 25 ha, there is a group of six camps (again Ardoch and Innerpeffray but also Scone Park, Lintrose, Forteviot and Longforgan) which, like the previous set, indicate the daily staging-points of vast battle-groups advancing inexorably through hostile territory. Too many variables exist to permit a precise calculation of the size of the respective armies housed by each set of camps but, accepting an allocation of 8–9 ha for the marching legion, the smaller camps could have accommodated 15–20,000 men, the larger at least 40,000. Such enormous forces, which could not have been assembled without either straining the military resources of the province or demanding heavy contribution from other provinces, point to campaigns of the utmost importance, requiring authorisation at the highest level.

A similar context must be sought for the camps at Dunning and Carey, a day's march apart on the south bank of the lower Earn. Only a little smaller than examples of the largest series at about 45 ha, they differ from the latter in being markedly less elongated on plan, a probable indication of a much earlier date. Such structural traits can be very important in helping the archaeologist to place these briefly-occupied enclosures in their correct period, datable artefacts being unlikely to be recovered from them. In this respect, the character of a camp's gateway can be particularly significant and special mention should be made of the camp at Dalginross. Here, at each gate, the camp's rampart terminals were extended in a quarter-circle (*clavicula*) – externally on one side, internally on the other – to impose an oblique approach to the narrows of the entrance, forcing a right-handed attacker to expose the side not protected by his shield. As an additional defence an outer traverse extended outward slantwise from the defences in front of the internal *clavicula*. Gate defences of this type, known as Stracathro gates after the camp-site in Angus where they were first recorded from the air, originated in the later 1st century AD and fell out of use in Britain shortly thereafter. They are thought to represent the 'signature' of one particular legionary battle-group, although the clustered distribution of Stracathro-camps and their variation in size (Dalginross at

about 9 ha has only half the capacity of its nearest neighbour at Callander)
make it clear that they mark the temporary bases of legions at varying
strength and different phases of operations.

Of the remaining camps, two groups call for comment: the first,
consisting of *c*. 5–13 ha examples, appears to represent evidence of early
probing operations in moderate force from the passes of the Ochils to the
upper reaches of the Earn. The latter is a heterogeneous group of temporary
works too small to have held a force of any size and perhaps, like St
Madoes, housing specialist units with specific short-lived tasks during the
campaign itself. Alternatively, they may have been associated, like the
smallest camp at Ardoch or Steeds Stalls, with constructional or extractive
activities in the post-conquest phase.

Communications and Surveillance Systems

The processes by which the army moved from active campaigning in
temporary works to stable occupation in forts and fortlets are as yet little
understood. If, as seems likely, there was an initial phase of tentative
deployment of garrisons, while the longer-term needs of the situation were
assessed locally, Perthshire offers only a few isolated instances and it is
difficult, if not impossible, to distinguish these from the changes that may
have resulted from gradually evolving frontier policy as a whole. Sooner or
later, however, a regular communications system would have been
required to link the various garrisons and once that was in place changes
would have been less readily entertained. The system comprised a
metalled road and a suitably disposed network of watch-towers and roadside posts manned by small detachments drawn from the adjacent
garrisons. Traces of the main trunk road that was driven north-eastward
from the Forth survive over much of its course from the regional boundary
to only a few km short of the crossing of the Tay at Bertha. The sector
which runs along the flat summit of the Gask Ridge, a little to the south-
west of Perth, is particularly impressive, its cambered alignment still
traceable along modern tracks and minor roads for more than 8 km.
Elsewhere, air reconnaissance has identified its path – especially clear
where the quarry-pits that produced the road-metalling appear as rows of
cropmarked dots on either side of the now-vanished causeway.

Throughout this sector there are also some splendid examples of roadside towers, in fact more here than yet discovered in any part of Britain,
their close spacing paralleled only on the Roman frontier in Upper
Germany. So far, about eleven such sites have been recorded on the Ridge,
seven surviving as visible earthworks; the rest are now betrayed solely by
the penannular cropmark, 15 m in diameter, that denotes their enclosing
ditch. Originally, a rectangular timber tower stood at the centre of the

interior, often protected by a rampart closely following the inner scarp of the ditch, together with a counterscarp bank. These towers, which are rarely more than a Roman mile (1480 m) apart, often much less, with each in full view of its neighbours, would have served to provide intensive surveillance along the road they adjoined. For signalling duties a much more widely spaced pattern of towers would have sufficed. The surveillance appears to have extended along the road to the south-west, between the River Earn and Strathallan. In that sector the towers appear to be set at regular intervals of almost exactly three-fifths of a Roman mile and, although of roughly the same size, some of them are enclosed by double ditches. One example of the latter type, which is overlain by the eastern defences of the largest marching-camp at Ardoch at a point where both structures survive above ground, provides an excellent comparison with those of the Gask Ridge group.

Surprisingly, both of the Perthshire watch towers representing isolated lookout points are also amazingly well preserved. That at the southern mouth of the Sma Glen serves the more lowly placed fort of Fendoch, while the tower occupying the summit of the Black Hill of Meikleour appears to be related to the security needs of the legionary base at Inchtuthil. An even closer functional link exists between certain watch-towers and the next largest type of roadside post, the small fortlet. The splendid example of the latter category at Kaims Castle, on the watershed between Strathallan and Strathearn, has long been known to archaeologists. Excavation of this double-ditched site in 1901 confirmed that it covered about 0.1 ha over the rampart but failed to discover structural evidence of its purpose. However, the tower which may be presumed to have surmounted its single gateway must have supplied a necessary link in the regularly-spaced system which extended south to Ardoch and beyond. Almost exactly ten standard watch-tower intervals along the road to the south-west, aerial survey in 1983 revealed the cropmarks of the closely comparable fortlet of Glenbank, subsequent excavation uncovering part of the wooden gate-tower that would have continued the chain of communication. Rarely can Roman archaeology furnish so extensive or so completely interlocking a system of installations as is illustrated here in Perthshire.

Larger Garrison Posts

The permanent structures which have been described above were manned by relatively small detachments. The maximum possible capacity of the fortlets was probably a century, about 80 men, for whose normal barrack-accommodation there is just enough space in the interior, provided that the building was constructed in two units, facing each other across a central street. In the towers, ten men would have been a crowd. Larger fortlets, garrisoned by slightly stronger detachments, are known in various parts of Scotland. In Perthshire, the example is the site at Cargill, on the left bank of the River Isla, immediately east of its confluence with the Tay. Discovered from the air as early as 1941, it is roughly four times as big as Kaims Castle and theoretically capable of holding a garrison of almost 300 troops, but without excavation that is impossible to determine. Its most significant feature is the curious fashion in which its double ditches unite at each gateway to form an inward-pointing 'parrot's beak', a device intended to provide extra defensive strength at the entrance. 'Parrot's beaks' are now known at many fort-sites throughout Scotland but, surprisingly, the nearest examples are to be found only 250 m to the north-east, at the much larger fort of Hatton of Cargill (discovered from the air in 1947). Covering almost 2.0 ha over the rampart (almost four times as big as the fortlet), the larger Cargill could have housed a garrison of considerable strength – one thousand men and more – but again, without excavation no definite statement can be made about either its garrison or its role. Traces of its street pattern indicate that it faced north-west, on which side the triple-ditched defences were continued down to the bank of the Isla – an indication perhaps that it guarded a bridge or ford across the river.

In contrast, much more is known about those permanent forts which have been excavated, although the earlier the examination the less useful the results. The multi-period site at Ardoch, examined in 1897–8, was found to have contained timber and stone buldings of three or four phases of construction but the incomplete nature of the evidence precludes identification of the garrisons, save that at one period legionary troops could have been involved. The importance of the site is impressively represented, not so much by its size, about 2.5 ha, as by the depth of its magnificently preserved defences, the multiple ditches on each surviving front emphasising the use and re-use of a crucial position at the crossing of the River Knaik. Combined with the remains of the temporary camps and the enigmatic enclosures immediately to the north, as well as the invisible earlier fort-site to the north-east, the earthworks of the fort at Ardoch constitute one of the most valuable Roman field monuments found on any frontier of the Empire.

In Fendoch (excavated in 1938) and Strageath (excavated from 1973–86), Perthshire offers a different kind of treasure, forts for which almost the entire internal layout can be reconstructed. Of similar size, each occupying 9 to about 1.8 ha and both reduced by cultivation to a levelled but distinctively shaped platform, the forts nevertheless differ sharply in plan and development. The elongated rectangle of Fendoch encloses only one period of occupation, during which, as its ten barrack-blocks suggest, it was the base of an infantry cohort one thousand strong. Strageath, on the other hand, almost square on plan, represents the superimposed remains of three periods of occupation with their defences. In the first period it contained twelve barracks housing elements of two auxiliary regiments (one of them part-mounted) and a detachment of legionaries. A similarly mixed garrison of almost 1000 men appears to have been present in the final period but in between the unit-strength was reduced to 500. Perhaps more impressive than the complex organisational changes which such details illustrate is the recurrent uniformity of building and street-plan of the larger installations: the tripartite division of the interior with barracks ranged tightly along the axial streets of the forward and rear areas and in the central range official buildings and senior officers' quarters fronting the main cross-street.

Sadly, no structural details can be seen within the largest example of this category, Bertha, at the confluence of Tay and Almond. That the 3.8 ha enclosure which guards the double river-crossing has never revealed, even to aerial survey, the slightest traces of internal structures invites queries about its character, specifically whether it may not be merely the annexe of a fort that once lay to the south-east but was almost totally swept away by a disastrous flood in the early 13th century.

Legionary Bases

Happily, exceptional size is not always combined with uncertainty. The largest permanent military bases in Scotland, both legionary fortresses situated in Perthshire, have been excavated in relatively recent times. Inchtuthil, on the left bank of the Tay some 10 km below Dunkeld and more than 20 ha in area, was designed to be the central strong point of the northern frontier at the end of the first conquest of Caledonia. Barely complete and in existence for only a handful of years, its standard plan embraces the sixty-four timber-built barracks, the workshops, hospital, stores and training-halls which were briefly home to men of the Twentieth Legion. On the plateau beside the fortress lie the remains of enclosures, construction-camps, senior officers' quarters and outlying defence-works that combine with the base itself to present an unrivalled vignette of the discipline and expertise of the Roman military machine.

The comparatively short-lived legionary base at Carpow on the south shore of the estuary of the Tay, to the west of Newburgh, represents by contrast the climax of the very latest Roman occupation of Scotland. Only 12 ha in area, it probably housed detachments, totalling perhaps 3000 men, from two legions, the Sixth and the Second. Only cropmark traces survive of their timber barracks but the buttressed granary, headquarters building and commander's residence in the central range are the most handsome examples of Roman masonry in Scotland.

HISTORICAL INTERPRETATION

Carpow represents an ideal location from which to begin a brief historical rearticulation of the foregoing structural bones. It was built *c.* AD 211 after about three campaigns directly commanded by either the emperor Septimius Severus or his son Caracalla. At the head of enormous armies, they had advanced from York to the Forth and thence past Stirling to Strathearn, Strathmore and Gowrie, as well as the coast of Angus; the initial ominously steady progress of their forces is marked by the 25 ha camps leading from Ardoch to Lintrose and from Forteviot probably to Longforgan, crossing the Tay opposite Carpow itself, the next phase by camps of 50 ha aiming solely for Strathmore. The legionary detachments later based at Carpow, with no Roman help closer than Cramond on the Forth, probably straddled the boundary between two subgroups of the Caledonian confederacy – the *Maeatae* to the south and the core of Caledonia to the north; both were shortly to become known to history as the Picts.

The previous period of occupation, the Antonine (AD 140–163) appears to have been preceded by no northern campaigning on the scale of that of Severus. But Lollius Urbicus, the governor of Britannia who won laurels of victory for the emperor Antoninus Pius shortly after his accession in AD 138, evidently based his overall plans on the same territorial assessment. Policy had determined that Roman and barbarian were to be separated by a wall of turf on the Forth-Clyde isthmus but practicality dictated that the peoples living beyond the frontier in Strathallan and Strathearn should not lack strong military control, hence the chain of forts whose links in Perthshire were Ardoch, Strageath and Bertha. The importance of the last site at the head of the trunk road, anticipating the role envisaged for Carpow, underlines the likelihood of it being a more complex site than has been previously imagined. The evidence of excavation at various sites indicates that these northern forts were drastically remodelled at some point within the Antonine period but precisely when and why cannot yet be determined.

The earliest occupation, the Flavian, is by far the most complicated to understand and, not surprisingly since new ground was being broken, it followed an elaborate series of campaigns. The main historical evidence is provided by the historian Tacitus, whose account of the life of the contemporary governor, Agricola, records five Scottish campaigns. The first, probably in AD 79, brought Roman troops to the banks of the Tay, an advance which may be marked by the 45 ha camps at Dunning and Carey, surely holding the bulk of the forces available in Britain. If this line of march continued to Carpow, as has been argued, its objective may have been the early establishment of a coastal base for the Roman fleet; in that case, somewhere in its vicinity we should seek the location of Ptolemy's *Orrea* (*Horrea Classis*, 'storebase of the fleet'). The construction of permanent forts in these parts would not have begun until AD 82, when we are told that Agricola, having temporarily confined operations to southern and central Scotland, advanced once more into Caledonia, his troops divided into three unequal battle-groups. It is just possible that the 9–14 ha marching camps at Dornock, Strageath, Ardoch and Dalginross indicate the theatre for this action (which included a close-run battle with the enemy).

The following year saw Agricola's total destruction of the confederate Caledonian forces at the battle of Mons Graupius, probably somewhere beyond the Mounth and with that the deployment of permanent garrisons could begin. Within Perthshire and on the northern frontier generally, the various structural elements are clear but their relationship to each other still has to be elucidated. Forming the central spine was the line of road from the Forth to the Tay, along which the close-set series of fortlets and watch-towers maintained a frontier-like system of surveillance. This system was stiffened (and in part manned) by garrisons of considerable strength at Ardoch, Strageath and Bertha and beyond them to the north-east a different pattern of strongpoints ensured the security of Strathmore, beginning with the fort and fortlet at Cargill.

In addition to these elements, the north-western flank was protected by a screen of glen-blocking garrisons (represented in Perthshire by Dalginross and Fendoch) and by the important decision to base a legion at Inchtuthil. There may be debate about precisely when or by whom these individual elements were built; forts displaying such idiosyncratic structural features as inturned entrances or 'parrot's beak' ditch-terminals may betray the identity of their builders (the 'parrot's beak' forts could have originated with the legion also responsible for the 'Stracathro' camps). But about their combined significance there should be little doubt. They and their successors exemplify the consistent Roman response, not only to the 'Perthshire' question but also to the perennial problems of dividing and controlling the peoples of any frontier area, at any period. Whether separating *Venicones* from *Vacomagi*, or *Caledonii* from *Maeatae*, whether representing the stability of a conquered province or the fluidity of the campaign, the Roman monuments of Perthshire provide in their rich diversity a microcosm of frontier dynamics throughout the Empire.

Four
THE DARK AGES

The centuries following the end of the Roman activity in Scotland saw Perthshire as an integral part of Pictland where Christianity was gradually gaining a fragile foothold. In the 9th century, perhaps with the help of Viking allies, the Scots were able to achieve political power with the establishment of the mac Alpin dynasty.

Early historians have presented the Picts as an enigmatic people, distinctive yet shadowy, who occupied eastern Scotland in post-Roman times. Many writers have portrayed them as woad-daubed savages battling against militarily superior Roman forces and have attempted to see them as a separate race with their own language and culture, very different from other groups in northern Europe at this time. This myth arose from the limited evidence available to the early historians, particularly the symbol stones and place-names which occur north of the Forth-Clyde line. Extensive research over the past forty years means that far more is known about the Picts than any other group during the Dark Ages in what is now Scotland. The Picts were the direct descendants of the Celtic populations who were moving into Scotland from as early as 700 BC. Furthermore, they shared many common features with other contemporaneous tribal groups in northern Europe and there can be little doubt that they were as advanced culturally and economically as these groups.

The first historical mention of the Picts occurs in the writings of Eumenius in AD 297, the term *Picti* being applied to the people living north of the Antonine Wall. No clue is given as to the origin or meaning of the term and herein lies the root of the enigma – a label has suddenly been put on a people. While some historians in the past have attempted to find origins for Picts in various parts of Europe, there seems no reason to do this. There is no evidence of new people moving into the area since the early pre-Roman Iron Age and it must be assumed that the people the Romans called Picti were simply the natural descendants of the pre-Roman local population. Whether Picti is a Latinisation of the name these people used themselves is an open question.

Other literary sources consist mainly of annals, genealogies and law books which need careful professional interpretation to separate fact from legend. Most are in Latin, often written far from Pictland and record an oral tradition from earlier centuries. Used intelligently, however, they can provide tantalising insights and pointers, as in the case of Forteviot, to Pictish times.

The most visible heritage of the Picts is the stone monuments bearing incised and relief symbols, hunting and battle scenes, Christian crosses and sometimes Biblical allegories. Although many stones have been lost in the intervening centuries and the destruction of these monuments at the time of the Reformation was unequal throughout the area, the present distribution (Figure 5) gives a general impression of the areas associated with Pictish activity. In the simplest classification these monuments can be used in an overlapping chronological sequence in three classes:

Figure 5

Distribution of Pictish Symbol Stones

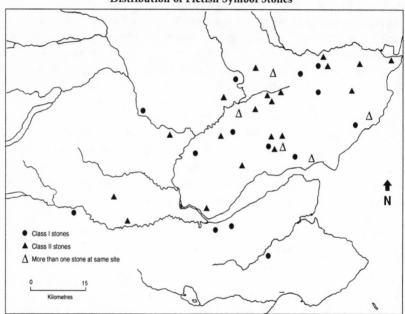

Class I	Rough, undressed boulders bearing incised geometric or zoomorphic symbols only.
Class II	Dressed stones with symbols, as above, standing out in relief and frequently incorporating a Christian cross on one side. Battle and hunting scenes are frequently a feature of this class.
Class III	Stones which do not include 'Pictish symbols'. In addition to the Christian cross they frequently include elaborately decorated motifs, which can sometimes be attributed to Biblical allegories.

The sequence is thus in three chronological overlapping stages, with Class I representing a pre-Christian phase. Class II is representative of the period when Christianity was becoming an increasingly powerful influence on society, although some of the ancient symbolism still remains. Class III covers a very broad group of monuments, some of which may date as late as the 12th century. By the Class III stage all Pictish symbols had disappeared and Christianity appears to have held complete sway. Considerable argument still arises over the dating of Class I stones. Many see the symbolism as unique to Pictland, but animal art was common in Europe in the 1st millenium. Artistic parallels to accurately datable evidence, such as the early Christian manuscripts, are somewhat tenuous and some authorities argue that Class I stones could commence as early as the 5th century, while art historians favour the second half of the 7th. The function of the stones is equally debatable and different stones may have had different purposes. Some may have been territorial markers; some may have been grave markers, although few have been excavated in direct association with burials; some may have had a commemorative function, notably the picture stones, while others may have played a religious role.

In contrast to neighbouring Angus, Perthshire has relatively few symbol stones (Figure 5). Excellent examples of Class I occur at Abernethy and Dunkeld (the Horseman Stone) with others from Cargill, Bruceton near Alyth and Struan. The most comprehensive collection of Class II and Class III stones dating from the 8th and 10th centuries is displayed in Meigle Museum. A brief description of two of the stones will indicate not only the range of information that can be gleaned from the study of the stones – Pictish dress, ornaments, weapons and equestrian equipment – but also symbolism which must have been well understood by the Picts but is lost to us today.

Meigle Stone No 1

Upright cross-slab. Cross richly decorated. Panels between the arms of the cross contain animals both real and fantastic. The other side of the stone incorporates six Pictish symbols, including the peculiar 'Pictish beast' as well as a serpent and Z-rod. A picture section shows five horsemen accompanied by a hound.

Meigle Stone No 2

Cross-slab. The cross consists of four equal arms set in a circle at the top of the stone. Below are three pairs of animals. The reverse side shows Daniel in an attitude of prayer with three horsemen above him. The upper horseman is most clearly defined as a bearded, cloaked figure with a sword hanging from his belt and carrying a spear. The horse is bridled and has a saddle cloth.

Three other stones merit individual mention. The superb 8th-century cross-slab at Dunfallandy (NO 946565) depicts a framed, finely decorated cross supported by fantastic animals and winged figures. On the reverse is a cluttered, framed assemblage dominated by two seated clerical figures facing a small cross above a horseman. Crowded around them are two crescents with V-rods, two Pictish beasts, a double disc symbol, a hammer, anvil and tongs.

At Fowlis Wester (NN 927240) a replica of a huge cross-slab over 3 m high stands in the centre of the village. The somewhat weathered original has been moved inside the church. It is the reverse side which is more interesting, with two horsemen and animals and an unparalleled depiction of a man leading a belled cow followed by six bearded men walking abreast. A late 8th or 9th-century date is suggested for this stone. A second better preserved 9th-century stone is also to be found inside the church. This shows a ring-headed cross with two clerics seated on ornately carved chairs. The standing clerics also have richly decorated robes. Note the Jonah and the whale motif at the top of the cross.

The Dupplin Cross (NO 050189), dating from the late 9th century, is one of the few free-standing crosses remaining in Eastern Scotland. Its historical importance is controversial in that in addition to the elaborately decorated cross it also displays horsemen and foot soldiers. Dating from after the establishment of the mac Alpin dynasty and within clear view of the royal site at Forteviot, some believe that it commemorates the Scottish ascendancy. At the time of writing the question of moving the stone to prevent further weathering is subject to debate.

Inscriptions on Pictish stones and related artefacts occur in a number of languages, including Latin, Gaelic and Pictish and in a number of alphabets including Latin, Runic and Ogam. The most important stone bearing an inscription from Perthshire is the Inchyra stone, now exhibited in Perth Museum along with the superb Class II stone from nearby St Madoes. Ogam is a monumental script, which was probably developed in Southern Ireland in the 4th or 5th century, the letters being formed by a series of strokes set against or across a line or stem. In Pictland the Ogams most likely date from the 7th century or later. The Inchyra Ogam is difficult to date as the stone, which appears to be associated with a burial, may have been re-used on more than one occasion.

While there can be no doubt that the Pictish symbol stones represent points of human activity, solid archaeological evidence of Pictish settlements remains extremely limited. The most numerous sites are souterrains – long, narrow, curving, stone-lined underground storage chambers which are the only surviving feature of larger complexes which consisted of one or more surface buildings making up a farmstead. Newmill (NO 084324), near Perth, is the best example of a modern excavation of such a site in Perthshire, where a souterrain was shown to be closely associated with a large timber house, some 17.6 m in diameter. Radio carbon dates suggest Newmill was built in the 1st century AD and abandoned in the late 2nd or early 3rd century.

If the interpretation of souterrains as storage chambers is correct, this suggests that they must have belonged to wealthy farmsteads generating a considerable seasonal surplus. As the known distribution shows (Figure 6), there is a close correlation between the distribution of souterrains and potentially rich grain-growing lands. Current dating evidence suggests that souterrains are characteristic of the 1st and early 2nd centuries AD, after which many of them seem to have been deliberately filled in. In this respect they are often seen as being proto-Pictish rather than truly Pictish.

Figure 6

Distribution of Souterrains

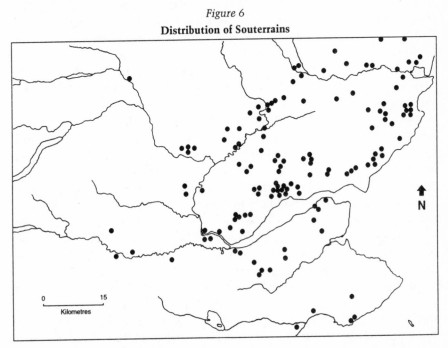

Three reasons may account for the paucity of domestic Pictish structures. It may simply be that they have not yet been discovered; that they were sited in the best quality land which has been cultivated throughout succeeding centuries, removing all trace of Pictish building or that they were largely timber-built, as in the case of Newmill and little trace remains. Further evidence of the extensive use of constructional timber comes from the numerous crannogs or lake dwellings in the area, notably on Loch Tay. These defended homesteads were sited on small islands, sometimes augmented natural features, sometimes entirely artificial and frequently linked to the shore by a stone or wooden walkway. Invariably, good quality agricultural land lies on the adjacent shore. Radio-carbon dates for the excavated site at Oakbank (NN 723442) suggest Pictish occupation in the 4th and 5th centuries.

Aerial photography has identified a potential large timber hall on the banks of the Tay near Scone and another in Upper Strathearn and while it is tempting to see them as the centres of substantial Pictish estates, this cannot be proven without detailed excavation, particularly as a similar site identified from aerial photographic evidence has proved to be Neolithic in date in an excavated example.

At a higher level, manuscript sources point to royal centres at Scone and Forteviot. Although there is no archaeological evidence for the precise location of the royal buildings at either location, Class II and Class III stones are recorded from Forteviot along with part of an arch richly carved with human and animal figures recovered from the river nearby and now in the Royal Museum of Scotland. The arch, presumably part of a doorway leading into an important stone building, dates from the late 9th or early 10th centuries, well after royal power at Forteviot had passed from the Picts to the Scots.

As in other parts of Scotland, Perthshire is beginning to produce some evidence of Pictish and later Scottish fortifications. Dundurn, a small hill fort in Upper Strathearn, guarding this major route to the west, is mentioned in the Annals of Iona for AD 683 and excavation has proved occupation from the 7th to the 10th centuries. It may have declined in importance after the union of the Picts and Scots. Without excavation it is impossible even to speculate how many of the other hill forts of Perthshire were either built by the Picts or are even early Iron Age forts re-used by the Picts. Small ring forts are a common feature of Glen Lyon and Strathtummel. Many are located on non-defensive sites and would seem to be little more than the fortified homesteads of wealthy farmers. Excavation suggests a range of dates. The site at Litigan produced radio carbon dates in the 9th and 10th centuries, suggesting occupation after the union of the Picts and Scots, while that at Aldclune suggested Pictish re-use of a pre-Roman structure. Aldclune, overlooking the River Garry, is also notable as one of the few Perthshire sites to have produced metalwork dating from the Pictish period, in this case a superb silver gilt penannular brooch. One, or possibly two hanging bowls are noted from Tummel Bridge and a silver-plated bronze strap-end from Dundurn. Although the few metalwork finds from Perthshire need to be treated with caution when taken with finds including hoards from other areas, they suggest that the Picts had metalworking skills and artistic abilities as sophisticated as any other contemporaneous groups in Northern Europe.

Current evidence suggests that Pictish graves took a variety of forms, most of which have an extensive distribution far beyond Pictland. The long cist enclosing an extended body in a slab-lined compartment was certainly part of the Pictish tradition as well as that of the pre-Roman Iron Age. Before modern dating techniques, many Pictish long cists may have been assigned to the latter period, in part explaining the relative paucity of Pictish graves. Long cists covered by kerbed, frequently now termed platform cairns, both circular and rectangular, are a feature of Pictland with several examples in eastern Perthshire. Earthen barrows surrounded by a circular ditch are another common form. Perhaps surprisingly despite the fact that the manuscript sources suggest considerable Early Christian activity in Perthshire, no typical Early Christian cemetery has so far been located.

Christianity was an extremely powerful force in the later Pictish and Scottish societies in Perthshire, as is clearly demonstrated by the quality of many of the Class II and Class III stones. However, little is known about when, from where and by what processes Christianity was introduced to Southern Pictland. The hypothesis that early Christianity was spread into the area by monks moving northwards from Ninian's AD 397 foundation at Whithorn no longer receives much support. This appears to leave the field open to Columban monks from Iona, founded in AD 563 or 565. However, it was Columban monks from Iona who founded Lindisfarne in Northumbria in 635 and Anglican influences spread northwards from there into Scotland until the Angles finally suffered a major defeat at the Battle of Nechtansmere, near Forfar, in 685. Could the monastery noted at Abernethy in the 7th century be a Columban foundation of Anglican origins? It had become an episcopal centre by the early 8th century, though this was of short duration as Dunkeld, also probably an early Columban monastery, became the ecclesiastical centre of the unified kingdom of Picts and Scots.

At this juncture it is worth noting the Perthshire distribution of the so-called Class IV stones – simply defined as cross-slabs bearing no other ornament. Without an archaeological context these stones are almost impossible to date, but there is no reason to doubt that at least some of them could date back to the mid 7th century. Apart from the example from Abernethy they have a distribution which relates to the routes through the Highlands to the west coast, *viz* three crosses at Balquhidder and single examples from Dull; St Bride's Chapel, Loch Lubnaig; St Blane's Chapel;, Lochearnhead; St Fillan's Chapel near Dundurn and Suie in Glen Dochart. While these Early Christian sites, on distributional grounds, would appear to be Iona foundations, it should be noted that by AD 716 Northumbria was regarded as the primary centre of the Columban Church, having displaced Iona. Indeed it was to Ceolfrith, abbot of Monkwearmouth, that King

Nectan wrote seeking advice about Easter and requesting masons to build a church in the Roman manner. Nothing is known of the scale of the Early Christian settlements. Many may have had only one or two monks, while others, such as Dunkeld, are likely to have been larger, wealthy communities. Dunkeld atracted Viking raiders and therefore knowledge of its wealth must have been widespread. Dunkeld also became the home for the Scottish share of the Columban relics (the remainder were sent to Kells in Ireland) in 849 when they were removed from Iona to protect them from the increasing Norse threat. A few years later they were moved to Kilrimont, later to become St Andrews.

The 8th century witnessed the spread of the *Celi De* (servants of God) or Culdee movement from Ireland. They developed as a reformed group and set out as a religious elite. Some groups, probably including those who established themselves at Inchaffray, lived a very strict, almost hermit-like existence, while other groups appear to have become little more than secular clerks serving bishops' churches rather than true monastic communities, perhaps reflecting the religious decline which appears to have affected Scottish monasticism by the early 10th century. Many of the high church offices had become the hereditary perks of the most powerful families. At Dunkeld, for example, Abbot Crinan, who was killed in battle in 1045, was married to Beathag, daughter of Malcolm II and was father of Duncan I. Later a son of Malcolm III and Margaret was both Earl of Fife and abbot of Dunkeld. The Culdee centre at Muthill appears to have been closely linked to the major ecclesiastical foundation at Dunblane.

Not all communities of secular priests were associated with diocesan centres. Many of these houses, often, but not always Culdee, served a considerable surrounding area. Certain identification of these centres is fraught with difficulty and one can do little more than suggest that Dull, Glen Dochart, Kilspindie, Kirkmichael (Strathardle), Madderty Melginch and Methven are strong candidates (Figure 7).

The Picts spoke a p-Celtic language related to that of Wales and Cornwall and distinct from the q-Celtic of the Irish and the Scots. Elements of that p-Celtic language remain in some of the modern-day place-names, including *aber*–confluence, *carden*–thicket, *lanerc*–clearing, *pert*–copse and, most common of all, the prefix *pit* as found in Pitlochry, Pitcarmick, Pitfour, Pitmurthly and many other Perthshire place-names. There is still some debate as to the exact period when *pit* was a place-name-forming prefix. It can be shown that it does not occur in areas of Scotland where the Norse language became dominant in the 9th and 10th centuries and that the suffix element is usually Gaelic in origin. This would suggest that the name-forming period was in the bilingual phase immediately following the political union of the Picts and the Scots. However, it is possible that many of the *pit* names could be earlier and only the descriptive part of the name in Pictish has been replaced by its Gaelic equivalent. It is generally agreed that pit itself means a portion or share, but there is controversy as to its significance in its place-name context. Some authorities hypothesise its use as a land division with the shire superimposed upon a series of *pit* units. Others argue that it simply means farm or settlement, while some take the view that many of them are associated with the taking in of new land associated with the rising population, possibly contributed to by immigration after the political union of the Picts and the Scots.

Figure 7

Possible sites of early Christian activity

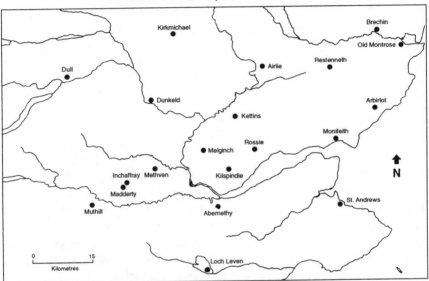

Whatever the original context of these names there is general agreement that they are related to land in use and, as such, may give a more accurate indication of the types of sites which were settled than do the sculptured stones, some of which may have been transported in post-Pictish times (it is possible that a number of *pit* names may also have migrated through time). *Pit* place-names are clearly related to the soils which would have had the greatest potential within the agricultural technology of Pictish and later Scottish times, suggesting that settlement was concentrated in well-drained, sheltered areas with considerable potential for grain growing within a mixed farming economy (Figure 8).

At the present state of knowledge, the historical, archaeological and place-name evidence all point to the emergence of a hierarchical structure

Figure 8
Distribution of *Pit* place-names

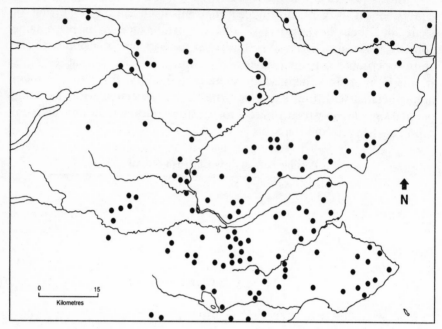

in social, land and settlement organisation during Pictish times. While Class I stones are widely dispersed, a distinct clustering, as at Meigle and Forteviot, appears with Class II and particularly Class III. Archaeology suggests powerful defensive centres such as Dundurn were in use by the 7th century. Thus it is argued that by the later Pictish period various foci of control or power centres can be adduced – Dundurn, Forteviot, Abernethy, Scone and Dunkeld being typical examples.

After the union of the Pictish and Scottish kingdoms under the mac Alpin dynasty in the mid-9th century the Scots became the dominant power, submerging the Picts in Perthshire. Gaelic replaced Pictish as the language of the people. It is perhaps surprising that when we know so much about the Picts we know perhaps less about the first 150 years of Scottish rule. As has been shown above, many of the trends emerging in Pictland flowed smoothly into the Scottish period. Class II and Class III sculptured stones continued to be produced and the church remained a potent force in the landscape. The role of hillforts may have declined as military techniques changed but some of the power centres continued to be the core of human activity, such as Forteviot, Dunkeld and Scone. Perhaps the most obvious change still visible today is in the place-names. Most Perthshire place-names today are Gaelic in origin, a process which started in the 9th century. Few can be dated within a narrow time-band, though the prefix *Bal* is believed to have been a name-forming element mainly between AD 800 and 1000 (Figure 9). These, like *pit*, are located in areas of good agricultural land suitable for arable cultivation and are presumed to represent large, mixed farming estates. The second element in the name frequently has agricultural connotations. The emergence of these large estates in the early Scottish period is suggestive of some land reorganisation, but at present there is insufficient evidence to prove it.

While the Picts and the Scots are the dominant characters of the Dark Age stage of Perthshire, the Vikings also play a small but important part. Indeed, Kenneth mac Alpin may have had the support of Viking groups from the west in his ultimate conquest of the Picts. There can be little doubt that the wealth of lowland Perthshire and its power centres was attractive to Viking raiders. In AD 839 Eóganan, whom legend says was based at Forteviot, was killed in a battle between Norsemen and the men of Fortrui (Strathearn). The slaughter was said to be beyond count and may have greatly weakened the Picts in their future conflicts with the Scots. The historical sources also record a major raid on Dunkeld by King Ivar II of Dublin in AD 903, showing its importance both as a religious and power centre.

Equally important is the evidence for Scandinavian trade and settlement. A late 8th – early 9th century Viking grave is recorded from Errol,

Figure 9

Distribution of *Bal* place-names

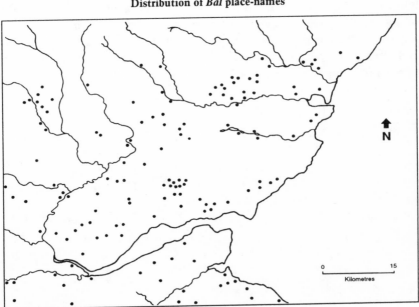

accompanied by a pair of tortoise brooches indicating a high status Norse lady – certainly unlikely to be part of a raiding group. A number of place-names also incorporate Scandinavian names indicating land holdings. Inchture (earliest reference Inchthore 1163X64) incorporates the personal name Thor, while Inchturfin is recorded near Coupar Angus *c.* 1150 and Incheturfy at Kinclaven *c.* 1310. Both the latter include the Norse personal name Torfinn. A further group of Scandinavian names occur as witnesses to charters in the Longforgan area between 1150 and 1200. These include Thor of Fowlis, Ulfechillus the Smith, Ketel of Longforgan, Svein of Longforgan and Magnus, son of Colban. These place-names and personal names confirm high-status people holding land, not only in the eastern margins of Perthshire close to Dundee but far inland.

When viewed in conjunction with similar evidence from Fife and Angus, there appear to be two periods associated with Scandinavian-type settle-ment – an early period in the 10th century when it is possible that grants of land were given in return for mercenary activities and a second period in the 12th century, which is more related to trading activities with the Anglo-Scandinavian settlers in north-east England. A related late 10th-century find from Perthshire is the hog-back grave cover in the Meigle collection. The origin centre for hog-back stones is thought to be in north-east England, possibly Yorkshire.

Perthshire lies at the heart of what is now Scotland and, though it was one of the formative areas of the emerging kingdom, the lack of documentary sources and limited archaeological excavation mean that knowledge of the period between the departure of the Romans and AD 1000 is fragmentary and the evidence often capable of more than one inter-pretation. There is a rich existing heritage of archaeological sites and finds and further excavation, supported by interdisciplinary teams, is needed to unravel the long list of questions which remain.

FIVE
THE MIDDLE AGES

INTRODUCTION

For the purpose of this chapter the period from 1072 until the Reformation of 1559 has been chosen as the most representative of the Middle Ages in Perthshire. The information presented is discussed, where possible, from an archaeological rather than a historical perspective and is an attempt to describe everyday life in medieval Perthshire.

ENVIRONMENTAL BACKGROUND

The landscape of Perthshire today has not changed markedly since medieval times although it is worth reviewing the evidence in order to describe it. The extent of the tree cover was fairly similar to that of today – the only difference being the types of tree present. There was less Scots pine and greater areas of oakwood, particularly on marginal land. The most marked difference from today was probably the extensive cover of bog and marshland.

The flooding of the Tay as experienced in recent years was also quite marked in medieval times. For example, in 1209 Perth castle was washed away and those burgesses attending a council meeting were forced to either escape in small boats or to retire to the upper floors of buildings on the High Street. This periodic flooding of Perth is one of the factors contributing to the high preservative qualities of archaeological deposits in the town (see below). Between AD 1000 and 1200 the climate was much warmer than it is today and therefore crop yields were much higher but after c. 1300 things changed for the worse with the onset of the Little Ice Age, which lasted for nearly five centuries.

HISTORICAL BACKGROUND

In 1072 William the Conqueror set foot in Scotland for the only time at the ancient round tower of Abernethy, in Perthshire. He was met by Malcolm III, king of Scots, who 'made peace . . . and gave hostages and was his man' (Lynch 1991, 75). This meeting of the two kings ensured that there was never a Norman invasion of Scotland as such. In some ways this is unfortunate as it means that we have no Domesday Book for Scotland

and our understanding of the country in the 11th and early 12th centuries is therefore very poor. It is not until the succession of David I in 1124 that the picture becomes slightly clearer. This is largely due to the appearance of the burghs and the influence of new religious orders, namely the Tironensians, Cistercians and Benedictines.

URBAN SETTLEMENT

Perthshire has only two medieval burghs, Auchterarder and Perth.

Auchterarder

Auchterarder is thought to have been a royal burgh from at least the mid-13th century. No charter of erection survives but it has been claimed that the proximity of the settlement to a royal seat (the castle) accounted for its status. The nature and layout of the burgh of Auchterarder remains unknown largely due to the lack of archaeological work that has been carried out there. Its position on a major east-west routeway is the reason for its existence and it is likely that in medieval times settlement may have simply been represented by ribbon development along the road rather like the 'Lang Toun' of today. The picture is completely different for Perth due to the large amount of archaeological work that has taken place there in the last twenty years.

Perth: the Early Centuries

There is no evidence that Perth was founded by the Romans. This idea was fostered by 19th-century antiquarians who insisted that Perth's distinctive gridded street pattern could only be of Roman origin, whereas it is actually the result of Norman-influenced town planning. It seems likely that before it was granted burgh status some sort of settlement existed in Perth if only because of its location at the highest bridging point across the River Tay, some 48 km from the North Sea. The nature of such a settlement has been the subject of much speculation and recently excavations on the south side of Perth's High Street have located a wattle-lined ditch which predated the laying out of burgage plots on the site and may be a boundary around an earlier version of St John's Kirk. A carbon date of between AD 998 and 1039 from the wattle lining is the best evidence so far recovered for a pre-burghal settlement at Perth.

The place-name Perth, meaning a brake, bush or copse, may provide some indication of the nature and topography of the original settlement site. St John's Kirk and the Watergate occupy the highest ground and at various intervals Perth has also been called St Johnstown in honour of

St John the Baptist, to whom the parish church is dedicated. These days this name is more commonly associated with the local football team.

THE FOUNDING OF THE BURGH OF PERTH

It is currently accepted that early settlement was focussed along the Watergate and around the early church. Following the granting of royal burgh status in the 12th century the focus shifted onto the High Street which ran as far as a suggested western burgh limit at the former line of Meal Vennel. The erection of a royal castle on the northern side of the burgh, where the museum currently stands, led to the insertion of the Skinnergate which, with the Kirkgate, provided an access route between church and castle. It was at the junction of these two streets that the market cross formerly stood. Following the destruction of the castle by the 1209 flood these streets lost their importance and the burgh began to expand both westwards and southwards. The westward expansion reached as far as the modern line of South Methven Street which follows the former course of part of the town defences. In the late 12th century South Street was laid out to the south of and parallel to the High Street and probably reflects the need for more space for new burgage plots. From the 14th century two suburbs began to develop outside the burgh limits, one on the former site of the castle and the other to the west of the burgh along New Row. By the mid-14th century medieval Perth had expanded to limits that remained largely unchanged until the early 19th century.

Buildings and Townscape

The oldest standing building in the modern city is St John's Kirk and it is probably only the tower which retains its medieval appearance. Perth's oldest secular building, The Fair Maid's house, is post-medieval in date and the last standing late medieval building was demolished in the 1960s. It is therefore fortunate that Perth is unique amongst Scotland's medieval burghs for having such remarkable archaeological preservation. In the core of the early town archaeological deposits can survive up to 3 or 4 m below modern ground level. These deposits are anaerobic (oxygen free) resulting in the survival of materials not normally found in other burghs. This means that vital evidence for the nature and structure of domestic buildings has been recovered. Present evidence suggests that up until probably the 15th century secular houses in the burgh were built of wood with thatched roof. Stone was used for the monastic houses and parish church and although there is a reference to a stone house in the 14th century it does not seem to have been a common construction material for domestic buildings until the later medieval period.

Figure 10

Location of Place-names

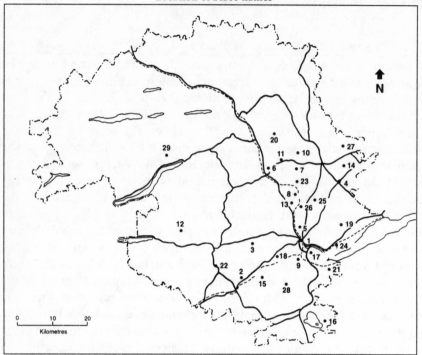

1. Perth	7. Clunie	13. Campsie	19. Kinnaird	25. Lawton
2. Auchterarder	8. Kinclaven	14. Coupar Grange	20. Pitcarmick	26. Cargill
3. Inchaffray	9. Dunbarney	15. Dunning	21. Abernethy	27. Alyth
4. Coupar Angus	10. Buzzart Dykes	16. Scotlandwell	22. Muthill	28. Ardargie
5. Scone	11. Laighwood	17. Moncrieffe Hill	23. Meikleour	29. Fortingall
6. Dunkeld	12. Glen Lednock	18. Forteviot Estate	24. Murie	

Perth still retains its basic medieval street pattern although at least two of its streets, Meal Vennel and Curfew Row, have been built over in modern times. Another street, the Argyllsgait, is only mentioned in one 16th-century charter granting land to the Loretto chapel and its former location is unknown. Recent archaeological excavations on the High Street have indicated that in medieval times it was much wider than today, maybe by as much as 2 or 3m on either side. This substantial width reflects its use as a market place with booths or shops extending into the street. Until recent times access to Perth from the south was through Craigie along Hospital Street and into the burgh through the South Port which stood at the west end of South Street. Professor Duncan pointed out many years ago that this unusual southern access route lines up with an early routeway to the river crossing. So far archaeological excavations have failed to back up this suggestion although recent trial work on the north side of South Street did locate possible property divisions that ran at right angles to the line of Hospital Street and not South Street.

The medieval layout of Perth was based on the rig system whereby each frontage building would have stood at the front of a long property which ran back from the street until it either met another property running back off another street or the common ground in front of the town defences. These rigs were still visible until recently and the Ordnance Survey map of the 1860s is still recording a largely medieval layout. A walk along a close from a major street would essentially provide a progress through the ordered hierarchy of a medieval burgh. On the frontage would be sited a merchant's house or shop belonging to the most privileged of burgesses who had formed their own exclusive guild by the 13th century. Behind this would be the workshop and dwelling of an ordinary burgess who may have been a master craftsman or a trader, then finally the buildings inhabited by the majority of the burgh's inhabitants, the so called 'unfree', who were journeymen or day labourers. Excavations in Perth have provided evidence of this type of layout although large parts of the rigs may have been open ground that was either in small scale cultivation or being used for rubbish disposal. On the latter point there are 16th-century references in the burgh's guildry book to 'pynnouris' or shore porters, who were paid to remove rubbish. There is limited evidence for domestic sanitation represented by a small shed containing a toilet on the back of a medieval building fronting the High Street at Kirk Close.

Town Defences

Perth's medieval limits were defined by a bank and ditch and, for part of the time, a stone wall. The first reference to a town wall is in a charter of 1153 x 1156 in which Baldwin the Lorimer (a Fleming) undertakes to work on the walls of Perth. It is possible that at this early period the defence line was actually a timber palisade and that it is not until a century later that it becomes a stone wall. References continue to be made to these walls right up to the 14th century and it would seem that both Edward Balliol and Edward III of England strengthened and fortified them. These defences seem to have fallen into disrepair after Balliol's failed attempt to win the Scottish throne and the last attempt to repair them was made by Cromwell's troops in the 17th century.

Although we have many references to Perth's town walls in documentary sources and on the first edition Ordnance Survey map of 1860 when fragments are marked as still surviving, they have proved very elusive in the archaeological record. Admittedly part of the problem is the fact that much of the defence line now lies under the modern streets of the town, namely Mill Street, Methven Street, Canal Crescent and Canal Street and, as such, is inaccessible. However, excavations in advance of Marks and Spencer's shop in the mid 1970s did discover the damaged remains of a well built stone wall on the right line. More recently excavations at the northern end of Skinnergate also located the foundations of a well built stone wall face directly adjacent to the town lade. There appears to have been common ground between the ends of the property rigs and the inside face of the town wall. This existed to allow access to the walls in times of war and documents survive that record the town council instructing people to keep this access clear as it was becoming blocked with midden and rubbish. Archaeological evidence for this common space beside the town wall was found in excavations at Canal Street in 1985. In effect Perth was surrounded by a wall and a moat as the town lade would have served that purpose. The lade would have been navigable for small boats which would have allowed for the transporting of merchandise to all parts of the town.

On approaching the town today from the south and looking down on it from the Edinburgh Road at Scoonieburn it is still possible to imagine what a strongly defended Perth would have looked like with St John's Kirk tower still being the most visible landmark. Captain John Slezer's 17th-century view of the town from the north east conveys some of the feeling of the defended medieval town.

RELIGIOUS HOUSES

Like many thriving medieval burghs Perth became a focal point for the foundation of religious houses. By the mid-15th century Perth possessed four, all of them beyond the burgh limits. The earliest foundation was that of the Dominicans or Blackfriars in 1231. This friary lay on the north side of the burgh to the east of Kinnoull Street at its junction with Carpenter Street, as recently confirmed by excavation. Following the destruction of the castle by the flood of 1209 the Dominican friary seems to have become the favoured lodging of Scottish kings when they were visiting the burgh. Indeed it was in the Blackfriars monastery that James I was murdered in 1437.

The second foundation was that of the Carmelite friary of Tullilum in 1262. This friary lay to the west of the burgh on the southern side of the Longcauseway (now Jeanfield Road). Why it is located so far away from the burgh limits is still not understood, although there is a chance that a church already existed on the site that was then granted to the Carmelites. The eastern end of the friary complex was excavated in advance of redevelopment in 1982 and some idea of the layout of the complex and the nature of the buildings was gained.

Perth's other two religious houses were the Franciscan and Carthusian friaries. The Franciscan or Greyfriars monastery was founded in 1460 and lay to the south east of the burgh in the area now occupied by Greyfriars cemetery. The Carthusian friary was founded in 1429 and lay to the south west of the burgh close to the site of King James VI hospital. Known as the Vale of Virtue it was the only Carthusian house in Scotland, which must reflect the importance of Perth at that time. James I and his consort, Joan of Beaufort, were both buried there. Both Franciscan and Carthusian friaries still remain archaeologically unexplored at the time of writing.

As well as the four religious houses detailed above, Perth contained at least eight chapels, several of which also had associated hospitals. All of these are now located below modern buildings or, in the case of St Leonard's, railway sidings. Across the River from Perth in the area now occupied by Bridgend the leper hospital was located.

By the 16th century every major Scottish burgh possessed a leper house and although not all the inhabitants of these hospitals may have had the disease, these institutions performed an important function in everyday life in the medieval town. The Scottish leper hospital is still poorly understood and only one has been excavated in recent years, just outside St Andrews.

Smaller hospitals or hostels also existed in the Middle Ages specifically to aid pilgrims who were en route to a holy shrine. One such 13th-century foundation existed at Scotlandwell on the north side of Loch Leven. This establishment was administered by the Trinitarians or Redfriars who only had eight houses in Scotland. It lay on the western pilgrim route to St Andrews.

It seems fair to say that religion played a much greater part in people's lives in the medieval period than it does today. This probably reflects the uncertainty of people's existence and the fact that, unlike today, they would have known very little about the rest of the world and its cultures. Religion therefore offered a common experience that people could relate to. The religious orders were able to exploit this and a thriving medieval burgh offered a substantial source of revenue.

Amongst some of the more personal objects from excavations in medieval Perth are pilgrim badges that people have brought back to prove that they actually visited the relevant shrine. Amongst the most unusual of these are the pierced scallop shells from the shrine of St James in Compostela in Spain. Badges from Canterbury and St Andrews have also been found. Perth's situation as a major port on the River Tay would have made travelling to these places comparatively easy. Perth also possesses its own saint, St William, who was murdered on the way to Canterbury and is buried in Rochester Cathedral in Kent.

There are no known religious houses associated with the burgh of Auchterarder, although the Augustinian priory of Inchaffray lies only a few kilometres to the north. Inchaffray was founded in 1200 and may have been colonised by monks from Scone. The site was the subject of an archaeological excavation in the 1980s which suggested that the abbey church was built on the remains of an early Christian monastic settlement surrounded by a banked enclosure.

Just to the south east of Auchterarder lies the small village of Dunning. This settlement was created a baronial burgh in 1511 under the control of Rollo of Duncrub. Its history, however, reaches back into the medieval period and a charter of 1219 indicates that St Serf's Church was founded between that date and 1300. Of particular interest is the square tower attached to the church which is defined by its two-light, arched windows as being of English influence. It is one of five similar towers, other examples being Dunblane, Muthill, Markinch and St Andrews. These towers have been dated to the late 11th or early 12th centuries and indicate sites of early Christian settlement, possibly by Culdee monks.

COMMUNICATION

The main reason for the location of the burgh of Perth was the fording point across the Tay. This allowed traffic from both the west and the south to cross the river and head up into Angus and Aberdeenshire. It seems very likely that the river offered the best and quickest method of transport both to and from the burgh as the road system may not have been very good. Although little work has been done on this subject it is likely that any surviving Roman roads such as the one along the Gask Ridge may have still been used during medieval times. The routes to the south and the north are harder to define.

THE HARBOUR

Perth's medieval harbour lay at the foot of the High Street and the tolbooth lay across the street controlling access into the burgh. By 1600 the harbour had moved to the end of Canal Street on the north side of Greyfriars cemetery. It then gradually moved downstream as the size of boats increased until it reached its modern location at Friarton in 1840. Tay Street was a 19th-century addition to the townscape and is built largely on reclaimed land that extends out from the former river bank. Effectively, this means that the early harbour and any associated wharfage is sealed below the modern town. Observations of underpinning work on the council chambers in the 1980s located sizeable jointed timbers some 3m below modern street level which implies that the medieval harbour frontage may still survive below the modern buildings. Archaeological excavations in the mid 1980s uncovered the later medieval harbour on Canal Street.

LIFE AND DEATH

From the many excavations that have taken place in burghs like Perth it is now possible to say a good deal about people's diet, living conditions and life expectancy. It seems likely that most of the inhabitants of medieval Perth existed on a largely vegetarian diet based on kail, porridge made from oats, bere and rye, broth and ale. Meat was available but how affordable it was to the mass of the population is another matter. Beef was the most common meat eaten, followed by sheep, goat, pig and very occasionally deer. The occasional hardship of medieval life is reflected by the discovery of butchered dog and horse bone, although the latter is still part of the staple diet in continental Europe. However some inhabitants were wealthy enough to eat imported figs and dates, as they were recovered from the Perth High Street excavation.

Fish played a large part in people's diet and was also a staple part of the country's export trade. Grain was available probably from the monastic estate centres (see below) and corn driers are a common find on excavations in the medieval town. In the excavations at Meal Vennel they were the earliest industrial structures located and may suggest where the street got its name. The Baxters (Bakers) of medieval Perth were some of the most important members of the Guildry Incorporation, a fact repeated in modern times when a recent Dean of Guild was a baker.

Excavations at two of Perth's friaries have located parts of their cemeteries and this has allowed for some analysis of the skeletal remains. It is important to realise that this is giving us a slightly biased view as a vast percentage of the burgh's inhabitants would have been buried in the town's cemetery, which lay around St John's Kirk until 1580 when it was moved to Greyfriars. In general the following statements can be made. People's life expectancy was much lower than now and men seem to have lived longer than women, unlike today. This was largely due to the dangers of childbirth. Children suffered the most from illness and malnutrition and there was a high level of infant mortality. There are traces of damage to bones caused by repeated exertions such as the lifting of heavy loads. One of the burials excavated at Blackfriars appeared to be that of a young woman who may have been buried alive by mistake. This may explain why the skeleton lay face down in the grave with its arms in the press-up position in a vain attempt to lift itself out of the grave. This problem of misdiagnosis of death was still common in the Victorian period, which is why many coffins were fitted with bell pulls so that those above ground could be informed of the mistake.

PERTH: TRADE AND INDUSTRY

Perth's situation as the furthest inland port on the Scottish east coast enabled it to thrive as a major trading centre, particularly with the Low Countries and Germany. From the available documents it would appear that the burgesses of the early town were largely made up of incomers from England and the continent. These foreign settlers brought very useful skills with them. In the case of the Flemings this included cloth-making, which in the late 12th and early 13th centuries brought a period of great prosperity to the burgh.

Perth can be regarded as a medieval burgh whose very existence was based on the different types of trades and industries that went on within its limits. It is Perth's unique archaeological preservation that allows us to discover so much about these different trades and their products. For example, leather-working seems to have been one of the burgh's major industries, presumably based around the Skinnergate. Excavations in the vicinity have located thousands of leather offcuts and hundreds of leather shoes, scabbards, pouches and other objects. Woodworking was also being carried out and many examples of turned wooden bowls, stave-built buckets and at least one piece of furniture have been found. It now appears that different parts of the medieval burgh may have been occupied by different craftsmen. For example, excavations in advance of the St John's shopping centre at Meal Vennel located the remains of smithies that were used for iron working. Excavations at Canal Street located the remains of structures that were related to malting. In both cases there are later documentary references for the 16th and 17th centuries to the same activities taking place in these parts of the burgh.

The Medieval Pottery Industry

The most common finds from medieval excavations in Scotland are sherds of medieval pottery. From the Perth High Street excavations alone there are c. 50,000 sherds of pottery. Until the post-medieval period, basic cooking equipment was made of ceramic material, although plates and bowls were exclusively made from wood. Whereas broken wooden implements could be burnt, pottery is virtually indestructable and is thus a common find from excavations.

At the time of writing the products of a native industry have been identified but very few kilns have either been located or excavated. The earliest Scottish pottery being made from the 12th century is white gritty ware, with production centres in the Borders, Lothian and Fife. From the early 13th century an East Coast redware pottery tradition seems to have developed and has been found in excavations from Stirling to Inverness. Up until that point asemblages are dominated by pottery from England and the Low Countries which have been imported into the town. It is possible that the prevalence of these imported wares reflects the nationality of a large percentage of the burgh's inhabitants.

The kiln sites producing these large quantities of pottery do not seem to have been located within the burgh limits. This is due to the enormous fire hazard that they would have posed to a town whose buildings were almost exclusively built of timber. In the case of Perth there are at least three possible sites for pottery kilns; at Claypots, Potterhill and Kinnoull. However no evidence for anything relating to such an industry has been found at any of these sites and it is possible that they may be further afield. A whole series of kiln sites situated in rural settlements may have been supplying the major burghs. In many cases this is where the resources – a clay and water supply – are located anyway. It is vital that some attempt is made to construct a chronology for the Scottish pottery industry as pottery is often the only dating evidence that is recovered from excavations and if it is a native product it is currently not possible to date it very closely. Some of the rural settlements described next in this chapter may hold answers to this vexed question.

RURAL SETTLEMENT

Despite the fact that a high percentage of the inhabitants of medieval Perthshire lived in the countryside, we still know very little about them. From an archaeological viewpoint, the main reason for this is the lack of opportunity to conduct any excavation on known rural settlement sites. All the information on urban settlement has been gained from excavations that were undertaken because the site was to be developed either for housing, shopping centres or supermarkets. Much of rural Perthshire remains undeveloped, which means that any excavation would have to be driven purely on research grounds.

In South East Perthshire the foundation of the abbeys of Scone and Coupar Angus transformed large parts of the countryside from royal demesne into monastic estate and much of the rest was converted into secular lordships often in hands of newly arrived Anglo-Norman families.

EARLY CASTLES

The centres of a number of early estates can be identified by the remains of earth and timber castles, often taking the form of a motte and bailey or, less commonly a ringwork. Individual mottes exist at Murie, Lawton, Meiklelour and Barton Hill, Kinnaird. The latter has been excavated and the remains of the foundations of a rectangular timber tower within a post and log fence was found. This castle may have belonged to Ralph Rufus, who was granted the barony of Kinnaird between 1172 and 1174. The only castle in this area specifically referred to in the documentary record is at Cargill, granted to Richard de Montfiquet between 1189 and 1195. The earliest stone castle in South East Perthshire is the one at Clunie which seems to have been established in about 1141 to accompany the royal forest of the same name. The royal castle of Alyth, first on record between 1196 and 1199 also accompanied a royal forest. These forests were owned directly by the king who could use them for hunting. Kinclaven Castle was founded between 1210 and 1236 and may have been a replacement of the castle washed away at Perth.

MOATED SITES

A number of estate centres were enclosed by broad ditches or moats and are also common in Perthshire. Remains of these moated sites are still visible as standing earthworks at Ardagie and Fortingall whereas the others only show up as cropmarks on aerial photographs. These monuments are little understood at present but should be the subject of future research and field-work. This picture of rural Perthshire being based on castles and estate centres largely in foreign hands, coupled with the nationality of many of the inhabitants of the burgh of Perth gives us a picture of a countryside inhabited by very few natives! Although it was stated earlier in this chapter that there was never a Norman invasion of Scotland it may have actually been carried out in a more surreptitious manner, by the king bringing Anglo-Norman and Flemish retainers and clients from his English to his Scottish estates to act as stewards or constables.

DEER PARKS

Perthshire possesses the remains of two deer parks at Buzzart Dykes which lies c. 3 km to the north west of Blairgowrie and at Laighwood on the east side of Butterstone. The bank and ditch surrounding the park at Buzzart Dykes is still visible except on its eastern side where it has been ploughed away. At Laighwood only a small part of its stone boundary wall is visible on its south eastern side and includes what may be an original gate into the park. Within the limits of the Laighwood park there survives the supposed site of a 14th-century castle belonging to Bishop William Sinclair of Dunkeld. These two deer parks are rare survivals of a common use of the countryside for leisure pursuits in the medieval period.

CHURCH LANDS

The biggest landowners in Southern Perthshire from the 12th century to the Reformation were the abbeys of Scone and Coupar Angus and the cathedral of Dunkeld. Of the Cistercian granges (farms) the only ones we know much about are at Campsie and Coupar Grange (5 km south east of Blairgowrie). At Campsie a group of five buildings is visible on the ground as wall footings arranged around a yard. At least one of these buildings was the holiday residence of the abbot of Coupar Angus. At Coupar Grange an extensive series of cropmarks appear to indicate substantial sunken rectangular buildings, possibly storehouses for grain or other farm produce, within a rectilinear ditched enclosure. The land holdings of the abbey of Scone are less easily identified, although cropmarks at Cambusmichael have been identified as probably those of a grange belonging to Scone. There is little documentary reference to the possessions of Dunkeld Cathedral, although Clunie did serve as a collecting centre for the estate.

SETTLEMENT SITES

Perthshire possesses known deserted medieval settlements, for example the burgh and abbey of Scone, both of which formerly stood to the east of Scone Palace. The village was moved to a new site by the Earl of Mansfield in the 18th century. The market cross still survives in the midst of forested parkland but little is known regarding the nature or layout of the settlement. A medieval village formerly existed at Dunbarney near Bridge of Earn but is now cultivated farmland, although traces of the village show up as cropmarks on aerial photographs. A lonely graveyard is all that survives to indicate where the church formerly stood. As elsewhere in Britain, it is the location of isolated churches that can point to the former existence of a settlement or kirktoun that failed to achieve burgh status.

Remains of settlement sites in the marginal areas of Perthshire may have medieval origins. For example in Glenlednock, which lies to the north of the village of Comrie, several of the deserted settlements are referred to in medieval documents and at least one has produced a small assemblage of medieval pottery. A great deal of valuable documentary and survey work was carried out in the glen by Elizabeth Bain in the 1970s.

Recent intensive survey work by the Royal Commission has provided us with valuable information regarding the rural settlements of Perthshire but, as with most things rural, a further programme of research excavation may be the only way of clarifying the situation. In the Commission survey of North Eastern Perthshire a new class of building type has been identified. The so-called Pitcarmick-type building is rectangular with rounded ends and is so far undated. It is possible that this new building type may be medieval in date and could represent the most common type of secular domestic building in the upland marginal areas. Remains of field systems possibly of medieval date are also visible in rural Perthshire. These belong to the narrow rig system of farming and can be seen within the policies of the Forteviot Estate and on the northern slopes of Moncrieffe Hill.

THE REFORMATION

Religion played an important role in everyday life in the medieval period. This was essentially based on many of the precepts of early Celtic Christianity which had been absorbed into the Catholic church. By the early 16th century dissatisfaction with the Catholic church seems to have been growing. The mendicant friars appear to have been the target of at least one of the public displays of this feeling in 1543 in Perth. The Blackfriars had their broth pot stolen by some townspeople who then paraded it about the burgh to prove that the friars who professed such poverty were eating better food than most of the townfolk. Around the same time part of the Blackfriars crop fields were sown with 'wald seed' which ruined the crop that was being cultivated.

The religious crisis of May 1559 was sparked by a sermon by John Knox in St John's Kirk which denounced the evils of Catholicism. According to documentary sources, the burgh's religious houses were all sacked following Knox's declamation. The extent of this destruction is still the subject of some debate. Following the excavations of the Carmelite and Dominican friaries, evidence for material destruction at this time is fairly limited. At the Carmelite friary, for example, there were limited amounts of demolition rubble overlying the friary buildings. However, a large amount of stone robbing had taken place in the 18th and 19th centuries which may have confused any earlier demolition horizons. As Whitefriars was some distance away from the burgh it is likely to have suffered less.

Rather than suffering total destruction of their monasteries at this time it is more likely that the friars were ejected from their buildings, which were then stripped of 'monuments of idolatry' and had their roofs removed. Over the following centuries the former friaries were used as quarries for building stone and gradually disappeared from the urban landscape. The

Carthusian friary may have suffered more immediate damage as it was close enough to the burgh to be very vulnerable. The archaeological evidence for events around the Reformation needs to be refined by further excavation.

It is convenient to describe the Reformation as marking the beginning of the end of the Middle Ages as it ushered in a different religious viewpoint that was to become the foundation of Scottish society up until the present day.

SIX

EARLY MODERN TIMES

In Scottish history, as elsewhere, the early modern age is an awkward period without accepted parameters. However, for studies of Perthshire there is a manuscript source that records some of the events of the 16th and 17th centuries which were of importance to the local inhabitants. The 'Chronicle of Perth' comes to a halt rather abruptly in 1668 but the events recorded by its several authors suggest that they would have acknowledged the Act of Union in 1707 as a symbolic point of departure for the locality, as well as for the country as a whole. Although much of the volume was compiled during the 17th century, the chroniclers looked back to the reign of Mary and plotted the troubled years which preceded the Reformation in Scotland. Thus, in this chapter, 'Early Modern Times' in Perthshire are to be understood as stretching from the era of the Reformation until the early 18th century. This was a period of appalling pressures for the inhabitants of Perthshire, years of political and religious upheaval, civil war, economic change and natural disasters.

NOTABLE EVENTS

The manuscript volume which is known as the 'Chronicle of Perth' was written between *c*. 1590 and *c*. 1668. The 'Chronicle' consists of just 28 leaves of paper but is full of information. Although it is an anonymous source, there is strong evidence to suggest that much of it was the work of John Mercer, the Town Clerk of Perth from 1623–42 and 1654–70. He and his assistants had access to a wide range of official documentation and would have had a particular appreciation of those events which mattered in Perth. The reason for the composition of the 'Chronicle' and its early ownership are not known. However, the volume is a varied source which might have been of use to both the civic and the kirk authorities in the burgh. It contains copies of official correspondence, material relating to the foundation of the King James VI Hospital in Perth, a register of deaths and, chiefly, a register of historical events of local and national significance. The 'Chronicle' is certainly not a comprehensive record of early modern times: it is biased towards affairs in the Lowlands and reflects the experiences of urban dwellers in an age when the majority of the population lived in the countryside. But the towns were the focus of political and economic affairs and within the historical register can be found indications of some of the defining events in early modern Perthshire.[1]

When the chroniclers came to record the Reformation, the riots in Perth in 1559 belonged to another time and a different generation but their effects were still being felt. The events of 1559 are rather glossed over in the 'Chronicle'. John Knox preached what proved to be an inflammatory sermon in St John's Kirk and elements of the burgh community went on a rampage, destroying the four monasteries which surrounded the town walls; shortly afterwards the nearby abbey at Scone was burnt to the ground by a mob which included people from the burgh. However, the 'Chronicle' notes abruptly, 'The reformatioun of the chart(er)house + Freiris besyde pth ye x day of May Im vc Lix yeiris' and, subsequently, 'The burnyng of Scone'. But although the chroniclers may have been disingenuous in seeming to pay such scant attention to the Reformation, it was a revolution which coloured the course of Perth's political fortunes for nearly a century and particularly the burgh's ambivalent relationship with the crown.

The tenor of the 'Chronicle of Perth' indicates that the departure of James VI for London in 1603 was an event of as much local significance as the religious changes which had occurred shortly before his birth. The town of Perth and nearby estates had regularly been places of royal residence and the Stuarts' traditional affection for Lowland Perthshire had brought prestige and economic benefits to its people. With the loss of such patronage, the seat of the Sheriffdom of Perth was diminished on the Scottish stage, at a time when Perth's economic status as one of the four great burghs of the kingdom was waning in consequence of the rise of Glasgow. Neither the murder of James I in the Blackfriars monastery at Perth in 1437, nor the Reformation riots, had tainted the burgh as a Stuart seat. The 'Raid of Ruthven' in 1582 did not drive James VI from Perthshire – although his relationship with its people was rather strained. The 'Chronicle' records six visits to Perth made by James VI between 1580 and 1617 but, famously, the latter was his *only* visit to Scotland after his coronation as King of England.

Given the political and economic significance of the crown's relations with Perth, one of the most important passages in the 'Chronicle' concerns the infamous affair of August 1600 which is known as the 'Gowrie Conspiracy'. The broad outlines of the incident are well known. John Earl of Gowrie, the Provost of Perth and his brother Alexander, the Master of Ruthven, supposedly attempted to murder James VI in the Gowrie House of Perth but were themselves summarily killed by the king's men. There was a history of antipathy between James and the Gowries and no independent witnesses to the killings. The earl was popular in the burgh and there were mass protests when news of his death became known. Records survive of the interrogation of 300 townspeople concerning their activities that day, after the king complained that he was 'assailyeit and persewit be a grit nowmer of the communitie and inhabitantis of the burgh of Perth, all in armes' and that the mob had 'environed his Majesteis hous on all pairtis, assegeit and persewit his Hienes within the same, uttering maist irreverent and undeutifull speiches aganis his Majestie . . .'[2]

Much has been written about the so-called 'Conspiracy'. Local historians have been particularly agitated by the killing of Gowrie and have exercised a lot of energy debating whether there could possibly have been a plot to kill the king. In contrast, the author of the account which appears in the 'Chronicle of Perth' was mainly concerned to exonerate the burgh community from any complicity in the Gowries' alleged plot. The lines which stand out were intended to emphasise the burgh's loyalty to the king: 'praisit be god ye king wes saiff fra yair intendit treasone'; 'praisit be god the king knew ye toun of pthis part to be frie'. The words 'conspiracie' and 'treasone' were employed without apparent qualification. The 'Chronicle' makes no mention of rioting townspeople and stresses that cordial relations were soon re-established between Perth and the king. James returned in April 1601 and was proclaimed a burgess at the mercat cross: 'Thair wes ane punscheone of wyne sett yair + druckin out he ressauit ye banquet fra ye toun + subsuit ye gilde buik'.

The townspeople of early modern Perth could be very dangerous – they did not baulk at destroying the royal tombs in the Charterhouse during the Reformation riots – and it is understandable that the 'Chronicle' is so carefully phrased. One of Perth's best local historians, the Rev James Scott, was well aware of the gloss which the chronicler had spread over the Gowrie affair. Scott was a keen defender of the Gowries and was convinced that the killings had been instigated by a deceitful king: 'How could the king immediately know that the Town of Perth was free of any traitorous combination, if he was persuaded of the Guilt of the Earl + his brother? The Expressions in the Chronicle seem to be artful + ambiguous'.[3] Despite the burgh's horror at the fate of the Gowries, the loss which was felt by the community when the royal court moved south may be reflected in the joy which was expressed at the king's return in 1617. Even radical Perth was capable of compliance with unwelcome royal impositions: when the 'Five Articles' were introduced at a General Assembly held in St John's in 1618, Perth paid lip service to their observance.

However, the 'Five Articles' did not last long. Although the 'Chronicle' provides evidence that Roman Catholicism was practised by the rural nobility and gentry, Perth was firmly Presbyterian. When Charles I's religious innovations met with strident opposition, the people of Perth welcomed the National Covenant of 1638 and worshipped in the 'auld maner'. With typical reservation, the chroniclers avoided overt criticism of the king and concentrated on troop movements in Perthshire during the Covenanting Wars, when Perth served as a strategic staging post for numerous Covenant forces.

The first battle of the Marquis of Montrose's campaign against the Covenanters took place at Tibbermore, near Perth, on 1 September 1644. The marquis had marched from Blair Atholl and his forces included at least 500 Perthshire Highlanders who had defected from the Covenanter cause.[4] The 'Chronicle' states that Montrose defeated a Covenanter force led by Lord Elcho, which was drawn from 'the haill s(|)reffdome of pth fyff +wthers + haill burrowis of fyffe nobill men and gentrie yairof'. Perth was occupied and was fortunate not to be sacked – as happened at Aberdeen later in that month. Not surprisingly, Highland soldiers seem to have been poorly received in Perth: in March 1645, 250 Highlanders who had been recruited into James, Lord Murray of Gask's regiment arrived in the burgh, 'The soieuris being hieland simpill bodeis naikit . . .'

The 'Chronicle' records that between September 1644 and March 1646, two armies and nine regiments or companies quartered within Perth. The forces of Montrose and Argyll caused damage to the land and the burgh in September 1644. These were perhaps the largest contingents which passed through Lowland Perthshire but accounts of the destruction of the castles at Kincardine and Aberuchill in March 1646 – seats of the Graham and Campbell families – are indicative of the disruption which the wars brought to the rural landscape.

Soldiers returning from the siege of Newcastle-upon-Tyne brought bubonic plague to the Lowlands in 1644, heralding a period of shocking mortality in the compact environments of the burghs. The countryside seems to have been comparatively untroubled by plague, although typhus was a potent threat to rural communities. However, such was the severity of the epidemic between 1644 and 1648 that there was widespread suffering in the Lowlands. About 3000 people died in Perth and its surrounding parishes between 1645 and 1647.[5] This figure may represent as much as half of the burgh's population – a devastating blow, which would in part account for Perth's poor economic performance in the second half of the 17th century.

The presence of an English occupation force in Perth in the 1650s was not popular and the construction of a massive citadel on the South Inch was an appalling inconvenience for a sickly urban community. 140 houses and several important public buildings were destroyed to provide materials for the fortress: a plan of Perth in the mid-18th century shows that the citadel was still a major feature one hundred years later, having been restored by the Jacobites in 1745.[6] When the citadel was first constructed, the

Cromwellians had cut turf from Perth's Inches to build the ramparts; this action ruined grazing land and in the following years the fortification was clearly an impediment to the South Inch, restricting its use as farm land.

Perth's Covenanting sympathies brought little fortune to the burgh but the Restoration receives only the briefest of acknowledgements in the 'Chronicle'. The years after 1660 witnessed rebuilding in town and country after the devastation of war, occupation and disease. Perth's manufacturing industries – notably in metal and leather working – were weak and the gradual silting-up of the Tay may have restricted maritime trade. Furthermore, in the later decades of the 17th century Perth faced strong competition in domestic trading from numerous market centres in the shire. By the time of the Union, the character of Perth and of Perthshire had changed substantially from the time of the Reformation, when the burgh had wielded national influence in politics and the economy. Once the residence of Scottish kings, by the early 18th century the burgh had become a military outpost for a monarch in London; formerly the dominant market in the sheriffdom, Perth was now encompassed by strong rivals.

THE MARKET ECONOMY

The burgh of Perth was vigorous in its attempts to assert control over the market economy of the sheriffdom but it was faced with the increasing strength of other centres. In 1692, the burgh complained of a loss of trade on account of competition from 'regalities, barronies, and other unfree places within ther precincts'.[7] Local produce, particularly foodstuffs and live-stock, were among the most important commodities traded in the towns.

The Perth Burgh Records indicate that the burgh authorities took measures to inhibit the activities of rival markets, restricting the inhabi-tants of Perth from trading with other towns and occasionally preventing outside merchants from entering Perth. But the most detailed information about Perth's local economic competitors comes from the report to the visitors of the royal burghs of 1692. This document was drawn up by the burgh and government commissioners and includes an estimate of the value of the trade handled annually by 'the regalities, barronies and other unfree places within the shireffdome of Perth'. The burgh worthies may have exaggerated the figures but the list points to those markets which Perth's authorities perceived to be their strongest rivals. By this reckoning, Dunkeld handled the largest volume of trade, accounting for £12,000 Scots. Dunblane, Doune and Coupar Angus all handled £8000 annually, whereas Crieff accounted for £6000. Abernethy, Dunning and Alyth handled trade amounting to £4000 per annum but most other market centres were smaller.[8]

In general, there was a preponderance of markets in Lowland Perthshire, mostly associated with the major rivers – although the significance of Dunblane and Doune was probably enhanced by their location on the over-land route between Perth and Stirling. There were hardly any successful large markets in the Highland areas of the sherrifdom; there was a cluster of failed centres in Strathardle, but Crieff thrived upon the Highland cattle droving trade.[9] The burgh of Perth certainly faced a concentration of rivals in Strathearn. In contrast, many of the markets on the east side of the Tay were relatively small; in particular, those closest to Perth at Scone and Bridgend only handled trade valued at £1000 per annum each. It might be supposed that the absence of a bridge over the Tay after 1621 would have bolstered markets in this area but this does not seem to have been the case. Ordinarily, ferries across the Tay were probably sufficient for traders coming to Perth from the Carse of Gowrie and Strathmore, although the ferry trade did need to be closely regulated. In 1730, the magistrates and town council of Perth heard complaints that the ferrymen were charging exorbitant rates 'upon the Towns passages on the water of Tay betwixt the Town + the Bridgend of Tay' and that as a consequence 'many of the country people to the eastward of the said water have been discouraged from coming to the town to the great disadvantage of the Retailing trade + commerce of this Burgh . . .'[10]

Tensions between leading market centres are illustrated in a record of January 1700, when the authorities at Perth complained to the Privy Council about the treatment of merchants who wished to use the market at Coupar Angus. Claiming to be the 'Second Burgh royall of the Kingdom', they asserted that Perth had lived in peace and quiet with its neighbours. Trading relations with Coupar Angus and the surrounding countryside had been good but the baillies of Coupar had recently introduced a stent on burgesses from Perth. Furthermore, the burgesses' goods had been impounded, 'upon this only pretence That these Burgess of pearth after they had presented their Goods in the sd Fares ≠ Marketts, where in use, to leave them in the sd Town of Coupar in privat houss to be kept until the next markett or Fair day . . .' Actually, it is probable that the Perth traders *were* engaged in some wrong-doing, by allowing their goods to be distributed by agents in Coupar Angus during their absences. Nevertheless, the Perth authorities argued that their burgesses were 'mast wrongousely stented + their Goods Pounded by the said Baillie ogilvie + his Complices And that not withstanding that the sd Burgess of Pearth doe pay stent in their own Burgh for all the Trade they Exercise in any place whatsoever . . .'[11] This dispute was in part a reflection of opposition to increasing levels of taxation. All of the local markets were under pressure after the famines of the 1690s and Coupar Angus was retaliating to the

Plate 1

Loch Tay from the north-east

Plate 2

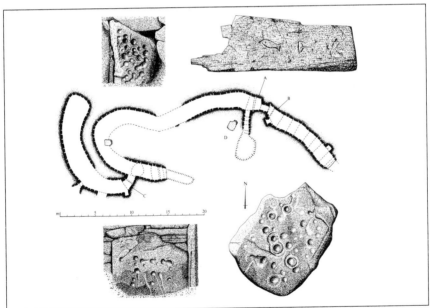

Pitcur

Plate 3

North Mains, henge and barrow

Source: RCAHMS

Plate 4

Drumturn Burn, hut circles and field systems

Source: RCAHMS

Plate 5

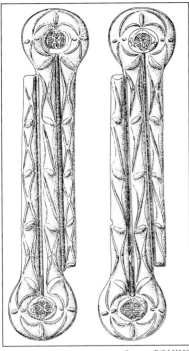

Pitkellony, Muthill. Two massive bronze armlets

Plate 6

= 5cm.

Source: Scottish Urban Archaelogical Trust Ltd.

Fourteenth century stave-built bucket

Source: RCAHMS

Plate 7

Source: Nicholas Bogden and Perth High Street Excavation Committee

Remains of medieval wattle and daub building. Perth High Street excavations, 1975–77

Plate 8

Strageath Roman Fort

Plate 9

Ardoch Roman Fort

Plate 10

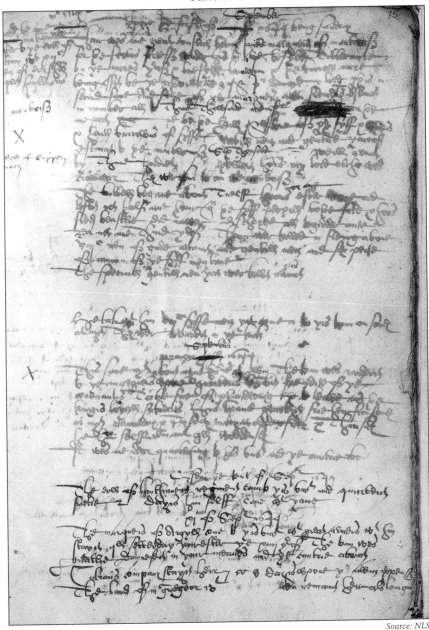

"TheChronicle of Perth" Adv. MS. 35.4.4. p.15. Account of the battle of Tibbermore, 1 September 1644

Plate 11

Palace of Scone

Plate 12

Perth Bridge and North Inch from Bridgend, *c.*1840

Plate 13

Blairgowrie Raspberry Pickers

Plate 14

Muthill War Memorial, 1919

Plate 15

Perth Station, *c.*1900

Plate 16

Dewars Distillery, *c.*1914

Plate 17

The Dunning Thorn Tree

Plate 18

Aberfeldy, Wade bridge over the Tay

Plate 19

Blair Atholl, Blair Castle

Source: John Foster

Plate 20

Loch Turret

Source: John Foster

Plate 21

Loch Ard, the Queen's View

Plate 22

Ben Venue

Source: DC Thomson and Co Ltd

Plate 23

Aerial view of Perth in flood

Plate 24

Source: Castellated and Domestic Architecture of Scotland, MacGibbon and Ross

Ruthven Castle from the south-west

Plate 25

Source: Castellated and Domestic Architecture of Scotland, MacGibbon and Ross

Drummond Castle, north side

Plate 26

Source: Castellated and Domestic Architecture of Scotland, MacGibbon and Ross

Elcho Castle from the north-east

Plate 27

Mausoleum, Methven Churchyard

Source: B Walker

Plate 28

Cottown

Source: B Walker

Plate 29

Flatfield

Source: B Walker

Plate 30

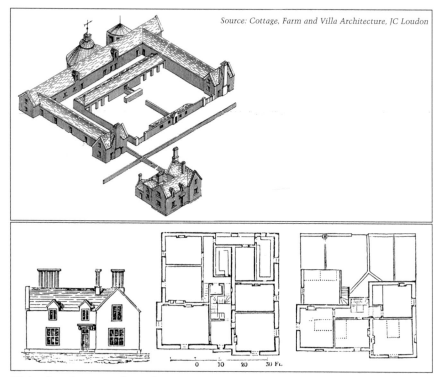

Source: *Cottage, Farm and Villa Architecture, JC Loudon*

Elcho farmhouse and steading

Plate 31

Jock Lundie, *b.* 1906

Plate 32

Belle Stewart, *b.* 1906

imposition of a national tax. However, the authorities of the royal burgh of Perth required the Privy Council to impress upon the baillies of Coupar the need for 'a better behaviour'.

Records made by two English visitors to early modern Perth include interesting observations concerning the burgh's economy. In 1655, Thomas Tucker was sent to Scotland by the English Parliament to produce a report on the settlement of customs and excise, prior to the proposed incorporation of Scotland and England within one commonwealth. The plan eventually came to naught but Tucker's report survives and is well known. He wrote that St Johnstone (Perth) was a 'handsome walled towne', with one customs official. This man was present 'not soe much because of any greate tradeing there, as to prevent the carryeing out wools, skyns, and hide, of which comodityes greate plenty is brought thither out of the Highlands, and there brought up and engrossed by the Lowlandmen'.[12] This rather tawdry impression of economic life at Perth is contradicted somewhat by the Rev Thomas Morer's account of 1689.[13] He described Perth as the 'second city of Scotland', and opined that the town was 'tolerable clean'; the local architecture was undistinguished, although he was impressed by St John's Kirk. He noted that vessels arrived regularly at the harbour and thought that the town's trade depended 'chiefly on linen, which the Highlanders bring thither, and which they export to the value of 40,000l. sterling per annum'. Morer seems to have enjoyed being quartered in Perth and was in no doubt that it was still the most important town in the locality. It is certainly interesting to consider his portrait of a burgh which was in a healthy condition, with a strong land and sea trade: other evidence points to intense competition amongst the markets of Lowland Perthshire and difficult living conditions for many people in town and country.

THE LANDSCAPE

The Advocates Manuscripts in the National Library of Scotland include a series of volumes associated with Sir Robert Sibbald, Geographer Royal, which contain detailed descriptions of the Perthshire landscape of the late 17th century.[14] These surveys pay particular attention to land-use and catalogue the important towns and houses of the sheriffdom.

Sibbald emphasised the diversity and size of the shire and summarised the land as being generally 'very well mixed the high grounds being propper for pasture and the lower very fruitfull in Cornes having many Lochs Rivers + Waters in it . . .' He also noted an 'abundance of woods, and much planting every where'. According to Sibbald, one of the largest woods was in Strathearn – the forest of Glen Artney – which was 'five or six myle in

Lentghe four myle broad', but this is not shown on John Adair's stylised map of Strathearn, Stormont and the Carse of Gowrie of *c.* 1685. Sibbald was generally vague concerning livestock in the upland regions but mentioned 'a great many deer and Roe and wild Horse and Cowes' in Strathearn and deer in the hills and glens around Blair Atholl. Cattle sales were of particular importance to the Highlands and drove-routes are still identifiable in the modern landscape.[15]

Sibbald described Strathmore as 'ane fertile country for cornes well planted and plenished w(t) many houses of ye nobility and gentrie'. Stormont was 'a mixed country the over part hilly being more propper for pasture ye Lower grounds are fertile in cornes + is well planted in the east . . . much Fishing of Salmond . . .' The Carse of Gowrie was 'a strong fertile Ground which produceth great plenty of the Best graines, wheat: Barly peas, Beans and oats and Rye.' The locals used peat for fuel but coal was also imported by sea for the gentry. In the west, the Stewartry of Menteith contained good pasture and arable land for corn. The Ochil Hills contained 'several ores as particularly copper . . .'

Of the river Tay, Sibbald wrote that it was navigable 'from ye Castle of Broughtie wher it Loseth itself in the German sea up to the Town of St Johnstoun to which small ships come wp yr is ane peer yr at which ye ships Load + unload and all along down ye River yr be upon each syde of the River severall places wher vessells lye to and load and unload'. This record actually implies that Perth's status on the Tay was in decline, with the emergence of new harbours and increasing navigation problems, for only 'vessells of Lesser Burthen' could make the journey all the way from Dundee to Perth. The proliferation of quays along the Tay must have compounded the pressure which was being exerted on Perth by the increasing competitiveness amongst landward markets. However, Sibbald was still able to describe Perth as the 'head Burgh of the shyre'.

Sibbald's description of the woodland and formal gardens at Drummond Castle, the residence of the Earl of Perth, is matched by the depiction on Adair's map. Indeed, legislation had been introduced in 1661 to promote afforestation and enclosure and the development of such wooded estates was a feature of the later 17th century.[16] Amongst the 'Chief Houses' of the shire, Sibbald noted Tullibardine, 'a noble duelling with large parks + much planting about it' and other Murray properties at Blair and Huntingtower. Indeed, Sibbald indicated that branches of families such as the Murrays, Drummonds and Grahams owned property throughout the shire.

Murrays exercised particular influence in and around Perth. There was a significant change in the structure of land ownership in Lowland Perthshire following the fall of the Gowries in 1600, as their lands were redistributed. One of the principal beneficiaries was Sir James Murray of

Gospetrie, a junior member of the Murrays of Blair Atholl, who succeeded to the Gowrie property of Scone. (The earldom of Gowrie had been erected out of the lands of the abbey of Scone.) William, Lord Ruthven and Earl of Gowrie had built a house adjacent to the ruined abbey in the early 1580s but Murray developed this building into a palace. The Gowrie property of Ruthven Castle (Huntingtower) passed into the hands of several branches of the Murray family – eventually becoming a property of the dukes of Atholl – and Scone was also established as one of the prominent secular estates in the vicinity of Perth.[17] Indeed, Scone's transformation from a religious community of national significance into the private estate of a titled landowner gave symbolic expression to cultural changes of the Reformation era. Sir James Murray became Lord Scone and later Viscount Stormont and often served as Provost of Perth. However, Scone did retain some of its former aura and the coronation there of Charles II in 1651 was a deliberate evocation of medieval tradition.

John Slezer's prospect of the 'House and Town of Skuyn', part of his *Theatrum Scotiae* of 1693, shows the 17th-century palace amongst a landscaped plantation.[18] The low buildings of the town are visible amongst the trees; the surrounding land is essentially arable. Scone is shown in isolation as a small but organised hamlet, dominated by the palace. This building is notable because it seems to have been constructed without a defensive function. In the previous century such an estate might have been vulnerable to attack and even in the 17th century the Covenanting Wars witnessed the destruction of prominent buildings such as the Grahams' castle at Kincardine, near Auchterarder. But Scone seems to have evolved as a splendid residence, rather than as a defensive domain. An engraving of the palace dated to 1775 indicates that the emphasis was on domesticity.[19] The architecture of Sir James Murray's palace was an expression of wealth and confidence and families such as the Murrays of Scone benefited both from positions of power in the locality and from the productivity of their lands.

Sibbald's portrait of Perthshire is unreliable in certain respects and his emphasis upon woodlands does not quite correspond with Adair's view of the Perthshire countryside. However, Sibbald's notes do provide useful information about land-use and Adair's map gives a valuable indication of the major overland routes along the Carse, through Strathmore and northwards from Perth to Dunkeld. Both men presented images of a densely settled, working landscape littered with the estates of prominent families.

NATURAL DISASTERS

Although the agricultural landscape of early modern Perthshire had rich potential, it was also prey to the disastrous effects of floods and heavy snows. The 'Chronicle of Perth' was written during a European epoch which has been termed the 'Little Ice Age' and Perth's chroniclers recorded a succession of debilitating floods and severe winters, particularly in the early decades of the 17th century. Bad weather, spoilt harvests and the concomitant problems of food shortages created condition in which infectious diseases such as typhus and smallpox could spread; urban communities were particularly susceptible to the spread of bubonic plague. The 'Chronicle' contains a litany of such woes.

The generally poor and erratic weather of the 'Little Ice Age' was punctuated by severe winters and wet summers.[20] The 'Chronicle of Perth' offers a portrait of intermittently freezing winters and summer dearths which fits the general trend and not only does the manuscript record the nature of bad weather but it also points to the effects which such crises had upon the lives of the inhabitants of town and country.

The 1620s were dismal years in Perthshire, beginning with a bad harvest and major flooding in 1621. The 'Chronicle of Perth' includes a lengthy, evocative account of the inundation which swept away the bridge of Tay:

14 october 1621

Thair wes suche ane inwnda(o)un of vater as ye luyke in no manes remembrance wes sene both in reguaird of ye hiche rysing in the most sorte As also of the sudane cumyng of it be(in)g setterday all day wating efter . . . IT semit ye wandowis of heawin and funtanes of ye deip wer opponit IT cariet away ye ellewin bow brig of Tay . . . The peopill of ye castil gawill hed died about iijc soules gif a boatt hed not bene borne be men from ye spey tour to it god lett ws nawer sie ye ellik of it againe . . .

In the short-term, the burgh and surrounding communities faced food shortages. The 'Chronicle' states that there was scarcity throughout the kingdom in 1621/2, somewhat alleviated by imports of foreign victuals. But there was 'great mortalitie' at harvest time in 1622 and in the following year 'x or xij deit ordinarlie euerie day from midsomer to mychaelmes wtin yis burt'. The longer term effects of such a catastrophe included large repair bills for the properties which had been damaged. New flood defences were not constructed until 1630 and – for a host of reasons – Perth remained without a bridge over the Tay until the second half of the 18th century.

At the height of the flood in January 1993, 65 sq km of rural land was under water and much of the inundated area was farmland in the straths of the Earn, Isla, Tummel and Tay. Smith has written that the characteristics of flood damage in rural areas include prolonged waterlogging of fields and grazing land; the destruction of buildings and land divisions; the spread of river deposits on the land; scouring and the removal of topsoil. The only tangible benefit of flooding may be the spread of minerals across arable land.[21] The 17th-century landscape of Perthshire was not as intensively cultivated or populated as modern Tayside but the experience of modern farmers probably mirrors that of their early modern predecessors. Thus there is likely to have been widespread dislocation in the late autumn of 1621, with damage to livestock and farmland which would have affected crop production in the following years. Harsh winters and a population weakened by diseases compounded this situation. Given that the trials of the 1620s were soon followed by the disturbances of civil war and military occupation, it is apparent that the first half of the 17th century was an era of concentrated hardships.

Floods, heavy snows, earthquakes and visitations of disease were all exceptional events but their effects were long-lasting and the inhabitants of early modern Perthshire were forced to endure some of these phenomena at least once in every generation. It should be no surprise that their written records are infused with a fear of such divine judgements.

One of the most serious epidemics of disease occurred in the mid-1580s, coupled with severe food shortages. According to the 'Chronicle', 'pest' arrived in Perth in September 1584 and lasted until August 1585, 'quharin) at the plesor of god deptit this lyff xiiij cc xxvij persones young and auld thby'. These are very high mortality figures and the 'pest' – probably bubonic plague – was also rampant in Fife and in Edinburgh at that time. The crops were 'universally corrupted' and in the St Andrews area the spread of disease was aggravated by wet harvest weather in 1585.[22] The records of the Perth Kirk Session include several references to the sufferings of the urban poor during the visitation. In November 1584, a list of poor people in Perth was presented to the session which detailed that there were over 550 in the High Street alone; a separate list was prepared of those people who were 'ashamed to be put in the Roll with common Beggars, + yet sustained great penury'.[23] Many of the needy are likely to have been itinerants from the countryside but the town dwellers were obviously suffering as well. Arrangements were made for distributions of food but by the New Year stocks were running out. In February 1585 it was recorded that 'Forasmeikle as there were sundry poor ones, within + without the Town in the Lodges, abill (likely) to perish . . . + the victual that was sent by the country for the support of the poor was all distributed, so that there was none left. Therefore it was ordained that ilk one who received meal, should have weekly for the peck 30 pennies. And these that received Bread, should for ilk loaf have 3 pennies; 'Till God moved the Hearts of the Gentlemen of the country to send more support for their Relief'.[24]

The Earl of Atholl responded to the crisis by sending some Highland cattle to Perth, which were sold for 8 merks and 10 pennies each and the burgh of Edinburgh sent financial aid for the poor and deprived. A large quantity of butter was sent from Stirling: 'The elders sold it to a merchant for thirty eight pounds current money of the realm to be bestowed by them on the poor & the merchant indemnified himself by retailing it in pounds & half pounds weight to all who could/would afford to buy it . . . It was a luxury in which none but the comparatively rich could indulge'.[25]

Records of public fasts to exhort God to bring good harvest weather, or to alleviate suffering in time of need, are commonplace in the Perth Kirk Session records. The urban community lived in fear of crop failure and rural communities were often suspected of hoarding supplies in the countryside against a poor harvest but in times of scarcity, migrant workers were the first to suffer. In the towns and in the countryside of early modern Perthshire, scarcity and disease was still a prominent feature of ordinary life. Foreign imports could not always counter the effects of domestic harvest failures, nor could dispossessed and hungry people rely on the generosity of wealthy landowners. Even by the time of the Union, the common people of Perthshire led blighted lives.

The picture of early modern Perthshire is thus a mixture of complex political and economic developments in an environment rich with natural resources, offset by social problems which derived substantially from hostile climatic conditions. The period between the Reformation and the Union witnessed changes in landownership in Perthshire: for example families such as the Murrays of Scone and the Hays of Kinnoull rose to replace the influence of the Gowries. The volatile burgh of Perth reflected the political and religious vicissitudes of the age: it veered from being a royal residence to the home of Covenanters, reaffirmed its loyalties to the Stuarts at the Restoration but in the 18th century was occupied by both Jacobite and Hanoverian forces. Inland trade was increasingly competitive but Perth fought hard to retain its prominence within the sheriffdom. Perth's links with maritime trade seem to have been curtailed by the silting of the Tay and rival quays emerged which were closer to Dundee and the open sea. However, the economy was stifled by civil war and constantly threatened by the severities of the climate. The 17th century concluded with serious subsistence crises in Scotland – the 'Seven Ill Years' of the 1690s. If political union in 1707 pointed to the beginning of a new era, so did the passing of the 'Little Ice Age' in the early 18th century.

Notes

1   The 'Chronicle of Perth' forms part of the Advocates MSS in the National Library of Scotland, ref. Adv. 35.4.4. An edition of the manuscript was published in 1831 by James Maidment for the Maitland Club of Glasgow, entitled *The Chronicle of Perth*. A full transcript of the 'Chronicle', together with commentary and notes, can be found in *The Chronicle of Perth: An Historical and Archaeological Study* by JLM Eagles, 1995 PhD Thesis, University of St Andrews Library; all of the quotations from the 'Chronicle' which appear in this essay are taken from the 1995 transcript.

2   *The Register of the Privy Council*, 1st Series, Vol. VI (1884), 159–160.

3   NLS Adv. 31.1.6, *A Register of Deaths at Perth* by Rev James Scott, (c. 1784), 49–50.

4   See EM Furgol, *A Regimental History of the Covenanting Armies 1639–1651*, (1990), 225–6.

5   See *Scottish Population History from the 17th century to the 1930s*, ed M Flinn (1977), p. 147. Other mortality estimates include c. 9-12,000 in the Edinburgh area and c. 600 at Brechin.

6   NLS Map Library 1648 Z3/1(c) 'A Plan of an Ancient piece of Fortification Near Perth Lately Repair'd by the Rebels Drawn and Survey'd by Jas Leigh Jones Feb the 9th 1745/6'.

7   'Register Containing the State and Condition of Every Burgh within the Kingdome of Scotland, in the Year 1692', in *Miscellany of The Scottish Burgh Records Society*, (1881), 60.

8   *Ibid.*, 59–60. This material has been analysed by ID Whyte in *Agriculture and Society in Seventeenth Century Scotland*, (1979), 190–2.

9   See Whyte, *Agriculture and Society*, 191–2.

10   Perth Burgh Records in the AK Bell Library, ref. B59/36/10.

11   PBR, ref. B59/25/2/23 (8 papers).

12   'Report by Thomas Tucker upon the Settlement of the Revenues of Excise and Customs in Scotland', in *Early Travellers in Scotland*, ed. P Hume Brown (1891. Fascimile rep. 1978), 171–2.

13   'A short account of Scotland . . .' by Thomas Morer in *Ibid.*, 285–6.

14   See particularly NLS Adv. 15.1.1 Map and Description of County of Perth, c. 1680, and NLS Adv. 15.1.5, description (c. 1695?) in 'Scotland, Ireland, and the British Islands . . .' 1733.

15   *North-East Perth an archaeological landscape*, RCAHMS (1990), 1.

16   ID Whyte, 'Early Modern Scotland', in *An Historical Geography of Scotland*, ed. G Whittington and ID Whyte (1983), 126–7.

17   For details of the Murray family's involvement with the property at Huntingtower, see RD Pringle's guide for Historic Scotland (HMSO 1989).

18   The plates from John Slezer's *Theatrum Scotiae* are reproduced in *A Vision of Scotland* by Keith Cavers (1993); 'The Prospect of the House and Town of Skuyn' appears on p. 52.

19   NLS Adv. 30.5.23 121b. This engraving of Scone Palace from the north by A Rutherford (1775) is reproduced in *South-East Perthshire an archaeological landscape*, RCAHMS (1994), 144. This volume also contains details about the building history of the site.

20   For information about the 'Little Ice Age' see ML Parry, *Climatic Change, Agriculture and Settlement* (1978), and G Whittington, 'The Little Ice Age and Scotland's Weather' in *The Scottish Geographical Magazine*, 101, (1985).

21   See R Smith, *The Great Flood*, (1993), Ch. 5.

22   Details in C Creighton, *A History of Epidemics in Britain*, (1891), 367–9, and R Chambers, *Domestic Annals of Scotland from the Reformation to the Revolution*, (1859), Volume 1, 154, 157–9.

23   NLS Adv. 31.1.6, 26–7.

24   NLS Adv. 31.1.1, *Extracts from Perth Kirk Session Register 1577–1620*, Rev James Scott, Volume 1 (1774).

25   See NLS Adv. 31.1.6, 28, and Perth Museum and Art Gallery Archive no. 346, *Account of the Plague in Scotland . . .* Rev James Scott, (1814), 2–3.

SEVEN

MODERN TIMES

The Jacobite movement came into being in 1688 when James VII and II, a Roman Catholic, effectively abandoned the throne to his daughter Mary and her husband William of Orange, both Protestants. Although frequently regarded as such, Jacobitism was not a single issue philosophy, the devotion of its adherents to James, if not its guiding principle, was at least a convenient cover for other causes of unrest. It embraced loyalty to the Stuart line (particularly after the death of Queen Anne in 1714), to the Roman Catholic and Episcopalian churches and was later linked to Toryism, a political grouping of natural supporters of the old order which had been politically sidelined through George I's preference for the Whigs. It was fuelled further by the deeply unpopular Act of Union of 1707 and, perhaps most importantly, by promises of practical support from France. If words had been backed by deeds and if the Jacobite leadership had been more effective, the movement might well have achieved its aims and the future of Scotland and the Union been radically different. Its failure, in fact, did more than anything to cement the Union and to bring about the speedy integration of the Highlands with the rest of the country. Perthshire, which dominates the centre of Scotland and which has a foot in both the Highlands and Lowlands, saw much of the Jacobite melodrama played out over its straths and glens.

John Graham of Claverhouse, Viscount Dundee, was the first, in April 1689, to raise the standard of King James. The exiled king, however, was not popular, particularly following his recent display of aggressive arrogance to the Scottish Convention, and few rallied to the cause. Claverhouse began his campaign in Dundee and then marched north-west to Blair Castle, the strategically important seat of the Marquis of Atholl, which guarded the main routes to the north and north-east of the country. The Convention army under General Mackay had the same idea and both sides met on 27 July 1689 at the pass of Killiecrankie, midway between Pitlochry and Blair Atholl. The Jacobite forces won the day though Claverhouse was killed at the moment of victory. Under new leadership the Jacobite army moved south towards the Lowlands but was checked at Dunkeld in August where both the town and the army were effectively destroyed. The *coup de grace* to the first Jacobite rising was delivered the following spring at the Battle of Cromdale in southern Inverness-shire.

Twenty-five years later, with most of Perthshire and indeed the north of Scotland now sympathetic to the cause, the hopes for Jacobite success were at their highest. John, 11th Earl of Mar, whose outward show of loyalty to George I had been snubbed by that monarch, raised the Jacobite standard in Aberdeenshire in September 1715. He proved himself to be a remarkably inept military leader whose hopes, like those of Dundee, were dashed on the soil of Perthshire. The Battle of Sherriffmuir was fought in the south of the county in November 1715 between Mar and the Duke of Argyll and, though tactically indecisive, was a strategic defeat for the Jacobites. James, the Old Pretender, arrived in Scotland at the end of December and briefly set up court at Scone. By early February, however, in the knowledge that Argyll was advancing along Strathearn towards Perth and that his own retreating followers had burnt and laid waste several villages, including those of Auchterarder, Blackford and Dunning, he and Mar fled to the coast at Montrose and took ship for France.

The government response to the '15 seems to have been both slow and comparatively mild, with few reprisals being taken against the rebels. The report on 'the situation of the Highlanders', compiled by General George Wade in 1724, recommended amongst other measures the construction of more roads and bridges to allow government forces to move around the Highlands more quickly and the raising of Highland companies, led by Gaelic-speaking officers, to keep a watchful eye over the troublesome Jacobite clans. Both suggestions were acted upon. Within fifteen years around 250 miles of Highland road had been constructed, along with about 40 bridges, and at Aberfeldy the Highland companies had been formed into the Black Watch regiment. Ironically it was the execution in 1743 of three members of the Black Watch, for refusing to serve abroad when in fact they were only obliged to serve in Britain, which gave added impetus to the Jacobite cause in the Atholl homeland. As could perhaps have been foreseen, the army which made the most of the new military roads was that of the Young Pretender.

The '45 began, as indeed it ended, with a mere handful of supporters on the shores of the north-west of Scotland. On 19 August Prince Charles Edward Stuart raised his standard at Glenfinnan and within twelve days, after side-stepping General Sir John Cope, arrived at Blair Atholl, ready to descend on the Lowlands. If the men of Atholl had been more resolutely Hanoverian in their politics or if the main route south had taken the Prince through the Breadalbane territories of the Whiggish Campbells, it is tempting to think that he might finally have been forced to see sense and turn back. Instead, the considerable, though not universal, support for the cause in Atholl allowed him an open gateway to the south. These divided political loyalties are well illustrated by those of the ducal house itself. James,

2nd Duke of Atholl, succeeded to the title on the death of his father in 1724 only because his elder brother, William, having been out in the '15, was deprived of his right to inherit. Their younger brother, Lord George Murray, was also staunchly Jacobite and with a wealth of military experience behind him was one of the Prince's most able commanders. When Charles and his army, including the Jacobite Duke William, arrived at Blair Castle, Hanoverian Duke James fled south.

It was a short march from the Atholl heartlands to Perth. The town had not fared particularly well during the '15 and many of the inhabitants would have been unhappy at the approach of yet another crowd of rebellious Highlanders. Those who could flee, including the magistrates and senior townspeople, did. After a sojourn of eight days the army moved south, heading for Edinburgh, Carlisle and the eventual turning point at Derby. Within months, of course, the tide of fortune had ebbed for Charles and he and his army again crossed Perthshire, drawing Cumberland with him, both destined for the final showdown at Culloden in April 1746.

From the benefit of hindsight the rout at Culloden marked the end of Jacobitism in Britain. At the time, however, a further uprising was felt to be a distinct possibility and it was this perception, together with a desire for revenge and punishment, which led to the repressive measures taken against Highland society and culture and the resultant general annexation of the Highlands to the rest of Scotland. The clamp-down was harsh. This was the first time that a British government had been able to stamp its authority on the Highlands and it was determined to ensure that never again did such a large part of the mainland defy Westminster rule. The bearing of arms was once again forbidden, Highland dress and the bagpipes were outlawed, rebel estates were forfeited (although this was often to the material advantage of the tenants) and the Heritable Jurisdictions (Scotland) Act of 1747 ended the vice-regal powers of many of Scotland's great landowners. Few suffered more under this act than the loyal 2nd Duke of Atholl whose Regality of Atholl covered a large part of north Perthshire. The effect of such measures was to sever the powerful bond between the Highlander and his distinctive culture and the loyalty of the clansman to his chief. Thereafter, the age-old filial ties between a man and his clan were replaced as the basis of Highland society by the new landlord-tenant relationship.

It is tempting but inaccurate to regard the failure of the '45 as the beginning of the end of the old Highland way of life. Far more subtle assaults on the isolation of the Highlands had already come in the forms, firstly, of an increasingly commercialised economy and, secondly, of a creeping anglicisation both of which predated by several decades the post-Culloden reprisals. The Campbells of Breadalbane, who were predominantly landowners without a strong clan following, were pioneering even in the early 17th century the move away from a self-sufficient economy to one founded on more commercial principles. The opening of the lead mines at Tyndrum in 1739 is but one example. The Society in Scotland for Propagating Christian Knowledge (the SSPCK) was founded in 1709 and aimed (in broad terms) to provide, through the medium of the English language, a sound Christian education for those in the Highlands and Islands. The establishment, within fifty years, of at least one such school in most parishes in Highland Perthshire undoubtedly hastened the retreat of the Gaelic from the county's glens. Although regarded by purists as a vulgar form of the language, the near extinction of Perthshire Gaelic in the 1990s marked the end of a linguistic era which must have spanned more than a thousand years. Bilingualism was a necessary attribute for the many agricultural workers who went south during the summer months to work in the fields of the Lowlands and for the whisky smugglers who maintained the steady flow of liquor out of the Highlands. English influence also penetrated the Highland line through the gentry and ruling classes who in many cases, having been sent to England for schooling, began to imitate English manners and English ways of thinking. When they returned to their Scottish estates they thought in terms of 'improvement' along English lines.

With their language and culture under threat and the social system of centuries dissolved in decades the people of Highland Perthshire, by the end of the 18th century, were no longer regarded as barbarian foreigners by their neighbours south of the Highland line. On the contrary, thanks partly to James Macpherson of Ossian fame, the Highlands were already being seen in a new light. Curiosity about ancient Celtic lore, a reassessment of the Highlands as an area of considerable natural beauty and the general *zeitgeist* of romanticism were inexorably drawing the Highlands closer to the mainstream of European culture.

The second half of the 18th century saw remarkable improvements in the agriculture of Lowland Perthshire which added significantly to the prosperity of the county. The transformation was graphically described by James Robertson in his *General view of the Agriculture of the County of Perth* which was published in 1799. He remarks 'What an astonishing change has taken place even in the memory of man! About half a century ago the country was uninclosed, the fields uncultivated and the farmers spiritless and poor . . . Then the farmer went on foot to market; now he rides well dressed and mounted: formerly he ate his food off his knee, and it consisted of meal, vegetables and milk: now his table is covered, his knife and fork are laid down before him to dine on meat . . . he sleeps comfortably on feathers with his curtains drawn snugly around him . . .'

Enclosures, the abandonment of the old infield-outfield system, the introduction of new crops such as potatoes and turnips, crop rotation and land
drainage (particularly in the Carse of Gowrie) all contributed to this
radical change in the basis of the Perthshire economy.

Beyond the Highland line, where poorer soil made arable farming difficult, the emphasis was on livestock production. The Highland economy in
the 17th and 18th centuries was dependent to a great extent on the rearing
of black cattle, many of which went to feed the great cities of England.
Crieff, situated at the edge of the Highlands and at the end of a huge
network of drove roads, had become the most important town in Scotland
for the sale of these cattle and in its heyday would have seen up to 30,000
beasts changing hands in the one week duration of the annual tryst. By
1770, however, Crieff had given way to Falkirk, though only temporarily,
as the cattle capital of the nation.

Agricultural improvements contributed to the evolving landscape as did
the work of the 'planting lairds'. Robertson described how, in a bid to
reverse the process of deforestation, forestry plantations had increased
rapidly both in size and number, 'thriving in almost every corner of the
county' from Stormont, Atholl and Breadalbane to Strathearn, Strathallan
and the Carse of Gowrie. The fourth Duke of Atholl alone,whose estates
covered vast areas of north Perthshire and stretched south to Dunkeld, is
believed to have planted a remarkable 27,000,000 trees of which
15,000,000 were larch. Descendants of these trees still soften the Atholl
landscape.

Townscapes changed too. Perth moved into a new era after the '45
although the process of change, in some ways just as rapid as that enforced
on Highland society, was rather more a regeneration from within than an
imposition from outside. The end of Jacobitism more or less coincided
with an upturn in the fortunes of the county town which, following its loss
of status towards the end of the medieval period, had struggled to find a
new role for itself. This finally came in the 1760s when the town broke free
from the confines of the old city walls and, in the spirit of the age of
enlightenment, gradually blossomed into one of the most elegant and
admired towns in Scotland. The completion of the Perth Bridge in 1771,
150 years after the destruction of the previous one, was one of the first
signs and a symbolic one too, of Perth's renewed openness to the outside
world. Most of the credit for the town's transformation should go to
Thomas Hay Marshall who, making use of his father-in-law's plans, began
the construction of the Georgian suburbs to the north and south. Rose
Terrace, with the magnificent Old Academy building in the centre, Atholl
Crescent and Marshall Place are some of the finest examples of Georgian
architecture outside the capital. The Victorian years saw expansion to the

east, on the lower slopes of Kinnoull and to the west in the shape of the ribbon development along the Glasgow Road and the growth of Craigie.

The town's architectural renaissance may have been envisaged by men of foresight but it was only made possible by an increasing prosperity, firmly founded on agriculture and textiles. In the 18th century the manufacture of linen at thousands of hand looms across the country was, after agriculture, Scotland's main industry. Perthshire was one of the five main linen-producing counties at this time, working with flax either locally grown or imported from across the North Sea and Perth itself according to the statistics of the period, produced almost as much linen as the rest of the county put together. In and around Glasgow, however, towards the end of the 18th century, cotton was the boom industry and the big firms of the metropolis were rapidly extending their network of outworkers towards the east, even to the extent of having infiltrated Blair Atholl by the 1790s. By the turn of the century it appears that most of Perth's weavers had made the change from linen to cotton. The most obvious sign of the successful establishment of the cotton industry in the east was the construction in the 1780s of the huge cotton mill at Stanley, powered by the Tay and built at the instigation of the Duke of Atholl and under the direction, initially at least, of Richard Arkwright. By the early 1800s Perth had developed into one of the most important textile towns in Scotland. Within easy reach of the town's cotton weavers could be found the rump of the nation's linen industry (still thriving in Fife and Angus), four major bleachfields (including Scotland's largest at Luncarty), a number of textile printing works and, at Stanley and Cromwellpark, two of the comparatively few cotton mills in the east. Linen and cotton were not the only textiles to come out of Perthshire. The Highland areas, where sheep farming predominated, concentrated in the main on wool while the mills of Blairgowrie abandoned linen production towards the middle of the century and turned to jute, now easily obtainable in the nearby city of Dundee.

Perth itself was known throughout Britain for its fine handkerchiefs and top quality waxed umbrella cloth. A considerable proportion of finished textiles, perhaps as much as half, also went overseas, so when the French blockaded British exports around 1810 about sixty textile businesses, suddenly deprived of their overseas markets, were forced to close. The industry later revived to a limited extent but the gradual introduction of power looms towards the middle of the century finally signified the end for the many handloom weavers of the city and indeed the county. Weaving was not the only industry to suffer. Several of the great printing presses of Perth fell silent in the early 19th century and many of the town's glove-makers became redundant. The 1840s – the Hungry Forties as they have been called – were such lean years for the people of Perth that the Town

Council resorted to various employment creation measures, including the laying out of the North Inch circular walk. The people of Perth were effectively rescued by companies on which, to a greater or lesser degree, the prosperity of the city still depends.

By the middle of the 19th century the mechanisation of the textile industry and the growing number of factories in the Lowlands had had a profound effect on the county as a whole. In 1831 the population of Perthshire reached its peak at 142,166, after which it went into a slow decline. These statistics, however, hide the significant change in the distribution of the population which, for example, saw the city of Perth double to just over 19,000 between the years 1755 and 1821 and the numbers in Blairgowrie increase almost tenfold during the course of the 19th century to around 4000. Swelling urban populations were paid for by the phenomenon of rural depopulation which began first in the Lowlands, with the agricultural improvements of the later 18th century and then, early in the following century and for much the same reason, in the Perthshire Highlands. The minister of Fortingall, writing in the *New Statistical Account*, stated that between the 1790s and 1838 the population had fallen by 50% in certain parts of the parish, with 120 families having emigrated across the Atlantic. In the neighbouring parish of Blair Atholl there had been a 25% decrease in numbers between 1755 and 1814, particularly from the parish uplands. The commentary on the 1831 census statistics frequently gave the same reason for the decline in both Highland and Lowland rural parish populations as could be found in the Statistical Accounts of forty years earlier, namely the 'enlargement of farms and consequent removal of cottars'. There were other reasons too. Blackface sheep were colonising the north-west of the county in ever greater numbers and although Perthshire escaped the magnitude of the Duke of Sutherland's clearances, the second Marquis of Breadalbane acted in a similarly inhumane manner in Glenquaich and in other parts of his estates. The above minister of Blair Atholl described the clearances in his own parish in the following terms: 'A system of more beneficial management has converted these dreary and comfortless habitations into sheep-walks; and greatly to their own interest, though not perhaps at first so congenially to their feelings, the people have emigrated to the large towns of the south, or to America'. The failure of the potato crop in the mid-1840s, particularly in the north-west of Scotland but also in Perthshire, was another factor contributing towards the drifting away of the rural population. Meanwhile the author of the *New Statistical Account* of Perth recorded the presence of Highlanders who spoke no English and a 'considerable number' who spoke both English and Gaelic – in a town where Gaelic is believed to have died out in later medieval times. From around 1786 Perth had a Gaelic

Chapel and even its own Highland suburb: the west end of the High Street was known as Glencoe, a name which survived until the mid-1970s in the form of the Glencoe Tavern.

Across Europe the 1830s and 1840s were decades of considerable political instability. Scotland, struggling to cope with Highland emigration and one of the highest rates of urban growth in Europe, did not escape the mood of unrest which came to be embodied in Chartism. This was a radical movement which demanded electoral reform and greater democracy in government and which tended to flourish in areas where life was particularly harsh. Perthshire, however, was enjoying one of the lowest rates of pauperism in the country at that time and it may have been for this reason alone that the Chartist leaders, in spite of rallying tours across the county, never succeeded in raising much support. Indeed the local press, even the Tory *Perthshire Courier*, regarded their attempts as pathetically humorous rather than subversive. Perhaps the only surviving monument to radicalism in Perthshire is the tiny village of Ardler (on the border with Angus) which was planned in the 1830s by George Kinloch, later MP for Dundee, as a collecting centre for the agricultural produce of Strathmore. He had intended the village to be named Washington, after the American president and the streets to bear the names of his political and philosophical heroes, including Jeremy Bentham, Benjamin Franklin and William Wallace. The project, conceived in the fine Scottish tradition of planned villages, was never completed.

Social improvement, not political reform, was higher up the county's agenda in this period. The growing awareness that man could fight back in the war against disease led to two beneficial developments for the people of Perth and later for the county. Perth's water supply was originally taken from both the Tay and the town's lade, the latter by the early 19th century becoming unacceptably polluted by the textile firms further upstream. The realisation too that a full regiment of soldiers in the barracks were using the lade for their morning ablutions at about the same time that many families downstream were drawing water for breakfast made the need for a clean water supply even more apparent. Adam Anderson, then Rector of Perth Academy and later Professor of Natural Philosophy at St Andrews, had already engineered a gas supply for central Perth in the 1820s and was commissioned to do the same with water. The finished result, in 1832, was the classically designed waterworks on the corner of Marshall Place and Tay Street (which now functions as the Fergusson Gallery) and a steady flow of pure water, taken from the Tay, extensively filtered and supplied firstly to street wells and eventually to many houses in central Perth. Blairgowrie acquired its own waterworks in 1870 and Crieff in 1872.

What may have given added impetus to the completion of the Perth system was the threat from the relentless progress of cholera which was then sweeping the nation. In February 1832, in the knowledge that the dreaded disease was on its way north from Edinburgh, a public meeting was held to discuss preventative measures during which it was decided, amongst others, to cleanse and whitewash the houses of the city's poor. On 7 March the first cases were reported in the city although the *Perthshire Courier*, in what seems to have been a blatant attempt to prevent panic, stated on 8 March that the town was still quite free from cholera apart from the fact that two people were ill showing all its symptoms! A variety of measures were designed to check the spread of the disease within the town, including the burning of tar barrels in the streets to purify the air, the setting up of a rudimentary health inspectorate and the feeding of the poor in soup kitchens. Even so, a total of 147 people had succumbed by the end of the year. Other parts of the county were affected to greater or lesser extents; Aberfeldy, with only a small fraction of Perth's population, lost 54 within the first fortnight while Comrie escaped completely untouched. High though some of these figures may seem, when compared with the estimated Scottish total of 10,000 deaths in 1832, Perthshire would seem to have weathered the storm remarkably well.

This visitation was behind the first attempts to provide Perth with a modern hospital. The idea was first proposed in 1832 and by 1835 funds were actively being sought for a building with the dual purpose of providing 'a place of refuge for the poor when seized with epidemic or infectious diseases' and of preventing the further spread of such disease. Three years later, in York Place, the County and City of Perth Infirmary opened its doors for the first time. Other towns waited before following Perth's lead. Aberfeldy, perhaps mindful of the ravages of cholera, had a Home for the Sick by the 1860s, while similar proposals were being put forward in Crieff a decade later. Public opinion felt, however, that even in the days of horse-drawn transport the infirmary in Perth was close enough and that the presence of a hospital in Crieff would change the town from a health resort into a centre for the sick. Crieff eventually built its own hospital in 1906 while the towns of Blairgowrie and Pitlochry achieved theirs at about the same time. Curiously enough, Perthshire was being served by two good mental hospitals, at Perth and Murthly, well before many of the county's cottage hospitals had been established.

Prior to the Education (Scotland) Act of 1872 the schools of the nation lacked a unified organisational structure. The *Old Statistical Account* for the parish of Fortingall records the presence in the 1790s of one parish school, four SSPCK schools and six small private ones. Added to this in other areas were Free Church schools, several other types of educational undertakings and, in the towns, the great burgh schools. Some parish schools had an excellent reputation and equipped the most able pupils to move on directly to university. The *Old Statistical Account* for Madderty parish stated that the school was 'attended by numerous boarders from different parts of Scotland, but chiefly England'. The schoolmaster there taught English, Latin, Greek, writing, arithmetic, book-keeping, mathematics and even land surveying.

The original Perth Grammar School is first mentioned in a charter of 1150 and for centuries served as the main burgh school offering a strongly traditional, classics-based education. Perth Academy was established in 1760 and, with its greater emphasis on mathematics and the sciences, was geared more towards the demands of everyday life and the worlds of business and commerce. In 1807 both schools, whilst retaining their independence, moved into what is now known as the Old Academy building in the middle of Rose Terrace. The advancement of a number of rectors and second masters of these schools to university professorships is a measure of the high academic standards found in Perth.

The prosperity and former primacy of Perth owed much to its excellent location on the Tay at a point where the river was still navigable at high tide and fordable at low tide. The opening of the Perth Bridge in 1771 (described by Pennant as 'the most beautiful structure of the kind in North Britain') and later the new turnpike roads radiating from it reinforced the town's central position in the communications network. Perth had also benefited economically from its long history of maritime trade, not only with the ports of Britain and western Europe but also with the Baltic and the Mediterranean. The town, however, had a major problem with the Tay which had a tendency to silt up, thus preventing larger ships from reaching the original harbour at the foot of the High Street. The harbour over many years was moved progressively downstream to its present location at Friarton, which dates from 1845, although since then, because of its inland location and dependency on tides, it has never been able to compete with the port of Dundee.

While the harbour was in slow decline the rapidly blossoming railway network gave Perth a much needed economic boost. The railway arrived in Perth towards the end of the 1840s and within ten to fifteen years had reached out to many parts of lowland rural Perthshire. Several of the city's well-known businesses of today rode to prosperity on the back of the steam engine, including Pullars, Dewars, Bells and Macdonald Fraser and indeed the railway itself was employing over 1700 local inhabitants as recently as 1964. Pullars began in a small and bold way in the 1810s when the town's textile industry was deep in crisis and yet, within eighty years or so, had grown into arguably the largest dyeing and dry-cleaning business in the world. The firm depended on the national railway network and an army of agents across the nation to bring work into Perth. In a similar way, following the decline of the Falkirk cattle tryst, the well-known firm of Macdonald Fraser (now a part of United Auctions) relied on the railway system to bring animals from all over Scotland into Perth for auction. The Perth firms of Bells and Dewars, both at the forefront of the art of whisky blending, used the railways firstly to bring in malt and grain whiskies from selected distilleries and secondly, once blended, to send millions of bottles out of Perth to all parts of Britain.

Travellers were visiting Perthshire in ever greater numbers from the later 18th century and by the early 19th, when the first guidebooks to Perth were being written, the individual traveller in the mould of Boswell, Johnson and Pennant had been replaced by the early modern tourist. Highland culture had been rehabilitated in the popular imagination by the bekilted George IV when he visited Edinburgh in 1822 and Sir Walter Scott's novel of 1828, *The Fair Maid of Perth*, with its lavish praise of Perthshire scenery in the opening paragraph, put the county firmly on the tourist map. While Queen Victoria's trip in 1842 confirmed Scotland as a favourite destination it was the creation of the railway network which allowed many others to follow in her footsteps. The village of Birnam, for example, developed into the attractive tourist village it is today, only after the railway arrived in 1856, and Pitlochry experienced a similar transformation from 1863 when it replaced Birnam as the terminus for the Highland Railway.

The early 20th century saw brief flurries of social conflict. Suffragettes, who were vilified locally at the best of times, succeeded in burning two Perthshire mansions to the ground in February 1914 while a third, Aberuchill Castle, was saved only in the nick of time. Ironically, 80 years later almost to the day, it was not quite so lucky. A number of suffragettes were held at Perth Prison which gained a certain notoriety for its rough force-feeding of women. Perthshire, lacking the usual breeding grounds of heavy industry and urban deprivation, escaped much of the industrial unrest of Red Clydeside. The huge Pullars firm, however, by far the largest individual employer in the county, had long endured a history of poor management-workforce relations which, exacerbated by war, finally came to head in 1917. Outside the company's dye-works an angry mob of 2000 besieged the gates and led to the mounted police being called in. By the following year the Pullar family had given up the struggle and sold the company. Many local workers, obeying the national call, were somewhat reluctantly sucked into the General Strike of May 1926. The shutting down of the railways had knock-on effects on Dewars and Pullars, both of which had to close temporarily, while the spring holidaymakers in Crieff, fearing a long strike, stampeded for the last trains home. All the staff of the *Perthshire Advertiser* laid down tools bar one young apprentice who was probably mortified to find himself featured in the same paper at the end of the strike, described glowingly as a future works manager.

With Perth being the home of the Black Watch and the county its main recruiting territory, the two world wars locally took their toll. The regiment, swallowed up by the Highland Division in 1908, was active in Flanders and the Middle East in the First War and suffered around 8000 deaths and a further 20,000 casualties. Little wonder that the local press reported 'no Mafficking' at the signing of the Armistice in 1918. Few, if any, towns and villages had remained untouched by the war and most quickly erected poignant memorials. The restoration of St John's Kirk in 1928 and the opening of the Bowerswell Memorial Homes in 1950, both in Perth, were particularly practical commemorations of the city and county war dead. Many Perthshire lads were amongst the 10,000 troops captured by Rommel at St Valery in Normandy in June 1940 and spent much of World War II in POW camps in Germany. Others, in the reborn 51st, later chased the same general across the North African desert in 1942 and 1943 and were allowed the privilege of liberating St Valery in 1944. The celebrations in central Perth in May 1995 to mark the 50th anniversary of VE Day were reckoned to be the biggest and best attended outside London and a worthy tribute to the fighting men of Perthshire.

Divisions in Perthshire are now focused on the ballot box where Conservatives and Scottish Nationalists vie for the local vote. The SNP claim that rural Perthshire, behind its Tory facade, has long been sympathetic to their cause and indeed have recently been enjoying considerable success at the polls. In May 1995 Roseanna Cunningham won the Perth and Kinross parliamentary seat for the SNP and in doing so gave the Conservatives, who had held both the county's seats for many years (apart from the SNP's tenure of Perth and East Perthshire between 1974 and 1979), a salutary reminder of the dangers of complacency. The Labour Party, going by local government election results, are strong only in Perth city.

In 1974 the old system of town and county councils, which had been the vehicle for the administration of local government since the 1890s, was replaced by district and regional councils. A large part of south-western Perthshire was hived off to form a part of Stirling District while the rest joined with Kinross-shire to become Perth and Kinross District, a part of Tayside Region. In 1996 the two-tier system was abandoned in favour of unitary authorities whereupon Perth and Kinross District, with the addition of Longforgan and Invergowrie, transmogrified into Perth and Kinross Council area. In its brief life, however and under various political administrations, the district council achieved a great deal, not least of its laurels being the much flaunted 'best quality of life' accolade. This resulted from a 1990 report by the Glasgow Quality of Life Group (funded by Glasgow and Strathclyde universities) which, in a comparison of 145 medium-sized district councils throughout the UK, placed Perth and Kinross at the top of the rankings and rated it particularly highly for its health services, housing, transport infrastructure and proximity to pleasant scenery. Other successes included, for Perth itself, a remarkable number of civic improvements and the Britain in Bloom title (large town category) in 1993 and 1995.

At the time of writing (1996) the Perth and Kinross Healthcare Trust supervises the health of the area, providing hospital and GP services in most of the larger centres of population. Perth Royal Infirmary, opened in 1914 and still the main hospital in Perth and Kinross, underwent a major extension and refurbishment in 1993. Housing stock is generally in good order with the council having successfully eliminated some of the worst housing blackspots in Scotland. Educationally, the council is now responsible for over 70 primary and 10 secondary schools. Perth College is the main institution of tertiary education, the town's bid to attract a brand new university in the 1960s having been pre-empted by Stirling. Perthshire is well served by a good road network with dual carriageway links to Edinburgh, Glasgow and Dundee. The Scottish Office, however, have been reluctant to upgrade the A9 north of Perth to a similar status and to approve the recent clamour for a third bridge over the Tay at Perth. Railway links with the rest of Scotland are a shadow of what they once were while conversely Perth Harbour has been enjoying a renaissance in recent years.

Perthshire's economic base seems secure. Agriculture is still one of the chief contributors to the county's wealth, with seed potatoes and soft fruit being the best known exports. Tourism is now the biggest income generator, contributing over £200 million annually to the local economy whereas about fifty years ago the figure was less than £700,000. The whisky companies remain, the blenders (no longer independent) in the city and the distillers in the country and have recently been joined by the UK's biggest producer of natural mineral water, Highland Spring at Blackford. Two Perth-based companies are now amongst the world leaders in their respective fields, the insurance giant General Accident and the public transport firm of Stage-coach. The development of hydro-electric power stations in mid-century across north Perthshire created much-needed employment and at the same time, with the building of dams and the creation and enlargement of lochs, changed in a small way the face of the landscape. The combined efforts of the Perthshire Enterprise Company, Scottish Enterprise Tayside, the Highland Perthshire Development Company (now under threat) and local initiatives such as the Aberfeldy

Locus Project have helped to stimulate the economic wellbeing of the whole area. It is no accident that unemployment figures tend to be well below the national average.

The flagship of the local arts scene is the Perth Festival of the Arts which celebrated its 25th season in 1996 and is reckoned to be the second biggest in Scotland after the Edinburgh Festival. There are several other smaller events throughout the county each year including Music in Blair Atholl and the Dunkeld and Birnam Arts Festival. Perth Theatre, recently renovated, is one of the best attended in the country, while the summer programme at the Pitlochry Festival Theatre continues to attract playgoers from a wide area. Sport and leisure facilities range from skiing at Glenshee to golf at Gleneagles, from professional football at St Johnstone's McDiarmid Park to swimming at the highly popular Perth Leisure Pool and from sailing on the Perthshire lochs to hillwalking in the Perthshire Highlands.

This chapter began with Jacobite and government forces chasing each other across the county. It ends with a picture of an area generally at ease with itself. The social, political and geographical divisions undoubtedly still exist, as indeed they exist throughout the nation, but they lie well hidden beneath the relative prosperity of a county which itself is situated in one of the most historic and scenically attractive parts of Scotland.

SECTION TWO

EIGHT

THE RURAL ECONOMY

INTRODUCTION

Perthshire's rural economy has been traditionally dependent upon resource based activities, particularly agriculture. Although these activities still play a vital role in the economic and social health of the rural communities their preponderance, in terms of employment and finance, is no longer as great as it once was. The continuing process of urbanisation combined with changing land use practices has led to the depopulation of many of the remote glens of the area due to lack of employment opportunities. This movement of people has been a factor in the rising population of the larger rural burghs. Another, with perhaps greater consequences to long-term stability, has been in-migration to Perthshire as a whole. The greater part of Perthshire lies within the Highlands and the concomitant remoteness has restrained industrialisation except in the larger towns of the area. Even here, with the exception of Perth and possibly Kinross, the vast majority of industries are orientated to serving local needs. The distance from large markets, difficulty in obtaining and retaining suitable labour supply and the continuing pressure of rationalisation into larger units makes the possibility of the expansion of the industrial base into the remoter areas unlikely. Examination of present day rural activity reveals a diversified economic landscape, with tourism and tourist-related developments to the fore and industrial activity confined to the larger country settlements. Study of the employment structure (Table 1) reveals that, similar to Scotland as a whole, Perthshire is heavily dependent upon the service industry for employment opportunities, with retail and hotels and catering nearly double the Scottish average.

This chapter will consider the mobility of the rural economy in the recent past and the transitions that continue to shape the reality of residence in a landscape subject to physical and commercial restraints.

AGRICULTURE IN PERTHSHIRE

The agricultural industry remains one of the most important activities in Perthshire's rural hinterland and includes numerous small manufacturers and service providers engaged in activities closely related to and dependent upon the agricultural practices of the area. The topography and underlying

Table 1

Structure of Employment Perth and Kinross

Scotland selected categories 1991

Employment	Employees	Percentage	% Scotland
Agriculture/Forestry/Fishing	1780	3.9	1.4
Utilities	652	1.4	1.4
Extraction Industries	114	0.2	5.5
Engineering	413	0.9	6.4
Retail	6050	13.2	7.0
Hotels & Catering	5458	11.9	6.0
Transport	2089	1.7	4.0
Services	17844	39.0	43.7

geology of the district provide for a wide range of agricultural enterprises that include intensive vegetable and soft fruit farms, along with cereal and potato production in the lowland area and a preponderance of livestock production on the hills and uplands. The number of people directly involved in farming has declined considerably from the early 1960s when approximately 8,000 were employed, to the present day when the combined total of those employed in agriculture, forestry and fishing is less than 2,000, or 3.9% of the working population. The loss of so many jobs would seem to suggest that the industry is of little relevance today but its continuing importance is evident when this figure is compared with the Scottish total of 1.4% engaged in similar activities. The impetus for the decrease in numbers can be ascribed to changing farm practices and methods and, since the 1950s, increased mechanisation, resulting in far greater output per man.

In recent years major changes in support structures, grant aid mechanisms, health scares and heightened environmental awareness have had serious implications for the viability of the traditional farming concern. Despite all these problems the agricultural industry in Perthshire remains

Table 2

Agricultural Production of Tayside as a percentage of Scotland

Livestock	%	Crops	%
Dairy Cows	3	Seed Potatoes	51
Beef Cows	8	War Potatoes	33
Total Cattle	6	Vegetables	34
Total Sheep	9	Soft fruit	77
Total Pigs	13	Combined Crops	20
Goats	6		
Broilers/Table Birds	25		

an important producer within Scotland especially in seed potatoes and soft fruit. It has also maintained lines of production in livestock, Blackface sheep and particularly Aberdeen-Angus cattle for which the area is justifiably famous (Table 2). These economic restraints have been a catalyst for the introduction of fundamental changes in landscape use. Around 40% of farms have become involved in economic activity not directly related to agricultural production. These alternative enterprises on agricultural land are dominated by tourism and include accommodation, field and other sporting facilities, horse riding and arts and crafts pursuits.

The afforestation of numerous sites that have been taken out of agricultural production has also been a feature of the changing Perthshire landscape in recent years. In Tayside total agricultural land fell by 2% between 1985 and 1990; of this 15,000 Ha, 90% was rough grazing, generally land over 300 m and it is probable that the majority, if not all, of this land was in Highland Perthshire.

The agricultural industry in Perthshire as a whole is dependent upon financial support from the European Union and national government and many of those farmers operating in the Highland part of the area, with its preponderance of hill farms and smallholdings, find themselves vulnerable to political as well as market fluctuations. Any major redistribution of subsidies would lead to profound economic and social consequences in the farming industry and surrounding communities. Many of these small towns and villages have low population levels and some are fragile to the extent that community viability could be threatened by the knock on effect to support industries and their related workforces of a reduction in spending by the farming community.

FORESTRY IN PERTHSHIRE

The planting and extraction of woodlands is not a recent economic activity in Perthshire; its history can be traced to the late 16th century when the Breadalbane estate forested Drummond Hill. Large scale planting was also carried out in the late 18th and early 19th centuries on Atholl estate. Newspapers of the later period indicate that the woodlands of the area were regularly coppiced to provide timber for the shipbuilding and mining industries, the latter still a source of revenue in the mid 20th century. In the modern era estates have continued to carry out somewhat smaller afforestation schemes than those noted, whereas the Forestry Commission has been at the forefront of replanting woods harvested during the war years and the afforestation of bare land, witnessed by the tree-covered hillsides visible from the routeways of the district. Perthshire's woodland coverage has increased over the last century from 38,298 Ha in 1883 to approximately 61,000 Ha in 1949. Tayside Regional Council's forestry strategy document indicates that in 1991 11% of the land, 825.2 km², within their administrative boundary was woodland totalling 85,800 Ha; the majority of this coverage, approximately 68,000 Ha, was in Perthshire.

The woodlands of the region are a mixture of coniferous and deciduous plantations and semi-natural woodland, with conifer plantations dominating the landscape. Broadleaved trees of all types account for 14.6% of coverage with birch, scrub and high forest, the most common species covering 5,612 Ha; this is followed by oak, scrub and high forest, with 2,635 Ha. Yet it is the preponderance of conifer trees that is the most notable feature of the forested landscape, accounting for over 85% of high forest cover, the dominant species being Sitka spruce and Scots pine with 40% and 20% cover respectively. The dominance of Sitka spruce can be explained by its fast growth rate on poor quality soil and its use in a wide range of processing industries, particularly paper making. It is unlikely that the make-up of the forests in the area will change dramatically in the near future. Figures for the decade 1980–90 show a decline of 4% in broadleaved planting along with a similar reduction for Scots pine. During the same period an increase of 3% and 9% in the proportions of Lodgepole pine and Sitka spruce planted has been identified. The continuing rise in overall coverage of coniferous trees may be arrested in the future by the integration of forestry with other land use, especially agricultural diversification. The expected increase of broadleaved species due to farm forestry will depend upon levels of subsidies and market demand, a situation which may lead to the planting of species that offer the most reliable income source; although it should be noted that the majority of broadleaved new planting and restocking throughout Scotland since 1990 has been carried out on private land. Integrated woodlands on farm units providing an additional source of income and employment is to be welcomed but the small scale nature of such changes may mean that the continued survival of individual units rather than increased employment in rural areas is the outcome of any such diversification.

Traditional forestry activity provides employment in two main sectors – the primary industry of planting, maintenance and logging and the secondary one where the timber is turned into saleable products via processing factories and sawmills. The former provides employment for between 450 and 500 people in Tayside, 90% of whom live within a 32 km radius of the forest in which they work. This workforce makes an important contribution to the local economy, one that could become of even greater significance if the Forestry Commission estimates of 50% growth, nationally, in employment over the next two decades (due mainly to harvesting and restocking of current forest cover) are correct.

There are no wood processing plants in the area. More sawmills outwith the administrative boundaries of Tayside than inside utilise the timber harvested, although the ten enterprises that constitute 10% of Scotland's capacity (if hauliers are included) employ some 200 people. The hauliers form an important link in the chain that connects the region's timber resources with the three processing plants – Caledonian Paper Mill, Highland Forest Products and Cowie Caberboard – that utilise the majority of the timber produced. There is great potential for expansion in forestry-related employment and industry within the area. As an indication of the possibilities, more than 90% of the woodland cover is capable of producing an economic return, nearly half of which has been planted in the last thirty years. At present, production from the whole of Tayside is estimated at 150,000 tonnes per annum. The expansion of forested areas since 1988 confirms that there is considerable scope for enhanced economic return and employment prospects with a doubling of timber output expected by the year 2005. In Perthshire the economic viability of forest cover is only one factor amongst many that must be considered concerning maintenance, expansion and viability of the rural economy as a whole and the continued survival of remote towns and villages. If blanket woodland coverage extends to the lower hill slopes and the better agricultural land, other important activities that contribute to the area's economic health could be affected, especially the tourist industry.

Figure 11

Tayside Region: Forest And Agricultural Land

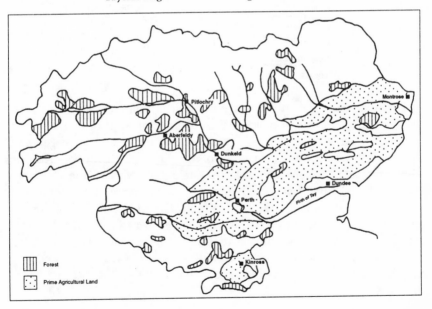

TOURISM AND OTHER RELATED ACTIVITIES

It is doubtful that any other author considering this topic 30 or 40 years ago would have included tourism as an important element in the rural economy; the possibility of expansion may have been related but the present day significance is unlikely to have been thought possible. Since then the expansion of leisure time and improvement in communications has made tourism an exceedingly important component of the continuing economic viability of many rural areas. Tourism in Tayside generated income of £155 million in 1987. The expansion of the industry is under-lined by the 1994 figures of £315.7 million, of which Perth and Kinross accounted for 70% or £221 million. A breakdown of the Perthshire figure reveals the true import of this industry to the rural areas where 70% of the income derived from tourism was expended – a financial input of approximately £155 million. It has been calculated that the revenue from tourism supports 7,680 full time equivalent jobs throughout Perthshire with 85% or 6,001 located outwith the city of Perth. The bulk of the expenditure and employment relates to retail, hotel and catering services, with accommodation accounting for nearly half of the total employment figures. Accordingly, the industry plays a particularly important role in the employment structure of rural areas, albeit variable and seasonal with fewer than half the number of jobs noted being supported in the winter months (Table 3).

Table 3

Income from Tourism Expenditure

Area	£ Million	% Perthshire
Perth City	35.8	16
Resort Hotels	30.6	14
Rest of Perthshire	155.0	70
Totals	221.4	100

The wide variety of free and paid tourist attractions in the area, from historic buildings to workplace visitor centres, make it difficult to deter-mine the levels of dependence that extend between tourist-generated income and the continued existence of related employment opportunities. That these connections exist is without doubt, witness the number of rural Bed and Breakfast establishments on farms or the camping and caravan sites on landed estates. Also indicative of the underlying import-ance of this revenue source are the amenities available at popular scenic spots, be it forest walks or the roadside mobile snack bar but perhaps the most perceptible link between traditional employment and the extra, possibly underpinning, revenue generated via tourism can be found at the distilleries.

There are five distilleries within the borders of Perthshire, three of which are situated in the Highland area, Edradour, Aberfeldy, Blair Atholl and two in the Lowlands, Glenturret outside Crieff and Tullibardine at Blackford. They were all founded in the late 18th or early 19th centuries and have been in more or less continuous production since. Most, if not all of these establishments cater for visitors in some form or another that varies from coach party tours to purpose-built visitor centres which depict the industrial history and process of whisky making as well as being a retail outlet for the finished product and other goods. It has not been possible to determine the exact number of overall employees connected with production and tourist-related activities but the figures for Edradour and Glenturret underline the importance of such activities to the local economy. Both of these distilleries invested in visitor centres in the early to mid-1980s and as a direct consequence began to employ staff, on a seasonal basis, to act as guides and shop assistants. The increase in visitors to these enterprises has led to the more than doubling of staff during the traditional tourist season between March and September. At Glenturret the seasonal rise is from about forty to eighty or ninety, whereas Edradour's production staff of three and related staff of four increases to seventeen during the peak of the season. The size of the distillery is not an indicator of its tourist potential; indeed Edradour is the smallest distillery in Scotland and attracts 95–100,000 visitors annually. The corresponding numbers available for other distilleries, during 1993, were 193,000 for Glenturret, 60,000 plus at Blair Atholl and just over 14,000 for Aberfeldy. When one considers that the most popular attraction in Perthshire during that same year was Blair Castle with 247,157 visitors, the numbers attracted to the various distilleries are not insignificant in providing revenue and job opportunities for their respective communities. This is also true for numerous other communities throughout Perthshire as the number of visits, nearly 1.5 million in 1993, to the ten most popular free and entrance fee tourist attractions, show. These attractions encompass museums, art and craft workplaces, wildlife centres, power stations and dams and serve to show the complex links that bind tourism to the rural economy. One further activity that demonstrates the ties between visitors to the area and traditional rural pursuits is stalking and fishing. In many of the remoter glens of Perthshire gamekeeping and field sports-related employment substantially exceeds those found in farming and forestry.

The Red Deer Commission has estimated that sporting revenue and venison sales from the wild deer cull is in excess of £1 million per annum to the estates within Tayside Region. The figure does not represent the full value of this activity to the rural districts. The spending power of over one hundred stalkers and gamekeepers is not included; neither are the benefits accruing to hotels and ancillary services, nor the employees of the five licensed venison dealers or those involved in the transportation of 80% of venison that is exported from the area. Also worth mentioning is the revenue accrued from visitors that include sighting deer as one reason for entering the remoter areas of the region; this activity is hardly quantifiable but the fact that red deer are an amenity in themselves should not be forgotten. The possibility of sighting deer has improved over the last thirty years with the doubling of the population between 1963 and 1989 due to the under-culling of hinds and increased shooting of stags. The increased numbers have contributed to two distinct but related areas of countryside conflict, regeneration of natural forests and environmental degradation. These issues impinge upon wider aspects of a rural economy that is increasingly dependent upon its visual impact as a visitor amenity. These problems and their potential solutions represent, in microcosm, many of the issues surrounding the economic viability and sustainability of remote rural areas and again emphasises the complexity and fragility of their economic situation.

The second and possibly the most important component of the rural economy associated with sporting activity is that of fishing. Angling is one of the most popular pastimes in Britain and Perthshire with its abundance of rivers and lochs has much to offer participants in this sport. There are two categories of anglers associated with the area, the first includes those who hire particular beats on the river from landed estates for a specific period of time and the second constitutes those that purchase permits to fish particular lochs and rivers. There is insufficient evidence to present a breakdown of relative importance concerning these two categories but it is without doubt that they contribute to the local economy in a variety of ways through buying food, renting accommodation and through the purchase of permits. Whatever the category, the value of salmon and sea trout angling on the Tay and its tributaries was estimated to be worth £4.8 million to the local economy and accounted for 320 full time equivalent jobs in 1994. The fact that the largest salmon caught by rod and line in Scotland was on the Tay, 64 lbs (29.03 kg) in 1922 by Miss GW Ballantine and that it is Scotland's longest salmon river, may be two of the inducements that bring anglers back time and time again.

It has been calculated by Perth Tourist Board that 25% of Perthshire's gross domestic product comes from tourist-related activities; the foregoing information indicates that it is substantially higher in the rural districts. The industry in Perthshire has its foundations in the character of the countryside, its beauty, culture and history; any activity that reduces this appeal would be detrimental to the economy of numerous communities. These same characteristics that enhance Perthshire as a tourist destination have also had an influence upon demographic changes of the recent past and are likely to continue to act upon them in the future.

POPULATION AND THE ECONOMY

The main problem associated with many of the rural areas throughout Scotland is the continuing drift of population to the towns. This process has been going on for well over a century, having serious effects upon the economic health and viability of some rural areas. Poor living and social conditions, low wages and lack of opportunity for advancement or full time alternatives to work in land-based industries have inevitably tended to force residents, especially the young and economically active, to leave rural areas. Perthshire has been no exception to these trends, although in recent times a complex demographic picture has emerged. The rurality of much of the greater part of Perthshire is demonstrated by comparing the population density figures for Tayside (0.51 pph, persons per hectare) and Scotland (0.64 pph) with Perthshire (0.24 pph), revealing that Perthshire is the least densely populated area of Tayside and that the comparable figure is considerably lower than for Scotland as a whole; the 7.0pph figure pertaining to the city of Dundee emphasises the stark contrasts between city and country within the regional context. Census data concerning age structure and population change within post code areas stress the economic fragility of some areas within the remoter parts of Perthshire and the growing commuter communities of those bordering industrialised central Scotland.

Overall, Perthshire has experienced significant in-migration in recent years which has contributed to the increase in resident population from 119,220 in 1981 to 126,346 in 1991. The breakdown of the official numbers reveals that births and deaths contributed a net decrease of 2.6% and migration an increase of 8.6%; further investigation provides evidence that many of those migrating to Perthshire are of pensionable age. This is particularly true of the Crieff, Auchterarder, Aberfeldy, Comrie and Pitlochry areas where the number of residents of pensionable age exceeds 23%. In comparison to Tayside's 20.4% and Scotland's 18.2% Perthshire's overall figure of 21.3% hides the fact that the retired population of outlying settlements is much higher; indeed the figure for Comrie is nearly double the Scottish average at 36%. In contrast to the ageing residents of much of the rural areas there is also a trend of out-migration from these same places by people in the 16 to 29 years age group. Official statistics also reveal that many of the market towns close to the industrialised belt have witnessed an increase in numbers by economically active individuals in the 30 to pensionable age range, mostly as commuters, but the overall trend for the remoter areas is one of an ageing and declining population base. Indeed, the preponderance of holiday and second homes within and close to rural towns indicates that the trends noted will continue for the foreseeable future. When these trends are combined with an overall decline in birth rates the figures do not bode well for the future economic health of rural Perthshire.

The pattern of change due to in-migration reflects the general quality of the environment found throughout Perthshire and the attractiveness of Perth, Kinross and their surrounding settlements as a central location within Scotland for commuters. They also highlight underlying problems associated with a rural economy that is supported by visitor numbers and a service economy whereby any development that may arrest the departure of young people may also conflict with the reasons for the influx of those with spending power. If these conflicting issues can be resolved then a larger proportion of young people could be retained in the rural areas and a more viable, economically stable situation would ensue.

CONCLUSION

It can be seen from the foregoing that the economic base of rural Perthshire has changed in the last few decades from one that is essentially land-based to one that relies heavily upon a mixture of tourism and visitor-related activities. The primary activities of the past are still relevant today but their continued existence is linked to a number of diverse economic activities that would have been seen as peripheral to the health and well-being of rural communities thirty years ago. This change in economic emphasis may save some of the less isolated communities from extinction but the viability of the more remote may be compromised by the continuing arguments over environmentally sound practice and a wish to retain the traditional character of those areas that promote the qualities and values which form the basis of the new enterprises that maintain the diversification of economic activity defining Perthshire's rural economy today.

NINE

STRATHEARN

A mere 65 km separate Lochearnhead from the River Tay south of the city of Perth but the contrast of scene between these two extremities of Strathearn could hardly be more dramatic.

In the west the narrow length of Loch Earn is gripped tightly between steep mountainsides, with the popular Munro, Ben Vorlich, just off to the south. From St Fillans, at the east end of the loch, to Comrie the hills become less high, though the strong sense of enclosure, combined with a remarkable variety of landform and vegetation, gives this part of the strath a very distinctive and attractive character. Its outstanding landscape quality merited its recognition as one of Scotland's 40 National Scenic Areas in 1979.

Downstream from Comrie the strath opens out, rising to woodland on more gentle hill slopes. By Crieff the intimacy of scale of Upper Strathearn has given way to the broad sweep of the lower strath, with its mix of fertile farmland and managed woodland. Behind the town the lofty southern outliers of the Grampians begin to drift away to the north as the strath broadens eastwards. To the south the long even skyline of the Ochils – lowland hills in appearance as well as location – mark the boundary of the strath till the River Earn enters the Tay, in character far removed from its upper reaches in the mountains.

Stratherne, as it was then known, was a well settled part of Perthshire by the 12th century. Today standing stones and other similar traces are in evidence around Crieff and in the upper strath. The camps at Ardoch (Braco) and Dalginross (Comrie), along with vestiges of lesser camps and signal stations, are reminders of the long, if tenuous, hold of the Romans here. When they departed, warlike incursions by Picts and Scots left their mark too, albeit lightly in terms of evidence on the ground.

The early centuries of the present millennium saw the rise of the Celtic earls and a number of powerful local families, not least the Drummonds and the Murrays. They, along with the clans in the glens to the north and west, were hardly less warlike than their forebears but they nevertheless did much to establish the settled pattern of the strath as we know it today.

Settlements such as Auchterarder, Comrie, Crieff, Methven and Muthill, then all spelt very differently, are on record as place names by the

12th century. Lesser clachans and fermtouns no doubt also existed where the nature of the ground made it possible to secure a livelihood.

Communication between these places must have been difficult, particularly across the River Earn and its flood plains. While the need to get to kirk and market had resulted in some improvement to tracks by the 17th century it was the coming of General Wade and Major Caulfield that made Strathearn accessible from elsewhere and helped communication within it for local folk. A military road from Stirling to Crieff was built in 1742 and one to Fort William by way of Lochearnhead opened up this hitherto remote corner of Upper Strathearn.

As roads improved through the 19th century and the first stage of a rail network was opened in 1856 (sadly long since abandoned) a whole range of traditional industries expanded for a time. Handloom weaving, dyeing and bleaching, paper and rope making and distilling and brewing all helped to raise living standards for local people. The 19th century too saw the development of tourism, today such an important element in the economic life of the strath. In 1860 a guide for visitors, *The Beauties of Upper Strathearn*, put Crieff on the tourist map of its day and described six excursions around it. The opening of the Crieff Hydro a few years later helped to provide accommodation for those wanting to put the guide to the test.

Today Crieff is the capital of Strathearn, strategically situated at the junction of the upper and lower straths and at the intersection of important east/west and north/south roads. Its protected position on a south west-facing slope, gives it an enviable micro-climate and a splendid outlook. Together, these have helped to make the town popular with visitors and increasingly with retired people who have moved into many of its fine Victorian villas or new housing estates recently developed on its outskirts.

Crieff has all the air of a couthy stone built place which has been around for a long time, although only relatively few of its buildings go much further back than the late 18th century. Sadly it did not fare well in the Jacobite rebellions. In January 1716, after the indecisive battle of Sherriffmuir, the Pretender ordered the burning of the town and in 1746 Cumberland's men destroyed the then recently built linen factory.

At this time, until the market moved to Falkirk in 1770, Crieff had a special significance at Michaelmas when as many as 30,000 black cattle, along with a substantial complement of sheep, were driven down the ancient drove roads of the Highlands to be sold at the tryst to dealers from the south and sent on to the fattening lands of Lincolnshire and East Anglia for eventual sale at Smithfield and elsewhere. Many of the Highland clansmen and drovers of the time had scant regard for the law but justice was swift and some paid the ultimate price on the 'kind gallows of Crieff' as Sir Walter Scott later described them.

For a town of a modest 6000 inhabitants Crieff has a remarkable range of positive attributes. At its heart is James Square, the shops grouped around it and along the High Street on either side, convenient both to residents and visitors alike. It is generously blessed with public parks, the main one a gift to the town by a local solicitor at the turn of the century. Much older is the delightfully named Lady Mary's Walk, by the River Earn, called after the daughter of Sir Patrick Murray of Ochtertyre who opened it up to local people as long ago as the early 19th century.

The Crieff Highland Games, held in August, are of national repute. For visitors of an enquiring mind there is paperweight, crystal and pottery manufacturing on the small industrial estate at the foot of the town. At Glenturret Distillery, one of the oldest in Scotland, a welcome dram awaits those who have toured the premises. Glenturret, however, has more claims to fame than its excellent malt. For 24 years it was the home of a cat, Towser, whose mousing prowess gained it a place in the *Guinness Book of Records*.

Crieff has two particularly interesting 19th-century foundations. One is Morrison's Academy which came into existence from a bequest by a local man from the nearby village of Muthill, one Thomas Morison (with one 'r' be it noted!), who had made his fortune as a builder in Edinburgh. Though he died in 1826, leaving instructions for an academy to be built either in Edinburgh or Muthill, it was not until 1860 that his bequest became a reality, in Crieff rather than in one of his two preferred locations. Over the years Morrison's Academy, now an independent school, developed a national reputation for its educational standards. Today it also has international links, with pupils drawn from countries of the Middle and Far East.

The other 19th-century foundation is the Crieff Hydro. Today it is the largest single employer in the town and a place known and loved by generations of guests, not infrequently with three generations of one family in residence at the same time. Built in 1868 and known then as Strathearn House, from the outset the Hydro had strong Presbyterian links. The early rule of a penny fine for being late for grace before meals is evidence enough of that. Though time has changed much and the establishment now has a sophisticated leisure complex and sports hall, as well as an equestrian centre and golf course, it still retains a uniquely dignified character which is much appreciated by its many regular guests from within Scotland and far beyond its borders.

Sarah Murray, who made her marathon 2000-mile tour of Scotland in the dying years of the 18th century, describes Crieff in her *Companion and Useful Guide to the Beauties of Scotland* as 'sweetly situated, just as it were without the jaws of the Highlands'. There can be few better places to appreciate the character of those 'jaws' than from the summit of the Knock, the hill which rises steeply behind the Hydro.

Looking west the high mountains which cradle Loch Earn also frame the twin peaks of Ben More and Stobinian on the far horizon. To the north and closer at hand the sharp V-shape of the entrance to Glen Turret and the peak of Ben Chonzie, another Munro, dominate the view. Off to the north east lies the Sma' Glen, the most dramatic gateway into the Highlands from lowland strath country hereabouts, never more so than when the heather is in full bloom on its steep rocky hillsides.

The summit of the Knock has the great virtue of providing a view round all the points of the compass. Consequently, to the south and south east the broad expanse of lower Strathearn is visible, stretching all the way to the foothills of the Ochils, except perhaps on those rare autumn days when the low ground is hidden under a vast blanket of dense white mist and the Knock floats high above it in brilliant sunlight.

West from Crieff, moving into Upper Strathearn, the substantial settlement of Comrie has long been a resort on a modest scale. It takes its name from a Gaelic word signifying the running together of streams, appropriately enough, for the Ruchill and the Lednock both join the River Earn within the village.

Although Crieff is barely 10 km away, not only does the countryside around have a distinctly Highland character, but in time past the common language of the Comrie folk was Gaelic, whereas in Crieff the 1799 *Statistical Account* records that 'the people fpeak the English language in the beft Scotch dialect'.

Comrie itself occupies flat valley land and is popular today with retired people anxious to avoid the effort needed to cope with living on Crieff's steep hillside. Nominally at least, however, there are risks in settling here, for Comrie sits squarely astride the Highland Boundary Fault. While there have been few tremors in recent years, in the late 18th and early 19th centuries the local inhabitants experienced some exciting times.

A contemporary account describes the most violent earthquake up till then as happening on the evening of 29 October 1839 when' for a second or two every house for miles around Comrie was shaken from top to bottom'. Fortunately casualties were light: only a few individuals fainted! According to the Rev John Macpherson, a Comrie minister at the time, 'most of the inhabitants spent the whole night in the streets, or in the churches, which were very properly opened for prayer'.

After a further severe shock in 1846 the number and intensity decreased significantly, but sufficient activity continued to warrant setting up a simple recording apparatus, probably the first of its kind anywhere in the world. It was installed in a small building which still exists today and is known locally as the Earthquake House.

Like Crieff, Comrie has a hilltop viewpoint, not as high but effective enough to make the short scramble up a rocky path well worth the effort. Dunmore Hill, just north of the village, is topped by a large obelisk of 1812 vintage, a reminder of one Henry Dundas, the first Viscount Melville, a powerful statesman in Pitt's time who had the doubtful distinction of being charged with misusing a large sum of money while Treasurer of the Navy. Having ensured the burning of any incriminating papers he was acquitted by the House of Lords. When he died this imposing monument was raised in his memory by his Perthshire friends.

From the top of Dunmore Hill there is a magnificient view in the round. To the west, Loch Earn lies deep in its mountain setting. To the east is the contrasting scene of the broadening strath away towards Crieff. Below, to the south, the streets of Comrie are laid out like a map and, beyond, the long sweep of Glen Artney, an ancient royal deer forest, runs deep into the hills. It may have been the knowledge that Mary, Queen of Scots and Darnley hunted there which led Sir Walter Scott to use the glen as the setting for parts of *The Lady of the Lake*.

The prospect to the north is of another glen, Lednock, once a busy place of small farms and summer shielings on the higher ground. Today, the long deserted remains of cottages tell a story of depopulation all too common in the Scottish Highlands. A large reservoir for hydro-electric power now dominates the upper part of the glen, reducing the River Lednock to a small stream compared with its character in time past. On the lofty ridge which encloses the west side of the glen a curious feature, known as the Deil's Footprint, was long held in awe by local children who would never dare put their foot into the impression for fear of dire consequences befalling them.

An unusual ceremony of ancient origin takes place at Comrie on Hogmanay to bring luck to the village in the coming year. This is the parade of the Flambeaux, six huge torches on wood poles with one end wrapped in canvas soaked in paraffin, in weight just as much as a strong man can manage to carry aloft. They are lit on the stroke of midnight and a piper leads the procession round the village on a time-honoured route with a following of guisers in a colourful array of unlikely costumes.

West from Comrie, Upper Strathearn assumes an ever more Highland character. St Fillans, at the east end of Loch Earn, is described in the 1860 *Tourist Guide to the Beauties of Scotland* as 'a pretty village, with its flower bordered cottages'. A century and more on it remains a small highland settlement, with a hotel or two and a few villas added. Less appropriate to its setting is a large permanent caravan park on the south side of the loch, for the present at least, fortunately screened to some extent from the village by a row of trees along the water's edge.

At the western extremity of the loch, Lochearnhead has added water ski-ing to its long standing role as a popular centre for sailing and walking. In July traditional Highland Games take place. Like St Fillans it has not expanded significantly in size and still sits comfortably enough in its mountain environment. On occasion odd artefacts do seem to appear in very unlikely places. Baddeley's Guide of 1908 records that in the then Lochearnhead Hotel there was a billiard table 'with fine marquetry work, remarkable as having belonged to the first Napoleon'.

The main road (A85) along the length of Loch Earn keeps close to the north shore with enticing glimpses of the imposing peak of Ben Vorlich across the water to the south. Another road, single track and tortuous in places but not heavily used, runs along the south shore, making possible an agreeable round trip of the loch by car. Some splendid specimens of mature pines en route provide a happy relief from the less attractive commercial plantations which here, as in many parts of the Highlands, make up much of today's woodland scene.

Towards the western end of this road the impressive shape of Edinample Castle, recently restored, can be seen down by the lochside. Built in the 16th century, for long it belonged to the Earl of Breadalbane and was an important element in the defence of the southern limit of Breadalbane country. Nearby, Ardvorlich House, seat of the ancient Stewart family, is said to be Sir Walter Scott's Darnlinvarach in his *Legend of Montrose*.

In 1620 Ardvorlich was the scene of one of many bloody encounters between feuding local clans. On this occasion a party of Macdonalds of Glencoe raided Ardvorlich to make off with their cattle. However the Stewarts prevailed and killed seven Macdonalds who were buried by the bridge near the entrance to the House. A stone still marks the spot nearly four centuries on.

In today's quiet countryside of Upper Strathearn it is not easy to envis-age the clan feuding which went on virtually incessantly for centuries in these parts, though perhaps no more so than elsewhere in the Highlands. In this scene the MacGregors were never far from any local fray. Those of Balquhidder were constantly at odds with the Drummonds of Glenartney and Strathearn, while the MacGregors of Breadalbane and Rannoch fought bitterly with the Campbells of Glenorchy. While cattle raiding was at the heart of many incidents, honour impeached and the imperative of revenge for real or imagined wrongs led to many a killing which, in turn, itself had to be revenged.

The broad fertile strath which opens out east of Comrie and runs all the way to the Tay is another world compared with the mountainous confines of Upper Strathearn. Though Crieff has long been the dominant settlement hereabouts, before that Auchterarder, at the foot of the Ochils, was the chief burgh of Strathearn. An enviable situation it might be thought, yet this was not so. In the 16th century so distressed financially were the townsfolk that an Act of Parliament appointed an annual fair to be held to relieve their plight. In the aftermath of the battle of Sheriffmuir the town, like Crieff, was burnt down, along with nearby Blackford, Dunning and Muthill.

All of that is a far cry from the Auchterarder of today. Although now bypassed by the main Stirling/Perth road, it remains a busy place, its prosperity closely linked to Gleneagles Hotel and the championship golf courses. Strangers entering the town at one end might be forgiven for wondering if they will ever reach the other end. With its main street over 2 km long, not surprisingly it is known locally as the 'lang toon'.

From Auchterarder to the rising ground which bounds the lower strath in the north there exists an intricate pattern of local roads and byways. Since the low land along the River Earn and its tributaries, particularly the Pow Water, was drained from the 17th century on, it has become ever more intensively farmed, though now by far fewer people than in the past. Many of the old steadings and cottages have either been demolished or converted into holiday homes or dwellings for people in other than farming.

Substantial areas of the lower strath still remain in traditional estate ownership. Abercairney, east of Crieff, has been occupied by the Moray family since the 14th century. Some of their farm tenants have been around for a long time too. Drummie, close to Fowlis Wester, has been farmed by the same family for over 250 years and, with another generation growing up in the farmhouse, three centuries of occupation is well on the cards.

Fowlis Wester possesses the remarkable 13th-century church of St Bean, built on the site of an earlier church possibly founded by St Bean himself who died in 720. Within it a carved Pictish stone cross, previously located on the village green, though much eroded by time presents a fascinating array of figures on horseback and on foot, along with animals and Pictish symbols.

This long settled nature of Lower Strathearn has produced a rich pattern of places of considerable antiquity and historic interest. Among the most impressive must be Drummond Castle and gardens on the way south from Crieff to Muthill. The castle commands a rocky eminence, the tall 15th-century tower standing remarkably comfortably alongside the much later mansion built following the deliberate demolition of an earlier building to prevent it being occupied by Hanoverian troops in 1745.

The great glory of Drummond, however, is its magnificent Italianate *parterre* garden, best seen in late summer from the high terrace in front of the castle. The present owner, Lady Jane Willoughby d'Eresby, daughter of the Earl of Ancaster, takes great pride in this garden, which has been open to the public since the middle of the last century.

About 3 km east of Drummond, by the Earn and the ruins of another castle, Innerpeffray Library's collection of books, established in the 17th century initially for the use of students, became the first free public library in Scotland with a borrowers' ledger dating from 1747. Apart from a pocket Bible of the Marquis of Montrose, one of the most intriguing volumes is a copy (one of only eight extant) of the 18th-century Treacle Bible, so called because of its reading of '. . . is there no balm in Gilead?' as '. . . is there no treacle in Gilead?'.

East of Innerpeffray, running through the ancient parishes of Trinity and Findo Gask, the line of an old Roman road and the sites of no less than eight signal stations along its length are identified on the OS map. This road was strategically located on land above the one time flood plains of the Earn to the south and the Pow to the north. Today it passes through an attractive mix of open farmland and enclosed woodland, the latter with some fine stands of birch. Eastwards the land rises gradually to form a broad whaleback ridge which towards Perth divides the strath into two distinct parts.

That to the north, where the finely restored castle at Methven and the ancient ruin of Huntingtower are situated, peters out quietly towards the western approaches to Perth town.

South of the ridge the Earn winds its course down an ever deepening valley under the shadow of the Ochils. East of Auchterarder, high above the road to Dunning, the three levels of the ancient Celtic ramparts of Craig Rossie command this part of the strath. Though now much weathered into their hilltop site over many centuries, they still manage to convey something of the tremendous industry and vitality of their builders and their ability to protect themselves against their enemies.

Today Craig Rossie makes a rewarding viewpoint from which to admire the richly productive character of Lower Strathearn, with the dramatic sky-line of the Highland hills beyond and, given good visibility, the distinctive peaks of Ben Vorlich and Stuc a' Chroin far to the west.

Although in many respects history is writ large in these parts, evidence of it still visible on the ground is all too sparse. The small village of Forteviot, beside the Water of May, is a quiet place today, betraying little of its importance as Fortren, capital of the Pictish kingdom following the Roman occupation. Here Kenneth Macalpin died in 860 after he had successfully brought together the previously warring Picts and Scots to defeat the Norse invaders of that time.

There is a local tradition, unsupported by material evidence, it must be said, that Malcolm Canmore was born here, his mother a miller's daughter. Nearby, in 1332, Edward Balliol, along with barons earlier disinherited by Bruce, defeated and killed the Earl of Mar at the battle of Dupplin. In cannier times Robert Burns dined at Invermay House in the birchwoods above Forteviot, recording in his diary afterwards that the lady of the house was 'gaucie, frank, affable and fond of rural sports'!

Forteviot possesses a feature which might well be emulated in some of the less distinguished villages of Scotland. Here the First Baron Forteviot of Dupplin in the mid-1920s completely rebuilt the heart of the village, setting the attractively designed new houses round three sides of an open green space. Immediately across the tree-lined avenue from them he added a substantial village hall. Today, an adjoining building is the workshop of a pipe-organ builder.

Just east of Bridge of Earn the old A90 road and the new M90 motorway cut across the strath as it opens out towards the Tay. Whereas the A90 sits low and is hardly evident in the wider scene, the M90 proclaims its existence to the world at large atop a high embankment. Beyond this highway engineering barrier the Earn pursues a meandering course across an expanse of level haugh land interspersed with farmsteads and a network of quiet minor roads.

This last stretch of the Strath of Earn is overlooked on the north by the wooded shoulder of Moncrieffe Hill from the top of which Thomas Pennant, the 18th-century Welsh naturalist, described the prospect as 'the glory of Scotland'. On the southern margin, at Abernethy, Malcolm Canmore is said to have paid his respects to William the Conqueror. What is beyond conjecture at Abernethy is its remarkable round tower, the lower part going back a thousand years. Older still by another millennium is the site of a Roman fortress strategically located to command the entrance to Strathearn from the Tay.

It is not without justification that Walter Scott, vying it would seem with Pennant, called Perthshire 'the fairest portion of the Northern Kingdom'. In its 65 km length of widely varied landscape and its colourful history, Strathearn must surely claim a substantial share of that reputation.

TEN

THE RIVER TAY

This chapter will take the reader on a historical and geographical voyage through space and time using the River Tay as its medium. The journey will extend beyond the political boundaries of Perthshire to include the whole length of the river. The river itself has been physically overcome by paddle, sail, ferry and bridge. Its natural resources have provided the raw materials of trade and manufacture, along with sustenance for the populace of its hinterland. The natural topography of the region, chiefly the Straths of Tay and Earn, aligns the area towards the estuarial waters of the Tay and especially the city and port of Perth from whence the area takes its name. The Tay has long been utilised as an artery of transport, communication and commerce into and from the heartland of Scotland to Europe and the wider world.

The physical dimensions of the Tay provide a clue to the environmental diversity encountered along its banks; thus the multiplicity of resources harnessed by man throughout the past. The River Tay is undoubtedly Scotland's longest river, although the claim is disputed. A number of observers have noted that it is only the Tay after it emerges from Loch Tay and that the 40 km of the estuary should be excluded due to its tidal nature. Whatever the arguments presented the received wisdom is that the river flows from its source on Ben Lui, as the Connish water, to the bar between Buddon Ness and Tentsmuir Point, where it enters the North Sea: a total length of 160 km, a catchment of 6,475 km² and a tidal volume calculated at 79,555 million litres per tide (Figure 12).

Human imprint upon the land throughout the historical and prehistoric periods can be located in numerous places on or close to the river. Mesolithic inhabitants of the Firth gathered shellfish at Tentsmuir and Stannergate in the lower Firth. They may also have been the users of the dug-out canoe found at Friarton, below Perth, in the upper reaches of the estuary. It is certainly true that few pre-farming societies lacked some form of water-borne transportation which would have been used to extend the foraging and fishing grounds of the local tribal populace. The refuse accumulated in the middens found in Tentsmuir, at Morton Lochs, indicates that the area was occupied, on a seasonal basis, for around seven centuries. These earliest occupants utilised the river in much the same way as their descendants would: as a means of communication and

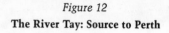

Figure 12
The River Tay: Source to Perth

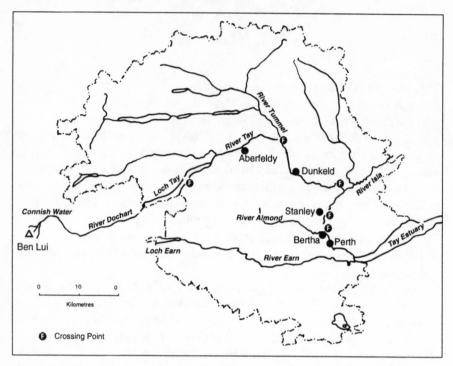

provider of sustenance. The archaeological record provides evidence of continued occupation of the area since that time.

Moving forward in time, Stone Age, Bronze Age, Iron Age and the enigmatic Picts have left a variety of structures for us to ponder. These include souterrains found close to the river inland of the lower estuary, along with their concomitant hill forts, while standing stones and *Pit* place-name clusters are found focusing upon the Abernethy–Scone–Perth district of the Tay. Further up the course of the river, at Loch Tay, crannogs have been located dating from the Bronze Age though it is suggested that some were still being used in the 17th century. These artificial islands offered a form of security to tenants over a period of two thousand years and must rank as one of the longest used of dwelling types in Scotland. Security was only one of the appeals of this area – the bounty from loch and hillside must also have been primary elements in the decision to locate here over such a long period of time.

Evidence of a Roman presence has been found in the Tay estuary and further north and west along tributaries of the river. It is debatable how much of an influence the presence of the Roman military had on the local population. One suspects that the presence of major fortresses at Carpow and Inchtuthil, along with forts, towers and camps stretching from south of the Earn to the lower reaches of the Isla resulted in some form of social/commercial contact between the legions and the local inhabitants. The location of these remains has led to speculation upon the use of water-borne traffic to supply these settlements. Without doubt the Romans did use vessels to transport men and materials and it is therefore likely that the Tay was utilised in such a manner. Arguments surrounding the inaccessibility of the river above Perth for vessels hinge upon the present-day river conditions. It should be stressed that during the period in question, the late 1st century, the configuration of the river would have been different due to continuing land recovery and concomitant lowering of sea level since the last ice-age. Thus a Roman port on the Tay could have been located above the present site of the city and port of Perth. A strong candidate for such a facility is Bertha, located at the confluence of the rivers Tay and Almond. This is also the place considered to be the crossing point of the main Roman road from southern Scotland into Strathmore. The remains of a fort from the Roman period and evidence of a wooden bridge at this location strengthens the view that this was a site of importance in the past. The site noted would be a logical port for larger craft to off-load cargoes that could then be transported upstream to the frontier outposts. This would have been achieved by either punting or towing, from the river bank, shallow draft vessels much the same as the Canadian open canoes that were utilised when that area was being explored and settled. The Roman remains at Carpow, near the confluence of the Tay and Earn, could also have been utilised as a staging port for the transportation of materials and supplies into Strathearn. If either of these locations were ports during the Roman period then they were the first purpose-built maritime infrastructures on the Tay but by no means the last. The movement of goods and materials up-river by the Romans cannot be proven but the use of the estuary as a commercial routeway throughout the historic period is without doubt.

One glance at a modern map of the river Tay reveals a number of places with a nautical connection: Tayport, Newport, Port Allen and Woodhaven are obvious candidates; however, these are but a few of the many sites with a maritime past. According to the minister of Longforgan the Pows of the Carse of Gowrie were the locations of the ports that shipped all the needs of the area. Again, these are not all of the sites on the estuary that have links to maritime transport. Newburgh, Balmerino, Friarton, Inchyra, Kinfauns and Carpow are some of the other places that have operated as ports in the past. It is difficult to specify when many of these ports were first built but it is possible to speculate about the origins of others.

There has been port infrastructure at Perth since the early medieval period, located further upstream than the present facilities. It can also be shown that the Pow of Errol, now Port Allen, was also utilised as a port during the 15th century. Other candidates for early maritime usage are Balmerino, where an abbey has stood since 1226 and Lindores Abbey, close to Newburgh, built in 1178 and situated on another small tributary of the Tay, the Pow of Lindores. Indeed the river, between its mouth and Perth, abounds with structures associated with trade from harbours and pack-houses to fishing bothies and ice-houses. The importance of Perth as a commercial centre in the past, and to a lesser degree in the present, is based upon its accessible location as an outlet and inlet for materials and commodities required by inhabitants of its hinterland – a hinterland that has seen the river harnessed for power and communication.

Upstream of Perth the River Tay and its tributaries are now the preserve of fishermen and water sport enthusiasts; there is no commercial traffic upon the river at all due to economies of scale and the advance of technology. In earlier times this was not the case. The floating of timber downstream and the harnessing of the natural power of the river to drive machinery, were two ways in which the Tay served the commercial needs of the local population. Although man had utilised water power to drive meal mills for centuries it was not until the mid 18th century and onwards that other purpose-built structures began to tap local rivers as a source of energy.

Perth and its immediate area has long been associated with the textile industry; the water resources in the vicinity of the city encouraged these developments. Between Perth and Campsie Linn three significant textile works were developed that encompass the range and importance of textiles to the development and expansion of the local economy. South of Campsie Linn are Stanley Mills, founded in 1785, originally as cotton spinning and weaving mills. This site also participated in the bleaching process and flax spinning. Luncartyfield is mainly associated with bleaching but cotton spinning was also carried out at this site during the late 18th century. The last site, Stormontfield also participated in cotton spinning during the latter part of the 18th century but is mainly recognised as a printing and bleaching location. Another concentration of textile manufacture occurred along the lower reaches of the river Almond. At least twelve mills were located here engaged in bleaching, spinning, weaving and printing of cloth. The mills stood along their respective sites primarily due to the power source available but the quality of the water, its softness and purity, was a factor as it made an excellent bleaching agent.

Elsewhere along the Tay and its tributaries other remnants of the textile industry can also be found. At Blairgowrie, on the river Ericht, there were at least six mills (dating from the early to late 19th century) associated with linen and jute production, a carding mill at Aberfeldy and a linen factory, dated 1767, at Spittalfield. Indeed throughout Perthshire the region's abundance of rivers has been a significant factor in the location of industrial complexes. The utilisation of this resource to generate electricity is just one further indicator of the significance of this natural resource for the industrial development of the region.

There is one other important activity associated with the rivers of Perthshire, especially the Tay, that has contributed to the economy for some consider-able period of time, namely fishing, especially salmon although trout, sparling and eels have also been important exports. The river Tay is known throughout Europe as a premium fishing river and Tay salmon is served as a delicacy on the menus of many famous hotels and restaurants. Few observers of the industry realise that the export of fish from the river has been an important industry for over two hundred years. Today the catching of salmon is looked upon as a minor industry, indeed as a sporting and tourist activity, but in the past it was a major industry and substantial source of income to the estates that border the river from Perth to the North Sea. Such was the value of this local resource that from the late 18th century a plethora of litigation was raised over methods of catching and the jurisdiction of adjoining estates over the river. The importance of the revenue accrued to landowners from the fishing cannot be understated. It is doubtful if many would have undertaken improvements to agricultural land and communications without it. Once export markets were assured during the mid-18th century the revenue from the salmon beats increased dramatically – nearly threefold during the period 1750 to 1800. Raw salmon has been exported to London since at least the early 18th century and probably long before; legislation to protect the 'fishing' is first recorded by the Scottish Parliament in 1318. Although the salmon trade was important as an export commodity in the 14th and 15th centuries it was not until new methods of preservation and transportation were introduced in the mid and late-18th century that the trade became an industry that was truly Europe-wide.

In 1740 the kitting method of preservation was introduced: fish par-boiled and soaked in vinegar and wedged into a box known as a kitt, thereby making the fish available for market throughout the season without the drawback of being preserved in salt. Later in the century, in 1780, the packing of salmon in ice made them even more widely available. It was during this period that salmon began to be exported to the major nations of Southern Europe. One of the most important exporters of salmon during this period of increased activity was the merchant firm of Richardson of Perth, later of Pitfour Estate in the Carse of Gowrie. This company leased the fishings of much of the estuarial waters during the latter part of the 18th century and early part of the 19th. They caught and transported salmon to the cities of Europe from Rotterdam to Venice and most ports in between. Until the advent of steam locomotion and a network of railways to London it was vessels belonging to companies like Richardsons that plied the trade from the Tay to continental Europe and beyond. It is not an exaggeration to note that without the initial trade in salmon other more lucrative connections with the growing commercial centres of Britain and Europe would not have been achieved at such an early period. Certainly intercourse with London would have been less.

It is only in very recent times that the netting of salmon has disappeared from the Firth due to over-fishing here and in coastal waters. Until then the commercial salmon trade remained an important component of the local economy. Rentals amounting to £22,000 and seasonal employment for three hundred individuals was not uncommon in the period after the Second World War. The stretch of river from Newburgh to Perth has always been the most lucrative but the fishing below here to the mouth of the Tay, centred upon Broughty Ferry, was also important during the 19th century. Now only the lower reaches of the Earn are fished in the traditional manner. All that can be seen today is the industrial archaeology of the industry that litters the foreshore of the Firth of Tay, from ice-houses to bothies and stumps of old wooden stakes that once held the nets.

Angling or sport fishing has been carried out in Scotland since the early 17th century. When it was established on the Tay is not recorded. An indicator of the importance that estate owners attached to their salmon beats is the significant number of court cases brought by them against the commercial operators on the lower reaches of the river throughout the 19th century. There is insufficient evidence to argue for an important sports revenue prior to the 1960s, a period when around three hundred men were employed as ghillies, boatmen and associated helpers. In 1994 the value of salmon and sea trout angling on the Tay and its tributaries was estimated to be worth £4.8 million, accounting for 320 full time equivalent jobs, to local communities that border the Tay. The fact that the largest salmon caught by rod and line in Scotland was on the Tay, 64 lbs (29.03 kg) in 1922 by Miss GW Ballantine and that it is Scotland's longest salmon river may be two of the inducements that bring anglers back time and time again. The foregoing provides an outline of the history and economic importance of fishing for salmon to the communities that border the Tay. Although the industry no longer sustains the levels of direct employment it once did, nor are the fish exported in such vast quantities, it has and still does provide valuable revenue and employment to residents of the area.

It has already been noted that the river itself has been an important link in the communications network of the past but it has also acted as a barrier to movement north and south, especially below Perth. To overcome this, man has built bridges and established crossing points for centuries. The ferry between Newport and Dundee is the most well-known crossing point and the rail bridge that was blown down in 1879 is probably the best known man-made structure that spanned the river. However, there is a long tradition of traversing the river by boat and spanning her by purpose-built structures.

Apart from the likely Roman bridge at the confluence of the Tay and Almond the first known bridge over the Tay was a wooden structure at Perth that was washed away in a flood in 1210. Its stone successor, built in 1329, suffered frequent damage by the river and was replaced in 1616, with a ten arch span. This new structure lasted only ten years before the power of the river removed it. It was not until one hundred and fifty years later, in 1771, that the river was bridged once again at Perth, by Smeaton. This construction was a nine-span bridge pierced by circular relief holes. Although cast iron footpaths were added to both sides in 1869 the structure in use today is essentially the same as the one utilised in the late 18th century. This century was a period of transport expansion and many bridges from that era survive throughout Perthshire. Forteviot (1766), Glen Lyon (1793), Kenmore (1774) and Inver (1740) are but a few. Two other bridges of this same period are worth special note. The first is the Wade Bridge at Aberfeldy which has been described as the finest bridge, architecturally of the 18th century Scottish military road system. Built in 1733, it has five spans and is 91.4 m long. The other crosses the river at Dunkeld. This bridge, seven spans and 209m in length, and its toll house were designed by Thomas Telford and built between 1805 and 1809 and like many of the others is still in use today.

In the latter part of the 19th century it was railway bridges and not road bridges that dominated the efforts of engineers to span the Tay. The most famous are undoubtedly the tow crossings constructed between Wormit, in Fife and Dundee. The present railway bridge at this location was opened in July 1887, six years after its construction was sanctioned. This bridge stands just a few feet from the location of its predecessor, the first railway bridge to cross the Tay and the brick piers of the original can still be seen, marching across the Firth. The first bridge was single track and nearly 3.2 km long. Built for the North British Railway Company, to a design by Sir Thomas Bouch, the mid-section of the bridge plunged into the river, taking with it a passenger train, during a storm on 28 December 1879. The resultant enquiry into the collapse of the bridge and loss of seventy-five lives led to Bouch shouldering the blame for the disaster. He died shortly afterwards. A further connection between the Tay and the first bridge concerns the crossing of the river at Caputh. The Victorian railway bridge that spans the river at this location was built in 1889 using trusses from the first Tay railway bridge. The bridging of the river has continued into the latter part of this century with the upgrading of the A9 trunk road through Perthshire and the construction of the final two estuarial crossings at Friarton, below Perth and between Newport and Dundee. The latter bridge replaced the last ferry crossing on the estuary in August 1966.

Ferries have crossed the river Tay at a variety of points for many centuries providing an important link in the communications network of the east of Scotland. Indeed, when Perth lost its bridge for one hundred and fifty years it was ferrymen, operating between the town and Bridge End, that provided the answer to the communications problem. Down river from Perth a number of crossings have operated over the centuries; the three most important were located at Ferry Port on Craig (Tayport), Newport and Woodhaven.

Figure 13

Location of Ports and Crossing Points on the Tay Estuary

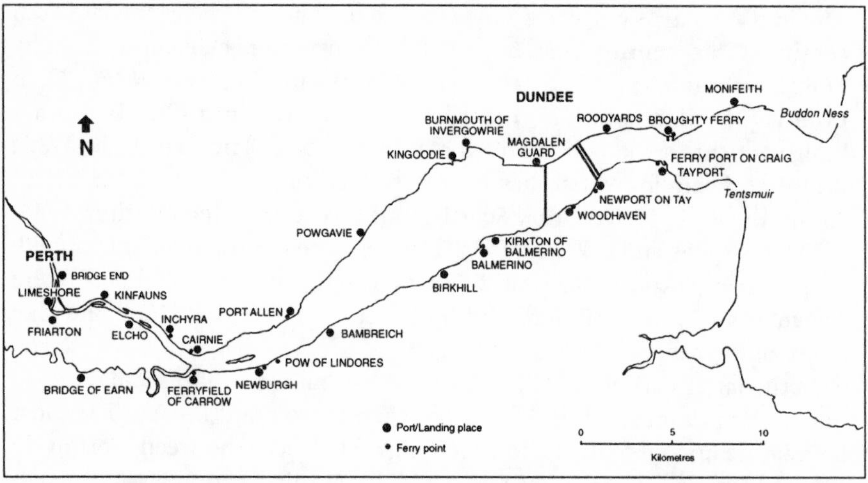

The most easterly of the estuarial crossings was between Tayport and Broughty Ferry. There is documentary proof of a ferry operating here since the early 15th century. The narrowness of the river here made it a natural place for a crossing and it is probable that a ferry service operated here well before this date. During the 18th and early 19th centuries it was mainly used for the transport of cattle from the north to markets in the south and west. The building of a new ferry terminal at Newport in 1822 and the introduction of steam ferries to the route led to a decline in business. In 1846 the construction of harbours both here and at Broughty Ferry, by the Scottish Central Railway Company, transformed the fortunes of the crossing. From this date until the opening of the Tay rail bridge the ferries plying between the two harbours were purpose-built vessels able to carry train wagons and their passengers. The collapse of the first bridge led to a further eight years of prosperity until the second Tay rail bridge was opened in 1887. A ferry crossing continued here in some form until the mid-1960s.

As has already been noted a new terminal was built and steam ferries began to operate from Newport in 1822. Not only did this reduce the services of ferries at Tayport but it also saw the demise of the ferry route from Woodhaven, a place that had been the foremost crossing point on the Tay during the 18th century despite its being the longest of the three main crossings. The main reason for this was that it had better communication links to Cupar and the Forth ferries and thus to Edinburgh. The shoreline at Newport, located between Ferry Port on Craig and Woodhaven, has a long history as a ferry crossing dating back to at least the 12th century. A combination of events led to the regulating of the ferries across the Tay and to Newport becoming the premier crossing point. An Act of Parliament, passed in 1819, began the process that led to Newport being selected as the main terminal for the Tay ferries. It was during this period that the trustees decided to invest in the use of steam boats for the passage due to there being 'no convenient or certain means of transporting cattle or carriages across, except at certain times of tide and in fine weather'. The lack of a reliable service led to investigations into the provision of low water landing places. Initially consideration was given to adapting Newport and Woodhaven harbours but the building of a separate pier, designed by Thomas Telford, close to the original ferry point used in the 12th century was decided upon. Shortly afterwards this service superseded both Newport and Woodhaven harbours as ferry crossing points. The 'new' terminal at Newport was operated as a ferry station from this period until 1966, when the Tay road bridge superseded the boats that had become known as the 'Fifies'. The terminal, with subsequent alterations and modifications, still stands, presently being utilised as the headquarters of the Tay Estuary Research Centre.

Although these three locations are the best known of the ferry points on the Tay there were many others, both on the estuary and the upper reaches, which allowed commerce and travel to be conducted throughout the area. Written documentation upon these crossings relates mainly to the other crossings on the estuary, but 19th-century maps show that there were at least five crossings on the river above Perth. These ferries were located between Hatton and Waukmill, below Campsie Linn at Stanley, at the confluence of the Tay and Isla near to Kinclaven Castle, at the confluence of the Tay and Tummel below Logierait and on Loch Tay between Lawers and Ardtalnaig. Many of them were still operating in the mid-20th century according to local reports. The other crossings on the estuary were located at Balmerino, where a ferry to Dundee operated twice a week and was latterly the stopping point for pleasure boats that operated on the Tay until the outbreak of the Second World War. The crossing between Newburgh and Port Allen had been the right of the abbots of Lindores when it operated from the Pow of Lindores to the Pow of Errol. During the 18th century West Newburgh became the landing place on the Fife side. Documents pertaining to this service indicate that it was operated on a regular basis from the 16th century to the early part of this century, when an irregular service operated. Other known ferry crossings on the upper estuary were located at Ferryfield of Carpow, where a service was maintained across the Earn and to Cairnie in the Carse of Gowrie and from Inchyra to Muirhead in the last quarter of the 19th century. Prior to that time a ferry ran between here and Ferryfield of Carpow. The last crossing point east of Perth was between Easter Rhynd and Kinfauns. When this service was instigated is not known but it was in decline by the mid-19th century. During this latter period the rowing boat stationed here was more likely to be ferrying passengers and baggage to and from local steamers than across the river.

On a journey from source to sea, built structures are the tangible evidence of human presence. However, one of the most noticeable features of the landscape bordering the Tay and its tributaries is the great variety of land use. The underlying geology and natural physical conditions give rise to a range of altitudes and soil types, each influencing man's activities in the landscape. The presence of the Highland Boundary Fault, a crustal fracture, splits the area into two main divisions – the Highlands, an area of heather-clad moors and steep sloped mountains and the Lowlands, an area of predominantly gently rolling arable land.

In the Lowlands, south of the fault line, the soils vary but they are mainly friable medium loams capable of growing a wide variety of root crops and potatoes. The outstanding exception to the medium soils is the low tract of alluvial land stretching from Kinnoull Hill to Invergowrie, the well known Carse of Gowrie, an area consisting of soils varying from deep clay to rich heavy loam which is ideal for combined crops, orchards and soft fruit cultivation. The Lowlands also includes part of Strathmore and Strathearn, both of which are renowned stock-breeding, dairy-farming and seed potato-growing parts of Scotland. The Lowland Straths and riverine areas of the Tay catchment have been transformed over the last two centuries from the pre-improvement landscape of bogs and wetland marshes, containing patches of cultivation, to the present agricultural mosaic that is basic to the economy of the area. The enclosure of land, the granting of long leases, the expansion of markets due to industrialisation in areas of

Scotland and England and the introduction of effective drainage systems enabling tenants to reclaim land were some of the important factors in the dramatic change that has taken place. The present Carse landscape is classified as category one (first class arable land) by the land utilisation survey of Scotland; indeed the majority of land on the Lowland region is covered by category one and two status. The remaining areas, the lower slopes of the Sidlaws and Ochils, are considered to be medium quality farm land (category 3), that is productive but not of high quality due to slope profile, climate or poor soil. Where these conditions have been identified cultivation tends to be pasture land or small forest plantations.

In the Highlands, north of the fault line, a landscape that has also undergone change can be traced. However, the changes witnessed here are of an altogether different kind from the improvements undertaken in the Lowlands. It is not true that all the land here is of poor quality, uncultivated and unimproved. The fertile Strath Tay, between Kenmore and Ballinluig, is but one of many similar fertile riverine areas located along the Tay and its tributaries that have increased productivity with the introduction of new farming techniques. Although small in comparison to the farm lands of the Lowlands these fertile belts, along with areas of sheltered low lying land in the glens, have been cultivated for centuries. Most of the land utilised for cultivation in the Highlands is below the 300 m contour; generally arable farming becomes precarious above this altitude due to excessive rainfall producing acidic peaty soils (category 4) which would require extensive improvement to render them even marginally viable as arable land. Due to the physical conditions hill sheep farming dominates the land use pattern of the Highlands, with the exception of the deer forests (category 5) lying on the highest ground and boundaries of the region. The last and most highly visible component of the landscape mosaic is forestry.

The forest cover of Perthshire is a mixture of semi-natural woodland and plantations comprising a wide variety of coniferous and deciduous trees. The practice of forestry is not a recent activity in the area. Planting on Drummond Hill on the Breadalbane Estate can be traced back to the 16th century and the Atholl Estates were extensively planted in the late 18th and early 19th centuries. In the modern era estates have continued to carry out somewhat smaller afforestation schemes than those noted, whereas the Forestry Commission has planted many of the hillsides seen from the routeways of the district. The once prevalent practice of planting only coniferous trees in very close formation has given way in recent years to include a mixture of deciduous trees and a more open and natural form of silviculture.

The tapestry of the rural landscape is again undergoing change, potentially as dramatic as the transformation from the pre-improvement period. In recent times the agricultural producers and growers of the region have had to rely increasingly upon subsidy payments and grant aid to maintain viability, resulting in diversification into a wide variety of non-farming activities. Alongside the economic restraints a growing awareness concerning environmental issues has led to a number of sites being designated as of scientific or natural importance. It is hoped by many that these protected sites will help sustain the diversity of land use noted; indeed, the protection of areas and habitats may lead to an even more diverse landscape throughout Perthshire from the estuary to the headwaters. Conversely, protection via widespread designation coupled with economic instability may lead to an accentuation of the contrasts already noted between the areas north and south of the Highland Boundary Fault; the northern landscape becoming predominantly forested with a few tourist-orientated diversified farming units, while the south re-orientates from large intensive arable and stock farms to smaller organic agricultural and horticultural units.

In the past man has utilised the Tay in a range of practices for a variety of reasons. Today that diversity of usage continues. Some are a modern extension of past practices: fishing and reed cutting are good examples as is the continuing use of Perth harbour as a maritime connection between the area and the wider world. Other uses and activities such as canoeing and white water rafting would bewilder our ancestors. The scenic grandeur of the river and its accompanying recreational and tourist value has replaced much of the industrial and commercial worth it once had. We should not forget that the communities residing along its banks and the people that depend upon it for an income are relying upon one of the most potent forces of nature. We may have crossed, bridged and utilised its resources but the Tay is not a benign stretch of water. A catalogue of floods and disasters associated with the river and estuary could be assembled, the last entries being dated 1990 and 1993. During these events residents of Perth and many other smaller communities in the catchment area were provided with a reminder of the destructive power the Tay can command. The proposed £20 million flood prevention scheme is just the latest of a number of projects to change the natural configuration of the river. Two of the most impressive schemes from the past were carried out upon the upper estuary and the catchment area of the headwaters. In the 1830s the trustees of the port of Perth instigated improvements to the upper estuary between Perth and Mugdrum Island. These works dredged the river to provide greater depth for the larger vessels that were entering the Tay but unable to reach Perth itself. The works also straightened the alignment of the river by connecting a number of small islands to the shoreline, thereby improving maritime access. In this century, since 1930, the building of dams to supply hydro-electricity has changed the volume and course of the upper reaches of the river and many of its tributaries. With the demise of industry along its banks much of the Tay has reverted to 'wild country-side' and it is this attribute that leads many to visit the area.

Environmental designations upon the river and its flora and fauna in diverse places, from the sand dune ecosystem at Tentsmuir Point via the reed beds of the middle and upper estuary to the shingle bars at Dowally and the fresh water mussel beds of the upper reaches of the river, provide evidence that much of what was once utilised for commercial gain or personal need is now part of the package that enhances visitor numbers, which in turn underpin the economy of the places that border the river.

There have been many reasons for settlement along the length of the river Tay throughout history. Today the criteria may be different but the central fact of the river remains.

ELEVEN
THE TROSSACHS

'A laugh was on every face when William said we were come to see the Trossachs; no doubt they thought we had better stayed in our own homes.'

Dorothy Wordsworth, *Journal*, 1803

Sir Walter Scott invented the Trossachs as, regrettably perhaps, the place is widely imagined and, so far as scenery is concerned, the Trossachs may sometimes seem like a figment of his imagination and be found disappointing on that account. The Trossachs might be described as several reservoirs separated by somewhat featureless afforested hills flanked by two scenically more interesting glens. Hugh Quigley, the travel writer born in Stirling, commented in Batsford's *Scottish Highlands* that it was not that the Trossachs were not sufficiently beautiful but that their beauty 'had become conventional and perhaps rather wearisome'.

Scott 'the great unknown' is now, in John Carey's phrase, the 'great unread'. He pretended, at least, to have a low opinion of his own poetry, but it has the virtue of striking a chord which hangs in the memory: after all, Scott wrote 'Ave Maria' and 'Hail to the Chief', both of which form part of *The Lady of the Lake* and, in another phrase, 'they can't take that away from him'. Perhaps he stole 'the scenery of a dream' from his friend Wordsworth but the picture-painting in the poem is memorable.

His invention was, perhaps crudely but nonetheless effectively, based on reality and tradition. He learned about the Trossachs, a district exceptionally rich in folklore and the scene of much historic incident, from Patrick Graham, the Minister of Aberfoyle and others. If no one since has succeeded in implanting such a powerful set of images as Scott, let us simply lament the poverty of the imagination of his successors.

The tourist resort of Callander is the 'capital' of 'The Trossachs' although the Trossachs proper – the country at and about the foot of Loch Katrine – is rather closer to Aberfoyle. The name is said to be derived from the Gaelic – now obsolete – for the 'cross-hills'. The whole of the district between Callander and Loch Lomond is now generally referred to as The Trossachs and the term is variously extended to include Doune, Strathyre and Balquhidder and even Lochearnhead, Crianlarich and Killin. However, it can safely be said that the further one travels from Loch Katrine, Callander and Aberfoyle the further one is from the Trossachs.

The country was eloquently characterised in the *Old Statistical Account* by the Rev James Robertson, Minister of Callander in 1791. It was he who did most to draw the attention of the world to the place: 'When you enter the Trossachs there is such an assemblage of wildness and rude grandeur, as beggars all description, and fills the mind with the most sublime conceptions.' Early accounts – *Scotia Depicta*, Lady Sarah Murray,' Dorothy Wordsworth and James Hogg – are all much indebted to him, as have been all of their sucessors.

The key to the Trossachs is the juxtaposition of two lochs, separated by low wooded ridges and dominated by two hills, the one, Ben Venue, massive and the other, Ben A'an, peaked, neither of which has any great distinction or look anything from any other point of view. The combination of the hills, woods and water is highly pleasing to the human eye but it cannot quite be satisfactorily apprehended by the camera, on a canvas or by mere description. Hence its appeal. Such combinations are not particularly unusual. It can be argued that the scenery of Strathard, next door, is superior to that of the Trossachs proper. There Ben Lomond, a much more impressive mountain, dominates the intricate Loch Ard and the Highland edge is marked by tumbling waterfalls in the pass of Aberfoyle. The Pass of Leny and Loch Lubnaig are equally attractive in their way and the Braes of Balquhidder, with Ben More and Stobinian more retiring than Ben Lomond, rightly have their adherents. Thus, within a comparatively few square miles, there are places which might be said to cut the Trossachs down to size. Glen Lyon or Glen Affric or Loch Maree may be considered far superior but no one attached so much magic and so much tradition to another place as Scott did to the Trossachs.

One reason why the Trossachs district is impressive is because of the contrast between it and the plain variously referred to as Flanders Moss, the Vale of Menteith and the Carse of Stirling. No sooner does the Forth tumble out of the Highlands than it starts to meander across its flood plain which, in geological time, used to be an arm of the sea. Nowadays some of the mosses have been drained to form rich farmland but, elsewhere, these flatlands, described by Scott as 'the coarsest and meanest covering which Mother Earth is ever arrayed in', are still impoverished. Sometimes ground fog gathers in this basin of the Forth to form another sort of sea. Southwards there is a rim of hills etched on the skyline which make the view of the plain from the road from Aberfoyle to Thornhill memorable. On the largest of three islands in the Lake of Menteith, lying about three miles (4.8 km) west of Aberfoyle, Cunninghame Graham is buried amidst the ruins of the beautiful Augustinian priory of Inchmahome where Mary Queen of Scots was taken as a child. At the Lake of Menteith there is a fine view towards Ben Lomond.

The hill country above this plain, straddling the Highland Edge, dotted with lochs and lochans is where *The Lady of the Lake* and some of the scenes of *Rob Roy* are set. Glen Gyle, at the head of Loch Katrine, was where the real Rob Roy MacGregor was born in 1671 and the famous cateran is buried at Balquhidder. William and Dorothy Wordsworth and Coleridge were among the first English visitors to the area. Stevenson touched the district and set a part of *Kidnapped* and *Catriona* on the edges of it. Carlyle, Dickens, Jules Verne, Nathaniel Hawthorne and Theodor Fontane were amongst those who alighted in the Trossachs after Scott. MacAulay complained that, however hard he tried, he had never succeeded in seeing the Trossachs in fine weather. Barrie, in ironic vein, pointed out that the fishing was bound to be good in August, provided you came in May and vice versa. George Eliot caused her heroines to discourse about the Trossachs and Trollope's Lough Linter in *Phineas Finn* was almost certainly in the Trossachs; Millais's famous illustration of Laura's reception of Phineas Finn's proposal has a hint of Loch Venachar about it. Scott undoubtedly started something.

Robert Cadell (1788–1849), Scott's publisher friend, arranged that Turner should illustrate Lockhart's edition of Scott's Poetical Works (1834) and he probably visited the Trossachs twice. There can be no criticism of Turner's exquisite drawings but his only oil connected with the district signally failed to attract the approbation of John Ruskin, who characterised it as: 'The worst picture I ever saw of this period'. Horatio McCulloch (1805–1867), the most evocative of Scottish mountain landscape painters, executed a masterpiece in his 'Loch Katrine' of 1866, a stunning picture of Ellen's Isle and Ben Venue from the same point of view as Turner chose for a drawing. Alexander Smith, in a *Summer in Skye*, commented 'As a view of Highland scenery we have never seen its equal, and no man but McCulloch could have produced it.' 'Loch Katrine' by James Docharty (1829–1878) of Bonhill, a painter of realistic pictures influenced by McCulloch may also be referred to. Pictures by John McWhirter (1839–1911), much praised by Ruskin, by Colin Hunter (1841–1904), pupil of James Milne Donald noted for his watercolours of the West Coast and the passionate John Smart RSA (1838–1899) were much praised at the time.

Ruskin was taken to the Trossachs as a young man and in 1853 took his bride and his protégé, Millais, to Brig o' Turk, the setting for the start of one of the great Victorian sex scandals. Perhaps the connection with Ruskin led 'the Glasgow Boys' to Brig o' Turk in 1879–81 but it was probably its character as the nearest 'Highland clachan' (in contrast to the estate villages of Luss and Gartmore) to Glasgow that attracted them. The summers they spent there were critical to their development as artists, not so much for what they produced as for their conversations about painting.

James Guthrie (1859–1930) drew a sketch of Crawhall, himself and Walton sharing a bottle of wine at Brig o' Turk which captured their fellowship. There is a beautiful oil by George Henry (1858–1943) of Brig o' Turk in the Glasgow Art Galleries. Arthur Melville (1855–1904), the leading 'Scottish Impressionist', followed them and he exhibited pictures entitled 'Loch Vennachar' and 'The Sheiling, Brig o' Turk' in 1884. John Lavery, who was friendly with Cunninghame Graham, executed a notable oil of Loch Katrine which is to be seen in Edinburgh. The Trossachs were, thus, both a birthplace of Scottish *plein air* painting and a place where Scottish artists began to paint real life rather than a romanticised vision of Scottish scenery; of these Guthrie's 'Funeral Service in the Highlands' is outstanding.

William Henry Fox Talbot (1800–1877), the British 'inventor' of photography, visited Loch Katrine in 1844 to make Calotypes of scenery associated with Scott and, in 1845, published *Sun Pictures in Scotland* which included six views of Loch Katrine, generally considered to be amongst his most interesting. There is an exhibition about them at the Water Board Information Centre, Trossachs Pier. George Washington Wilson (1823–1893), of Aberdeen, became Photographer Royal to Queen Victoria and is usually regarded as the first landscape photographer who exercised an influence comparable with that of Scott on the development of tourism in Scotland in the second half of the 19th century. His earliest photographs were of his native Deeside but his views of the Trossachs are amongst his earliest subjects. He established many well known photographic points of view but he frequently adopted interesting and original standpoints. His views of the Pass of Bealach nam Bo and the Goblin's Cave are notable in this respect. An edition of *The Lady of the Lake* published by A & C Black in 1863 had photographic illustrations by GW Wilson.

The Trossachs Tour was an objective of a very early excursion organised by Thomas Cook in 1846 and tourism rather than travel may be said to have begun then. The principal sights were Ellen's Isle, an attractive island, mis-named by Sir Walter Scott; the Silver Strand, a fine quartz beach submerged by the Glasgow Corporation after 1859; the craggy Ben Venue, denuded of its trees by the Duke of Montrose shortly after Scott made it famous, Coire nan Uruiskin, on the opposite side of the loch from the beach and a high promontory from which the whole could be viewed, Roderick Dhu's Watch Tower. A sail on the loch from the pier could be undertaken in the *Rob Roy*, the first steamer, later the *Sir Walter Scott*. Connoisseurs of loch scenery will grant that the scene is grand but not that it is unsurpassed.

The district was popular with visitors long before Thomas Cook for several reasons. It was possible to complete the tour from Glasgow or Edinburgh relatively easily. The Trossachs provided what HV Morton described as 'a traveller's sample of Scottish scenery' or, what the North British Railway, with rather less restraint, called 'the most entrancing single day's journey in the two hemispheres'. Most importantly, the district was associated with Sir Walter Scott and Rob Roy.

In the 17th century the parishes of south west Perthshire were over-whelmingly Gaelic-speaking; it was not simply their geology, but their culture which made them a part of the Highlands. When Robert Kirk, the Minister of Balquhidder and of Aberfoyle, wrote *The Secret Common-wealth of Elves, Fauns and Fairies*, he described genuinely held beliefs among his parishioners, who were at the same time as devout in uphold-ing Christian beliefs. His successor, Patrick Graham, gave Scott the folklore which established Coire nan Uruiskin on Ben Venue as such a romantic spot. Scott called it the Corrie of the Satyrs, drawing attention inadvertently perhaps, to the universal and timeless nature of folklore. The eerie tales of divination and of succubi in Glen Finglas which Scott wove into more than one poem were Graham's too.

The population, almost as great in the 17th century as it is now, depended largely on raising black cattle and a few sheep on small estates recovered from Royal hunting forests where deer and wild boar had been taken. In addition to the remnants of these forests, there was much uncul-tivated heath and poor coppices, with a scattering of meadow ground and patches of corn here and there. There was some iron smelting in the woods and a little urbanisation. The population of Glasgow was modest then in comparison with that of Perthshire and the intimate connections which there now are between Highlands and Lowlands did not exist. In Cromwell's time the garrison at Stirling experienced as much difficulty in maintaining law and order in the Trossachs as in more remote places. Indeed, John Graham of Duchray was the last to formally surrender to General Monk following the Earl of Glencairn's Rising and, even so, he was permitted to maintain a private militia as long as it was engaged simply in the protection of his own estate.

One hundred years later Nichol Graham of Gartmore described a situa-tion which was little changed:

> The lands at the head of the Parish of Buchanan lying betwixt Loch Lomond and Loch Katrine, are, of all these in that country, the best adapted for concealments, and the most conveniently situated for bad purposes . . .'

The country between Loch Lomond and Balquhidder became known as the Rob Roy Country. Wordsworth's worst Scottish poem likened him to Robin Hood. There is, indeed, a story of a widow whose rent Rob Roy paid, telling her to make sure she got a receipt. He then relieved the factor of the money. However, many of his exploits and those of his sons were much more disreputable. Graham explains blackmail in the following amusing way, although, of course, it was not amusing at the time:

> A person who had the greatest correspondence with the thieves was agreed upon to preserve the lands contracted for thefts, for certain sums to be paid yearly out of these lands. Upon this fund he employed one half of the thieves to recover stolen cattle, and the other half of them to steal, in order to make this agreement and blackmail contract necessary.[2]

The *Scottish National Dictionary* suggests that 'blackmail' may have been so-called because of the black beasts involved and the 'Black Watch' gave the name of a famous regiment a singular resonance.

The surprising of the Barracks of Inversnaid by Gregor MacGregor of Glengyle was the first military event of the '45 and there were many Stuart supporters, overt and covert, in the district during the uprising. After it, while the exiled Court was in France, Stewart of Glenbuckie was prominent amongst those who gave sustenance to envoys who visited the Highlands, including Alan Breck Stewart who appears in *Kidnapped*. The district was the scene of a last sad episode in the story of the Jacobites when Dr Archibald Cameron, Locheil's brother who was in the Highlands in connection with the abortive Elibank plot of 1752, was finally caught. He was in hiding with Stewart of Glenbuckie when he was betrayed. Calum MacLeod states that Cameron was discovered because his presence was suspected when a child who was ill made a surprising recovery and Cameron was reported by a jealous rival. Other sources state that he was given away by a kinsman, yet others implicate James More MacGregor, Rob Roy's disreputable son. We have an account of his arrest by soldiers from Inversnaid but whether that took place at Glenbuckie or at Brenachoil on Loch Katrineside is also in dispute. Cameron was executed in London and Dr Johnson famously condemned the execution as a barbarous act.

After the '45 there were 1000 sheep in the parish of Callander. By the end of the 18th century there were 18,000. The clearances which affected the district were not so dramatic as those elsewhere in Scotland, but they took place with the same deleterious effects: the population declined and the landscape was much altered, as trees were felled and replaced by sheep. It was to this depopulated country that Walter Scott, an apprentice Edinburgh lawyer engaged in superintending an eviction at the head of the Braes of Balquhidder, came.

The present character of the Trossachs owes a great deal to the Corporation of Glasgow whose principal water supply was secured from Loch Katrine in 1859. The scheme was begun with a ceremony on the ridge between Loch Katrine and Loch Chon in May 1856 and, remarkably enough, finished in 1859. It was declared open by the Queen and the Prince Consort, who arrived via Callander, in October of that year. Details were given in the local papers of the various routes by which dignitaries would arrive at the remote spot chosen for the opening and the fine mileposts put in along the way can still be seen. 'Royal Cottage' was refurbished for the occasion and, to look at it, one might suppose that the party were to stay for at least a week. In fact they had lunch there. The weather was appalling with thick mist and heavy rain. There was a predictably pompous address from the bailies of Glasgow and the Queen responded in a simpler fashion. The proceedings then concluded with, as the *Stirling Journal* put it, 'a long prayer' from the local minister. It was not until 1869, when she stayed at Invertrossachs, that Queen Victoria saw Loch Katrine under favourable conditions.

The engineer JF Bateman (1810–1889), at a banquet given in his honour, gave an eloquent account of the works which at the time were the most considerable of their kind in the world. It is still well worth walking the first part of the 'Pipe Track Road' in order to see the achievements of these Victorian engineers who built fine stone aqueducts in the heart of an inhospitable countryside:

> The rock, especially the mica slate, proved extremely hard and difficult to work. At several points along the side of Loch Chon the progress did not exceed three lineal yards in a month at each face, although work was carried on day and night. The average progress through the mica slate was about five yards in a month: in drilling holes for blasting, a fresh drill was required for every inch in depth on the average; and about sixty drills were constantly in use at each face. The cost of gunpowder alone consumed in the contract was £10,540, and there was about 175 miles of fuse burned in firing it.[3]

One intriguing legacy of this period is an arcane place name: Sevastopol, the site of an encampment at Loch Chon occupied by the navvies engaged in the waterworks. There is no doubt, either, that during this era the Teapot, an inn which sold illicitly distilled whisky, enjoyed a period of prosperity. This old cottage still stands beside a hump-backed bridge between Kinlochard and the Dubh Lochan on the military road to Inversnaid.

The waterworks scheme was expanded between 1885 and 1914 by raising the level of Loch Katrine, providing a second pipeline, utilising Loch Arklet and, after the Second World War, including Glen Finglas. What is remarkable is that in spite of the changes, which involved the submerging of 'the Silver Strand', the landscape which attracted the Wordsworths and Scott has been preserved rather than spoiled and continues to attract visitors from all over the world. The pleasure steamer, the *Sir Walter Scott*, which still affords the best means of visiting the loch, is the last steam-driven vessel of its kind in Britain precisely because Loch Katrine is Glasgow's water supply and a motor vessel might pollute the loch.

Loch Katrine was chosen in preference to a scheme using Loch Lubnaig the winding loch. This loch, drained by the tumultuous Leny, presents the visitor travelling northwards with a variety of interesting prospects, the more so because it is difficult to decide on which side of the loch the various hills which dominate it are situated. It is the scene of the start of *A Legend of Montrose* and St Bride's Chapel, near the foot of the loch, is in *The Lady of the Lake*. Nearby, at Tombea, the poet and travel-writer Alexander Campbell was born. At the head of the loch is the village of Strathyre where nowadays there is considerable employment in forestry. A little further on is Balquhidder where the kirk sits at the foot of a glen with a charming waterfall. The beautiful dressed stone church of 1853 is associated with St Angus, Balquhidder's saint. Above the church is a magnificent view of the long narrow glen occupied by Loch Voil and Loch Doine. The old kirk, beside the new, dates from 1631; Robert Kirk ministered there and his first wife, Isobel, is buried in the kirkyard. Beside the old kirk are the graves of Rob Roy and two of his sons.

The Trossachs were never totally deforested, although the Duke of Montrose outraged Scott by grubbing out the trees on Ben Venue. The largest landowners recognised the enduring value of trees and the char-coal industry was succeeded by the use of bark for tanning. The Duke extended his woodlands and throughout the 19th century they were a significant source of employment. After 1858 the slate quarries in the Duke's Pass above Aberfoyle prospered and provided roofing material for perhaps a third of the houses in Glasgow.

The railway reached Callander in 1856 and in the succeeding years it crept northwards as far as Glen Ogle, eventually going on to Oban. From Stirling the line went to Dunblane and thence Doune, a tiny burgh once famous for pistol-making and for cattle and sheep fairs. Callander owes its reputation to its situation on the Highland Boundary Fault, marked by the fine crags above the town. It is at one of the principal gateways to the Highlands, the fine Pass of Leny. Like Crieff and Dunkeld it would have been a popular place of resort without Scott or Rob Roy. It was laid out as a planned village in 1739 and developed with impetus from commissioners for the forfeited estates after 1745. The principal hotel in the place, the Dreadnought, gets its name from the motto of Francis McNab who built it in 1801–2. With Ben Ledi looming over a bridge crossing the rapid River Teith, the situation of Callander is extremely romantic. It enjoyed even more prosperity than Aberfoyle as a result of *The Lady of the Lake*. The narrative could be followed almost word for word by approaching the Trossachs from Kilmahog. Four-in-hand coaches conveyed passengers from the train. They crossed the Leny by the 'Roman Brig', an 18th-century bridge designed by John Baxter, even then altered and widened. They then went by Bocastle Hill with the giant erratic boulder, 'Samson's Putting Stone' perched on its shoulder, passed Dunmore, the site of an Iron Age fort and reached Coilantogle. From then on the passengers could enjoy an undiluted diet of Sit Walter Scott as the scenes encountered in the poem were successively revealed to them.In 1820, as part of the improvement of his extensive estates, the Duke of Montrose constructed a road of sorts between Aberfoyle and Loch Achray for the followers in Scott's foot-steps. In 1824 John MacCulloch, in a letter addressed to the author, was deploring the effects of Scott's works which included, as a by-product, an adaptation of *Rob Roy* for the stage:

> The mystic portal has been thrown open and the mob has rushed in, dispersing all these fairy visions, and polluting everything with its unhallowed touch. Barouches and gigs, cocknies, and fishermen and poets, Glasgow weavers and travelling haberdashers now swarm in every resting place and meet us at every avenue. As Rob Roy now blusters at Covent Garden and the Lyceum, and Aberfoyle is gone to Wapping, so Wapping and the Strand must also come to Aberfoyle. The green-coated fairies have packed up their awls and quitted the premises, and the Uriskins only caper now in your verses.[4]

The building of the Forth and Clyde Junction Railway from Stirling to Balloch, opened in May 1856, transformed the accessibility of Aberfoyle which was reached either from Port of Menteith Station near Arnprior, enabling the visitor to see Inchmahome, or from Buchlyvie by Ward Toll. The stationmaster at Arnprior wrote what is still one of the most in-triguing guides to the district with tales of Rob Roy more elaborate than Scott's and of witches and hobgoblins and the Reverend Robert Kirk. The railway reached Aberfoyle in 1882. The company improved the Duke's Road and, thereafter, there were two four-in-hand coaches daily between the Baillie Nichol Jarvie Hotel and the Trossachs Pier. With steamers on Loch Lomond and on Loch Katrine, the 'Trossachs Tour' became a highly sophisticated trip.

One hundred years later the track-beds of these railways were being turned into footpaths and cycle tracks. One of the first long-distance cycle tracks in Britain is from Glasgow to Killin, using the Callander and Oban railway which crossed and recrossed the roaring Leny and then ran along the shore of Loch Lubnaig. The cycle track eliminates the railway bridges but generally follows the old line.

The government had sanctioned the further improvement of the Duke's Road to provide work for unemployed miners in 1931-32. Perthshire landowners opposed the scheme as they had opposed Glasgow's water scheme, on the grounds that it was a waste of public money and would lead to a loss of amenity. An intriguing feature of this project was that in order to make it labour-intensive as few mechanical aids as possible were used. The structures which were afterwards used as the Youth Hostels at the Trossachs and at Ledard were part of a camp built at the head of Loch Achray to house the workers. Great attention was paid to amenity: heather borders were laid out and there was a 'hiker's path'. The Trossachs provided many young people from the cities with an escape to the countryside in the 1930s.

The road, formerly restricted to horse-drawn vehicles and cyclists, soon became a favourite, as a testing route which ordinary drivers could tackle, with the rapidly increasing number of private motorists in the 1930s. It was one of the few in Britain where hairpin bends suggestive of the Alps could be found. The four-in-hand coaches were succeeded by motor coaches engaged in the Trossachs Tour. Nowadays this era is recreated by a post-war charabanc, the Trossachs Trundler, plying between Callander, Aberfoyle and Stirling.

Near the foot of the Duke's Pass above Aberfoyle is David Marshall Lodge, the visitor centre for the Queen Elizabeth Forest Park. The Forestry Commission purchased the Renagour and Gartloaning estates in 1928–9 and gradually acquired 16,800 hectares between Loch Venachar and the headwaters of the Forth which constitute the Forest Park, named in celebration of the Queen's coronation. From the first there were critics of afforestation – of the Sitka spruce in particular – but as Tom Weir who grew up with the forests has pointed out the wildlife was enriched. The Park was always expected to be the forest visited by the greatest number of people and only three-quarters of the Commissioners' estates were afforested. If, in places, they have a certain bleakness, they did provide significant local employment and are now highly productive. It is interesting, too, that after the war Scotland eschewed National Parks and some ideas about 'visitor management' in the countryside were worked out in the Forest Park: nature trails, an orienteering course, a forest drive and now cycle routes have been established.

Recent developments have included a Safari park at Blair Drummond, by which the famous improver Lord Kames, whose residence it was and who drained the mosses in the basin of the Forth, would probably have been startled but of which he would probably have approved; the Rob Roy Centre in Callander, employing the latest multi-media technology; a charming and disarming Farm Life Centre near Thornhill and, in Aberfoyle, the Scottish Wool Centre where there are daily shows about sheep and wool as well as concerts and plays and outdoor sheep-dog demonstrations. One of the first time-share developments in Scotland was established at Forest Hills, Lochard, without overwhelming either the old farmhouse of Ledard, behind which is the waterfall described in *Waverley* and *Rob Roy*, or the relative quietness of this charming loch. At the Trossachs itself, the old Trossachs Hotel with its 'candlesnuffer' turrets where so many distinguished literary visitors stayed has also been converted into a luxury holiday complex, Tigh Mor. This is not to say that the district is entirely given over to visitors. Parts are congested but elsewhere, even in the Forest Park, there are places where seclusion can be found and, beyond the head of Loch Katrine, wilderness.

David Marshall Lodge was built as early as 1958 and it provides access to a tributary of the Forth which tumbles down from Craig Vadh in a waterfall which was for long known as MacGregor's Leap, giving the place a spurious association with Rob Roy. Another waterfall on the Duchray, the Black Linn of Blairvaich, was used in the Richard Todd film *Rob Roy* which can serve to remind us that the district's popular appeal continues to be bound up with the media. In August 1962 Callander took on new life when it became 'Tannochbrae', the equally doubtful but as memorable setting for the exploits of AJ Cronin's Dr Finlay in the first television series. Doune Castle is so authentically medieval in its appearance that it was used as the location in *Monty Python and the Holy Grail*. More recently, the scenery of Liam Neeson's *Rob Roy* was sewn together in Inverness-shire and more distant parts of Perthshire. However, the image was of the Trossachs. Local people have always regarded such associations with a degree of ambivalence; they generate pride but they imply disturbance. However, the district retains its reputation and, in comparison with these modern visions of the Trossachs, Scott's images seem more authoritative. In reality the district attracts visitors for the best reasons: it is both attractive and accessible but it is also highly evocative and, in some respects, elusive. The combination is irresistible.

TWELVE

THE CITY OF PERTH

The 'Fair city' of Perth is sited astride the River Tay about 1.6 km south of its tidal limit. It was on the right or west bank that the original settlement took place on a rectangle of river terrace between two former islands, the North and South Inches, which were damp areas in early times, a circumstance that has endowed the town with two large and grassy open spaces on either side of its early and its contemporary core.

The river was fordable at Perth and at the lowest place on the Tay early routeways from east, south, west and possibly north converged at a short inlet of the river near the eastern end of the present High Street, where a landing area developed for small boats. The original settlement developed round it and on the line of the present Watergate. By the 11th century, on the sloping bank to the river, boats could be pulled up on to the gravels; the 'coal shore', a pier for the discharge of coal at the river's edge, was later developed there.

As early as the 13th century, a wooden bridge across the river was washed away in a severe flood in 1210. One of King Alexander I's sons was drowned; the elderly king escaped in a small boat. In 1621, a ten-arched stone bridge which had been recently built was destroyed and in 1814, the highest water level was recorded, 7 m above average level. Smeaton's bridge, which was opened in 1771, survived that flood and another eighteen floods of at least 5m above average level and is still carrying heavy traffic. The second highest flood at 6.5 m above the average level occurred on 17 January 1993, when the greatest depth of flood water was recorded in the town. Many houses and commercial premises were flooded and damage estimated at over £12 million was sustained in Perth alone. Since then, plans to protect Perth by the creation of 10 km of a near-continuous series of embankments and flood walls on the west bank of the river, 4 km west of the mouth of the River Almond to Perth Harbour, have been approved and should be completed by the year 2002.

The trading area grew westwards along the High Street from the original settlement. Before 1124 Alexander I granted permission to foreign merchants to trade with the monks of Scone Abbey, by which date Perth had the highest customs yield of all the Scottish towns. Both Alexander I and his son, David I, encouraged trade and the convergence of the routeways and the river brought merchants from Britain and Europe to Perth. Its trade flourished and in 1124 Perth was created a royal burgh by David I, the fifth oldest in Scotland. The Crown would thereafter have appointed a sheriff who, besides dispensing justice, acted as a collector of the king's customs. He also collected, stored and sold produce from the king's estates in the castle, which stood on rising ground near where Perth Museum is now located and when the king was in residence he supplied victuals from the store.

By c. 1150 a mill lade from Huntingtower Haugh on the Almond had been excavated and was turning the water wheels of the town's mills. The lade may have continued down the present line of Mill Street and possibly been diverted along the line of South Methven Street. From there it ran along the line of the present Canal Crescent and Canal Street back to the River Tay, thus enclosing much of the broadly level area between the Inches and later formed part of the defences of the medieval town.

It is thought that a church existed in Perth in Pictish times. However, it is known that in 1128 a church was built on the present site of St John's Kirk from where a lane, the Kirkgait (the way or walk to the kirk, now spelt Kirkgate), linked the church with the High Street and another lane the Skinnergate which in turn linked the castle with the High Street and St John's Kirk. The castle was probably a wooden structure, enclosed by an earthen rampart, which may have been washed away in the 1210 flood. By 1180 the Turret Brig, which crossed the lade at the High Street Port (the gate at the west end of the High Street) and the South Street Port were both in existence and also the streets associated with them, including a small suburb beyond the lade and west of the High Street Port, the New Row. The two main streets, High Street and South Street, were linked by vennels or lanes west of the Kirkgate, St John's Kirk and St Anne's Lane. There is no evidence for a town wall before the defensive wall constructed at the bidding of Edward I of England, but thereafter the lade also served as a moat through which Robert the Bruce and Randolph waded to scale the wall and retake Perth. At right angles to the two main streets, burgage plots were laid out and allocated to the burgesses. As early as 1126, David I gave to Dunfermline Abbey the revenues of St John's Kirk and a house it possessed on a plot of land on the north side of South Methven Street, suggesting that all the plots inside the town lade had been allocated, although they may not have been completely built up by 1126.

If royal favour was already evident in the grant of royal burgh status, it was extended further by the endowment of the Dominican or Blackfriars monastery on a site at the junction of Kinnoull Street and Carpenter Street by Alexander II, who used it to house the court on its peripatetic rounds of Lowland Scotland. The monastery was also a most important teaching seminary. Another small surburb grew in this area. Alexander III founded the Whitefriars or Carmelite house west of the town, near the junction of the Longcauseway and Rigg's Road, in 1462. The Carthusian monastery, the only one in Scotland, was founded by James I's queen, Joan of Beaufort, in 1429. It lay to the northwest of the South Street Port, probably near where the King James IV Hospital stands today. The Franciscan or Greyfriars monastery was established in 1460 by Lawrence Oliphant on a site south of the lade at the end of the Speygate.

Parliament met at the end of the 13th century in the Augustinian abbey of Scone founded by Alexander I in 1113 on the site of the present Scone Palace, some 8 km north of Perth and convened on at least twelve more occasions between 1318 and 1445, more usually in the Blackfriars monastery. The Exchequer Audit was carried out in Perth on several occasions and church councils also met in the town.

The North Inch was the location of a strange incident, the Battle of the Clans, which was viewed by Robert III and his court from the Dominican monastery. This was a very bloody tournament between 29 Members of Clan Kay or the Macintoshes and a substitute, a Perth armourer called Hal o' the Wynd and 30 members of Clan Chattan or the Macmillans (once of Clan Chattan and later of Clan Cameron. Both groups had been at odds with one another). One MacMillan and 11 Mackintoshes survived. Recent work, however, suggests that the tournament represented the two sides of a very divided court, the Macintoshes representing the Earl of Fife and the Lindsays, while the MacMillans supported the Queen, the Earl of Carrick (the heir to the throne) and the Dunbars.

After James I's assassination in Blackfriars monastery in 1437, the king and his court ceased to visit Perth, which had been favoured and advantaged by these visits. Perth had become a very central location in Scotland and the presence of the court led to considerable business for the merchants of the town, one of whom, John Mercer, acted as the king's envoy and negotiated King David II's ransom.

A church court held in Perth in 1407 led to the conviction and burning at the stake of John Resby after a heresy trial. Resby was a follower of Wycliffe, whose ideas about civil power were of concern to the ecclesiastical establishment. Undue pressure was exerted by the abbot of Dunfermline Abbey on Perth Town Council to take responsibility for repairs to St John's Kirk, although the abbey had received the teinds from the Kirk for three centuries. Disapproval of such greed increased after a performance of Sir David Lyndsay's satire *The Three Estates* in Perth in the presence of James V. A dispute between a citizen and the Blackfriars in 1543 resulted in an attack on the monastery and the parading of a monastic cooking pot through the town. Cardinal Beaton's heresy trials resulted in the hanging of five men and the drowning of one of their wives. Beaton's nominee for the office of provost was not elected and the successful nominee and his supporters had to repel an attack by the unsuccessful candidate! John Knox preached a fiery sermon in St John's Kirk in 1560 after further trials of Protestants by the Queen Regent had taken place in breach of assurances previously given. As a result, all four monasteries and Scone Abbey were destroyed. The monastic lands and property were transferred to the burgh in 1569 to provide a hospital for the disabled, distressed persons and fatherless children. The King James Hospital was erected on the site of the former Carthusian abbey. Recently it was converted into flats for single people.

The departure of King James VI and I to London after a visit to Perth in 1600 nearly cost him his life through a possible assassination attempt in Gowrie House. In 1621, a new bridge built in 1617 collapsed. The Covenanting and Cromwellian periods brought little relief; Cromwell destroyed about one third of the buildings in the town including the remaining piers of the 1617 bridge. He used the stone and tombstones from the Greyfriars monastery site to build a citadel on the South Inch near the foot of the present Marshall Place which was later turned into stables and finally razed to the ground. To compound all these disasters, two ships built by the burgesses and others and a third carrying cargo belonging to Perth merchants were lost, as well as money invested in the Darien Scheme, a total of some £35,000 (Scots). The Jacobite Rebellions brought no relief, except the establishment of a permanent garrison in Perth which helped increase trade in the town. However, the revival of Perth was about to begin.

In 1758, two textile factories were founded by the New Row Company and the Mill Wynd Company and began to produce fine sheeting, creating work for handloom weavers and employing some of the rural craftsmen who came into Perth from the surrounding areas to work in the factories. Weaving of Silesias, a medium quality cloth, bleaching it, shipping it to London in Perth sailing craft for export to the West Indies, continued to flourish. By 1774 this development had also stimulated ship repairing and shipbuilding in the harbour area and brought in ships carrying flax and flax seed from Danzig and Riga in the Baltic as well as from The Netherlands. Textile manufacture became the principal business of Perth for the next half century.

In the early 1760s, when the population had reached 7500, the walls were taken down, a sign that expansion of the town was required beyond the lade. About the same time the government was encouraging bridge building in order to facilitate trade and transport in the more densely popu-lated parts of the Highlands and Islands. The lack of a bridge at Perth was holding back trade until the Earl of Kinnoull opened a subscription list to fund a bridge and raised some £5000 to which was added £13,800 from the funds of the Forfeited Estates: in all some £35,000 was raised and John Smeaton was commissioned to design and build the bridge at the southern edge of North Inch. It was opened in 1771 and, after widening in 1872, still carries much of the traffic across the River Tay.

Perth started to expand westwards and a weaving surburb developed at Dovecotland on the site of the former Carthusian house, and further expansion took place in Thimblerow and Mill Wynd where sheeting and later cotton cloth was woven. Perth became an important textile town which was not surprising as the clear, soft waters of the Almond and Tay were most suitable for textile manufacture. Bleachfields for linen first developed at Tulloch on the lade in 1735 followed by a site at Luncarty on a low terrace, using water drawn from the Shochie Burn in 1736 by the Sandeman family. Both fields had the expert assistance of Alexander Christie, an experienced Ulster bleacher and in the case of Luncarty there was also financial assistance from the Board of Manufacturers for expansion of the bleachfield.

By 1794 there were some 1500 handloom weavers in Perth. Mill spinning and cloth printing arrived from Glasgow and together changed Perth from a linen weaving town to cotton working. Cotton mills were built on the Lower Almond at Cromwell Park and also on the left bank of the Tay, at Bridgend and 3.2 km to the north at Stormontfield. In addition, by 1792, there were two cotton spinning mills on the lade. Other textile mills were built at Tulloch, at Ruthvenfield, on the lade and on the Annaty Burn on the left bank of the river about 1.6 km north of Bridgend.

The peak years for Perth's textile industries were from 1780–1820, although they continued till about 1850. Competition from Glasgow, in particular, had brought about Perth's decline. During its halcyon years not only bleaching and finishing but also dyeing was developed. Luncarty became the largest bleachfield in Scotland with some 300 staff and a capacity to bleach 549,000 m of linen, with cloth coming from Dunfermline and from England. Bleaching ceased at Ruthvenfield in 1976 but continued at Luncarty until 1996 when the site was razed. However, the staff cottages are still occupied. In 1851 John Shields started a linen factory on Dunkeld Road which continued until the early 1990s.

The textile operation which remained in Perth long after production of cloth ceased was dyeing and dry cleaning. Dyeing developed with the opening of Campbell's dyeworks in 1814 in New Row Green, with John Pullar, perhaps as their apprentice employee. Originally he was a linen handloom weaver who later had a factory producing cotton cloth, umbrella gingham and muslin. His son, Robert, began buying and selling umbrella gingham and later became a cotton manufacturer. In 1823 he brought his son back from London and set him up in business as a dyer in Burt's Close off the

Figure 14

A Plan of the Town of Perth 1774

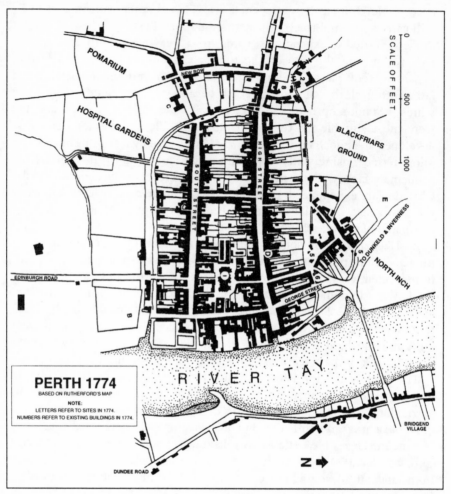

Rutherford, who was art master at Perth Academy, offers us an excellent portrait of Perth at the beginning of its regeneration after sterile years from 1600 to 1730. The town wall has gone, but the mill
lade still constrains growth except where the medieval suburbs of New Row and northern suburbs on
the former Blackfriars ground and the area round the grain mills and baker's granaries are beginning
to expand, for example, the Pomarium, a growing handloom weaver settlement. George Street has
been added leading to Smeaton's Bridge, opened in 1771.

Within the town there are two main streets linked by vennels. The burgage plots are evident. The
role of the lade as a water power provider is evident from the mills recorded on the plan. Bridgend village is a growing settlement. The first significant expansion took place in the area marked Blackfriars
Ground, but not till twenty years later.

High Street. John Pullar Silk Dyers obtained a royal warrant after the Great Exhibition of 1851 and a large, modern factory was built between Mill Street and Carpenter Street.

Pullars commenced dry cleaning operations c. 1870 and became one of the leaders in this sphere, using the cheap parcel post and the railways to great advantage so that by 1900 they had a workforce of some 2000 and some 1100 agents all over the United Kingdom. Competition from other British dry cleaners and the death of three partners in the family business led to it being bought over by Eastmanns of London in 1918. The Pullar family were also benefactors to Perth, providing baths and wash houses on the site of Dr Anderson's Gas Works on Canal Street at a period when few houses had running water or bathrooms.

Perth's population rose from 7500 in 1766 to 14,878 in 1801 and the first large expansion of the town took place on the Blackfriars ground which faced on to the North Inch. It was bought before 1797 by Thomas Anderson, a linen merchant, who secured an agreement in 1795 that no other houses would be built on the north side of Charlotte Street, leaving good views across the North Inch from houses he planned to build in Atholl Crescent and Rose Terrace. His son-in-law, Thomas Hay Marshall, bought the Blackfriars ground from his father-in-law and built houses in Atholl Crescent; the central one, a Masonic Lodge, has superb Georgian features, particularly the plasterwork. In 1802 Marshall donated the central site in Rose Terrace to Perth Academy for a new building, completed in 1804 and built what is now called Corner House on the junction of Charlotte Street and Rose Terrace. The architect for all these buildings was Robert Reid, who later designed the buildings in Charlotte Square in Edinburgh.

An enormously energetic man, Marshall became Town Treasurer in 1791 and a merchant baillie in 1792. He successfully approached the Earl of Kinnoull with a proposal to exchange parcels of land which doubled the size of the North Inch by adding the North Haugh. He also took charge of the negotiations for land to create a cavalry barracks in the then wooded Drumhar area, now a housing estate near the District Police Headquarters on Dunkeld Road. Marshall secured ground at the edge of the South Inch for building houses with Georgian frontages in what is now Marshall Place and also succeeded in feuing part of Burghmuir estate. Unfortunately he died in 1808. The domed Library of Perth Museum was built in 1822 in memory of all he had done for Perth, as not only had he started the expansion on the north side of Perth, but saw the construction of St John Street, Mill Street and Canal Street which paved over the lade that had powered some of the early industries in Perth. Building thereafter continued northwards and Barossa Street, Barossa Place, Melville Street and Stormont Street were added to the town.

Another key person in the development of Perth was Dr Adam Anderson (c. 1780–1846), Rector of Perth Academy from 1809–37. With Marshall's extension of Perth, well-water was proving insufficient for the town's needs and Anderson provided a secure water supply by taking and filtering water from the gravel beds at the northern end of Moncrieffe Island and having a deep trench dug from there to the waterworks he designed at the foot of Marshall Place as well as the engineering which included pumps and a cast iron dome above the cistern, in the building now occupied by the Ferguson Art Gallery. He had 8 km of water pipes laid making a domestic water supply available to householders, a hotel, Pullars Dye Works and Wright's Brewery. Anderson also built a gas works to provide lighting in factories (enabling them to extend the hours of production in winter) and for domestic and street lighting certainly by 1831.

In 1837, this extraordinary Rector of Perth Academy was appointed Professor of Physics at St Andrews University but his expertise was still called for in Perth in discussions about improving navigation on the Tay and the construction of a tidal harbour. When the railway from Dundee reached Barnhill on the left bank of the river, Anderson identified the best site for a railway bridge, with a swing section to enable ships to reach the coal shore, crossing the river just north of his waterworks, thus preserving the South Inch from encroachment.

If the invention of steam power initiated a decline in Perth as an industrial centre, the coming of the railway from Dundee in 1847, from Glasgow, Aberdeen and Inverness in 1850 and from Edinburgh direct via the Forth Bridge in 1890 along with steam boats on the river, re-emphasised the central location of Perth and brought a new expansion in commerce and services. The railways were the largest employer of labour with 2000 staff in 1951. Even after the Beeching 'axe' there were still some 1750 in 1964. Today the railway remains one of the largest employers.

The consumption of wines and spirits from 323 outlets was noted by the authors of the *New Statistical Account* in 1837. The proximity to the Highland malt distilling led to the establishment of several notable firms, one of the first of which was TR Sandeman in 1825. Arthur Bell was a travelling salesman with this firm and became a whisky blender on his own account. His son, AK Bell, who became one of Perth's outstanding entrepreneurs, took over his father's firm in 1900 and bought both Blair Atholl Distillery and Dufftown-Glenlivet in 1933 and Inchgower in 1936. He then bought Buckie Distillery. The Dufftown-Glenlivet purchase was enhanced by the acquisition of an adjacent farm, woodlands and shootings. Earlier in his career, in 1924, AK Bell had bought the farms of Gannochy and Muirhall between Perth and Scone and by 1932 had built 150 bungalows for renting cheaply to artisans. When John Shield's linen factory was in danger of closing, he bought, re-organised and re-equipped it.

Having developed a very fine business, AK Bell turned to charitable activities. He was a keen cricketer and created a cricket gound at Doo'cot Park. In 1933 he purchased Quarry Mill Den on the Annaty Burn at the limits of Perth (on the road to Blairgowrie) and presented it to Perth 'to be kept as a place of public resort'. It has recently been developed as an excellent amenity Woodland Park, Visitor Centre and MacMillan Coffee Shop, with woodland walks in a shallow valley earlier used for cotton spinning and the extraction of starch for use in the textile industry. Perhaps most significantly of all AK Bell set up The Gannochy Trust, a charitable foundation to aid organisations for young, old and disabled people. It has contributed much to the Bell's Sports Centre on the North Inch as well as helping to fund a new sewage system for Perth. AK Bell's generosity has provided many of the finest facilities in Perth, not least the National Heather Collection at what was Bell's new headquarters near Cherrybank, now a part of the spirits conglomerate Diageo.

Another major whisky firm had a similar origin when John Dewar began his career in 1828 working in a relative's wine and spirit firm in Castle Gable and establishing himself in the wholesale trade in the High Street. The next generation started blending and bottling in the Speygate. They then moved to purpose-built premises on the corner of Glasgow Road and Glover Street and finally to a location close to the northern limit of the town at Inveralmond near the by-pass leading to the M90. The firm of Dewar closed in the 1990s after becoming part of United Distillers. The Glasgow Road and Glover Street site now houses Dewar's Leisure Rinks for curling and skating. In an adjacent building are Perth Leisure Swimming Pool with its Ozone Fitness Centre and Health Suite.

Lord Forteviot and Lord Dewar were also very charitable men. They bought Kinnoull Hill with its splendid views of Perth and District and presented it to the town, helped finance the restoration of St John's Kirk, added a wing to the Royal Infirmary and contributed to the building of the Men's Lodging House in Skinnergate and another trust for disadvantaged townspeople.

Matthew Gloag and Peter Thomson started in similar ways, Gloag importing wine – hence the name of their premises, Bordeaux House. Gloag evolved *Famous Grouse* whisky, while Thomson had a port speciality. Like Bell's and Dewar, these firms have been absorbed into bigger concerns: Highland Distilleries and Waverley Vintners.

One other most remarkable firm, based on insurance, was founded in Perth and retains a key significance as one of the largest employers in the town. Consequent on the Employers' Liability Act of 1880, a small group of leading businessmen started an insurance venture and recruited as manager Francis Norie-Miller, who perceived a niche for specialist insurance, identifying burglary in addition to fire and accident policies and adding motor vehicle policies in 1896. Later, comprehensive household policies and no-claims bonuses were pioneered and branch offices and 800 agencies were established. Sir Francis was succeeded by his son, Stanley, in whose memory a riverside walkway and garden has been created. General Accident now employs some 15,000 staff worldwide. The firm was based at the foot of the High Street, virtually on the site of the earliest quay and trading place in Perth. Here a shell midden and the remains of a prehistoric hut were found at 7 m below the surface during excavations of foundations of General Accident's first World Headquarters in 1956. Nowadays, offices of Perth and Kinross District stand on the site as General Accident has moved to Cherrybank, with ready access to the motorways.

Agricultural machinery and supplies are part of Perth's business fabric. One firm whose name is well known among cattle breeeders worldwide originated in Perth. The auction mart of Macdonald Fraser began when a young member of the family joined an established auctioneer in 1864 when the mart was held around St John's Kirk, a usual European site for a medieval market place. He became a partner and eventually managing director when the firm specialised in annual national auctions of Aberdeen-Angus and Shorthorn cattle at the mart which was built in Caledonian Road near the railway in 1875. The mart also attracted American and Argentinian buyers. The original mart became a supermarket and a new mart was built as Perth Agricultural Centre which includes a visitor centre. The firm Macdonald Fraser is now part of United Auctions.

A more recent industrial firm established in Perth was John Moncrieffe Limited, the North British Glassworks founded in 1865 to manufacture engineering and laboratory glass. In the 1880s the firm moved to premises in St Catherine's Road. During the Second World War a new product, borosilicate glass called Monax, was manufactured and, perhaps more significantly, Salvador Ysart came from Barcelona to Moncrieffe's and began to make Art Deco glassware. Mrs Isobel Moncrieffe's artistic influence was also important and soon Salvador and his sons were producing hand-blown decorative glass, distinctive in style, colour and decorative techniques called Monart. It was sold principally in Watson's China Hall in the High Street and Wyllie and Lochheads in Glasgow as well as being advertised in Liberty's catalogues and exported to Australia and new Zealand.

In 1946 Salvador and two of his sons left Moncrieffe's and started to produce Vasart. Paul Ysart remained in Moncrieffe's and made Princess Elizabeth's wedding present, a 33-piece set of Monart. He continued to

Figure 15
Perth: Stages in Growth

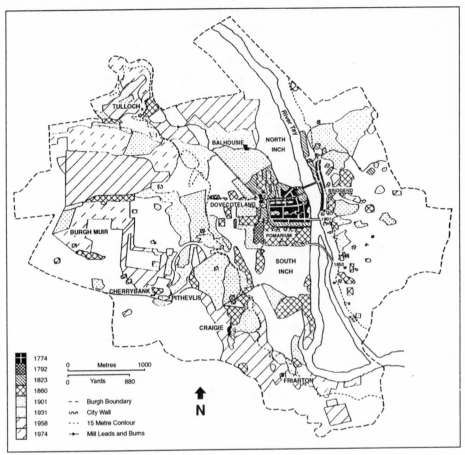

make paperweights until 1961 and joined Caithness Glass in 1962.
Paul's assistant went to the Strathearn Glass Factory at Crieff until his
retirement in 1970. Monart and Vasart glassware are now most collectable
and there is a fine exhibition of both in Perth Museum and Art Gallery.
Moncrieffe's was bought over and its successor, Monax ceased to manufacture glass in Perth in 1996.

CONTEMPORARY PERTH

Perth, with a population of 41,490 in 1991, was recently identified in an
academic report as 'the best place to live in Britain' and from 1991 to 1995
the population of Perth and Kinross District increased by nearly 6400,
almost as many as the total increase from 1981–90. Furthermore, the

district is now predicted 'to experience the highest level of in-migration of any Scottish District Council between 1991 and 2013'. Some reasons for this influx which has a considerable proportion of professional people (only 10 per cent are pensioners) could be the pleasant character of the town and its people, the environmental beauty of the setting, with large expanses of open space in the Inches and Kinnoull Hill, the high standard of recreational facilities in Bell's Sports Centre and Dewar's Rinks and Perth Leisure Pool. Additionally there are fine countryside walks in and around Perth and many cultural activities including a fine Repertory Theatre and excellent musical events. Perth has been most fortunate over the centuries, with businessmen and a Rector of the Academy of stature, including Thomas Anderson, TH Marshall, Dr Adam Anderson, the Pullar family, AK Bell, the Dewars and the Norrie-Millers, gifted men of great vision and business acumen who not only provided employment but endowed Perth with high quality planning and fine caring, leisure and cultural facilities.

The hillslopes of the Sidlaws, Friarton, Craigie Hills and the Burghmuir have given scope for housing expansion, although the North Muirton over-expansion has proved liable to flooding. Perth has retained its original core within the confines of the medieval lade still running unseen under Mill Street, South Methven Street, Canal Crescent and Canal Street and the sites created by the burgage plots have been recycled through the centuries. Archaeological excavations on sites being developed in the High Street have yielded much evidence of the physical and social fabric of the early town. The findings are well displayed in Perth Museum and Art Gallery. Two main streets in the core are distinctly unusual and in most European cities the wall has been replaced by an urban motorway. Perth, however, has retained the original layout.

Perth has reverted to its historic role as the county town for Perth and Kinross District and the market centre. It has an extensive shopping centre mainly on level ground with shopping malls and a wide variety of shops, a partly pedestrianised High Street and a reasonable number of parking-places. Perth draws many visitors and is also a popular Conference Centre which reinforces the dominance of the service sector in its employment profile, with distribution and catering accounting for over one quarter of employment, government and other services almost one third, banking and financial services 16%, manufacturing 11% (including Caithness Glass and a company assembling electronic components) and transport 9% in 1991. The largest employers are General Accident (Insurance), the Railway Companies, Royal Mail, Tesco Stores Ltd, Diageo and Waverley Vintners Ltd, Perth College and also on the national scale, Stagecoach. Perth and Kinross District's percentage unemployment is low at 4.5%.

As a result of the attractiveness of Perth, there is now little space left for housing development and the District Council have had to address the population forecasts for the period 1999 to 2013. They have proposed sites outwith the town but close to the existing motorways and dual carriageways which facilitate commuting to all four Scottish cities. Three self-contained sites for communities, rather than commuter suburbs, have been identified within 16km of Perth. Oudenarde on the other side of the M90 and almost 1.6km from Bridge of Earn, is currently the site of a dis-used hospital which could accommodate 1200 houses. Errol Airfield, a wartime facility which did *not* become Dundee's airport, has space for 2000 houses. A spacious greenfield site, where some 350 houses have already been built, in the Lower Almond Valley on the present northern edge of Perth could accommodate a total of some 1100 houses. Railways pass near these sites and stations could be built enabling local or longer journeys to the cities to be made with less pressure on the motorways and other roads. Each of these communities would need a primary school and an additional secondary school, possibly built to the east of Perth.

In addition, certain communities, also within 16 km of Perth, including New Scone (1991 population 4502), Stanley (1267), Errol (1125) and Inchture (840) have been identified as capable of expansion, along with other smaller communities. For example, Bankfoot (1000), St Madoes (754) and Forgandenny (281) have been identified as 'small opportunity sites'. All of these locations are in attractive rural countryside, with sufficient space around them. These proposals provide an innovative and interesting plan for Perth and its environs for the early 21st century.

Perth would retain its attractive characteristics without overcrowding and its immediate rural hinterland, which is also pleasant countryside, would be reinvigorated but not swamped by an additional 10,000 people located in discrete communities. Some of the smaller settlements would also revive and Perth would remain a central place and continue to be one of Britain's most attractive towns.

THIRTEEN
CASTLES AND MANSION HOUSES

The early castles of Scotland were timber and earth-built structures that survive as archaeological features in the landscape. The earliest stone castles are castles of enclosure, comprising a stout masonry curtain wall enclosing a courtyard. Openings in the curtain wall were kept to a minimum and the accommodation was provided in a range of stone or timber buildings built against the inside of the curtain wall. Doune Castle, formerly in part of Perthshire, is the most complete example of this type of building in east-central Scotland. Built at the end of the 14th century and therefore more sophisticated than many of the West Highland examples, Doune Castle represents a transitional stage between the great-keep gate-house castles of the border counties and the towerhouse constructed with a substantial enclosing wall. The main defences come from the high curtain wall which, in the absence of firing slits, must have been defended from the parapet walk alone, although careful planning and the substantial solidity of the fabric combine to make the castle a formidable defensive stronghold. The Lord's Hall and the Retainers' Hall are situated over the main gate. The Retainers' Hall with its central hearth and open timber roof abuts the Lord's Hall but is not connected internally. The kitchen block stands apart, served by its own stair but communicating, through a service room, with the Retainers' Hall.

Detached kitchens are reasonably common in medieval and post-medieval buildings as cooking on an open fire constituted a considerable fire hazard. Over the centuries, the kitchen changed from being in a detached building to being incorporated into the vaulted ground floor of the towerhouse and then, in the mansion house, to being in a service wing. Each stage served as a fire precaution. However, it was perhaps more for the comfort of the household to make sure that the bustle involved in the day to day workings of the mansion house and the cooking smells were kept away from the principal rooms.

The most common form of surviving fortified dwelling is the towerhouse, a building type found at one time in almost every European country but particularly popular and long-lived in Scotland and Ireland. The towerhouse with its passive fortification, stacked accommodation and compact form, struck the correct balance between physical security, domestic comfort and modest cost in a country economically straitened and politically unstable. The towerhouse dates from the 11th century but the majority of the early houses were of half-timbered construction. A major rebuilding from the late 15th to the early 17th centuries saw the replacement of many of the earlier structures with masonry towers. The half-timbered structures that did survive were either demolished to make way for new structures or were incorporated into the new structures leaving little that can be immediately recognised by even a trained observer. The feature that did survive was the timber-framed aesthetic where the timber-frame forms and details are transferred to the masonry replace-ments producing some of the most interesting masonry structures in Europe. Corbel courses imitate the jettying of timber floors, dental courses represent exposed joist ends and stone brackets replace timber to carry projecting balconies and parapet walks. Regarding building form, the creation of a square planned cap-house, corbelled out to cover a supporting drum, is comparatively easy to achieve in timber but requires considerable expertise to copy in masonry.

Previous studies have categorised towerhouses into types according to the plan form. The plan types include circular, square, L-shaped, Z-shaped, E-shaped, T-shaped and elongated. This is convenient as a descriptive tool but gives no clue as to improvements in domestic arrangements. Throughout the entire period of towerhouse construction domestic arrangements were changing, with the introduction of innovative features to improve comfort, safety and the standard of luxury experienced by the occupants. Many of the new ideas resulted in cosmetic change such as new methods of painting wallls and ceilings, the introduction of richly decorated plasterwork, changes in the style of mouldings, sculptural decoration, panelling, use of tapestries and furnishings. Others involved practical con-siderations that required pre-planning, such as the provision of garderobes, slop sinks and urinals; bathouses, private chapels, the eviction of animals from the ground floor, the introduction of ground floor halls, bakehouses and breweries, increased window sizes, design of yetts and grilles and the provision of smoke chambers, originally in the kitchen flue but occasion-ally as free standing structures, for preparing smoked meats, fish and poultry; herb gardens and so on. Some of the arrangements appear to 20th century observers to be ridiculous. The detached kitchen at Kinnaird Tower made it necessary to carry the prepared food across the yard while rising about a storey's height to the ground floor entrance to the tower. A mural staircase then had to be climbed to the first floor, where the food would be served in the hall. This was not considered excessive and up until the period after the First World War, kitchens continued to be remote from the dining room, partly as a fire precaution and partly to prevent unpleasant kitchen smells affecting the appetite of the diners. The shortage of servants after the War made proximity between kitchen and dining room desirable.

The L-plan towerhouse known as Balvaird Castle has a vertical soil stack serving garderobes in each of the chambers in each wing. This is supplemented by a series of square niches, each having a shallow-dished sole with central drainage outlet. The outlet discharges into a stone channel within the thickness of the wall. This in turn discharges into the vertical soil stack under the seat of the garderobe. The height, size and location of these niches combined with the shallow dish forming the sole suggests that these are urinals rather than some form of slop sink.

The provision of smoke chambers within the volume of the kitchen flue was recorded by MacGibbon and Ross in their five-volume work *The Castellated and Domestic Architecture of Scotland*, published between 1887 and 1892. They cite three examples in Fife towerhouses where in each case the smoke chamber was entered from the floor above the kitchen to allow access to the meat and fish being smoked. Further work on this subject in recent years has established that this is a common feature in 16th and 17th-century houses in all parts of Scotland but normally the access to the smoke chamber was via the kitchen hearth rather than by a door in the floor above. Tell-tale signs of this provision are two rows of joist sockets on the front and back of the flue; heavy, widely-spaced joists about 8 ft (2.4 m) above the hearth and light, closely-spaced ones above that. The heavy joists were designed to carry a floor with an opening to allow the smoke to rise into the flue and the lighter joists above supported the meat and fish being smoked. Occasionally the smoke chamber contained a salt box and, most unusually, a window opening to admit light to the operatives resalting or repositioning the food to ensure an even distribution of smoke over the surfaces. The provision of a window in the smoking flue possibly gave rise to the concept of a blocked up room as there was an additional window opening on the facade but no means of access. The introduction of more sophisticated recipes demanding a specific type of smoke for particular foodstuffs or cures resulted in the introduction of self-supporting smoke chimneys built in close proximity to the house where the type of smoke produced was totally independent of the day to day cooking requirements. Many of these chimneys were designed to be decorative features with battered sides covered with thatch. There was often a detached boiler-type arrangement to one side of the main kitchen fireplace with the gathering of the flue above the boiler discharging into the kitchen flue. The reason for this is not fully understood but it may be some form of brewing pot or still as these occurred only in kitchens where there was no oven. Where an oven was provided the brewhouse was usually linked to the baker's area as baking and brewing were considered to be linked trades.

Unfortunately, classification of towerhouses by the services and facilities provided has not been attempted. This has possibly been hindered by the excellent work published by MacGibbon and Ross but, with modern facilities, this type of information should be easy to extract. However, since the original researchers were not specifically looking for evidence of this type of building, the towerhouses would have to be revisited and reassessed. This is no simple matter as many of the houses, freely accessible when MacGibbon and Ross were surveying, have now been remodelled as dwelling houses, often without the detailed survey of the existing features that might provide the missing evidence.

Evidence has also been altered on many towerhouse sites. Towerhouses traditionally formed part of the home farm of the estate. The fermtoun tenants' buildings stood cheek by jowl with the towerhouse. This is illustrated in a 19th-century engraving of Huntingtower on the outskirts of Perth, where vernacular buildings with smoke coming from the chimneys stand against the east side of the towerhouse. The fermtoun may also have contained office houses related to the servicing of the towerhouse but this is not easy to prove. Certainly garderobe chutes would have discharged into middens to be utilised as fertiliser in the laird's fields or gardens. This type of planning lost favour in the 18th century when new concepts of privacy and landscaping were adopted. This resulted in many fermtouns being relocated away from the towerhouse and the removal of substantial enclosure walls to provide a more romantic setting for the tower. Where towerhouses did remain on the farm steading they were often used to provide accommodation for farm labourers before being allowed to decay.

Just as the towerhouse setting was changed, the nature of the fortifications also changed. Towerhouses are not castles in the true sense of the word but are passively fortified dwellings designed to withstand the initial attacks of guerrilla fighters rather than to withstand armies. Parapet walks gave way to normal eaves details. Windows became larger, particularly in the upper portions of the walls. Arrow loops developed though a series of combinations into gun loops. Special grilles were devised for door and window openings based on quartered patterns of vertical through horizontal and horizontal through vertical to make very strong barriers. These are often considered to be peculiarly Scottish but they are also found in buildings of the same age in the north of Italy. Many fine towerhouses survive in Perthshire, particularly the Historic Scotland properties of Elcho Castle and Huntingtower, both open to the public, though even more were demolished to make way for mansion houses in the 17th, 18th and 19th centuries.

Elcho Castle can perhaps be considered as one of the earliest mansion houses in Scotland. The numerous chimney stacks and the increase in the size of the windows were typical of the time and emphasise the new concern for domesticity and spacious and well-lit rooms. The wall of the basement is still pierced by seventeen gunloops designed for hand-held swivel guns. The windows up to second floor level are protected by substantial iron grilles, similar to those at the Palace in Stirling Castle. The defences of the main building and the outer walls were never expected to be effective against contemporary methods of siege with artillery but had the much more limited purpose of discouraging lesser threats, from private enemies and intruders. While the loops were certainly intended for use in anger if necessary, all of the warlike paraphernalia was seen as fitting ornament for a gentleman's residence. These features can be seen in the Scottish baronial mansions as pure decoration.

Mansion houses began to replace fortified houses towards the end of the 17th century. The earliest examples were Palladian in influence and were introduced into Scotland by Sir William Bruce. Bruce, a landowner and diplomat, was also a capable architect who saw the need for an architectural profession in Scotland. He altered a number of towerhouses to make them more symmetrical and in keeping with the taste in northern Europe before embarking on his first new house, Dunkeld House, 1676-1684, a simple symmetrical cubical block of the plainest description, distinguished externally by a cupola over a piend roof with a low attic story sandwiched under the eaves. This house was demolished in 1830. The formula was repeated at Moncrieff House, 1679, destroyed by fire in 1957. The only survivor of these early Bruce houses in the vicinity of Perthshire is Kinross House, 1672-1693, built as his own residence.

William Adam (1689-1743) was the most successful of the second generation classical architects in Scotland. A pupil of Sir William Bruce, his style was at odds with the English neo-Palladian School. His buildings were inventive, sometimes bizarre but never dull. His houses in Perthshire include the reconstruction of Lawers House, 1724-1726, with further works in 1737-1744; Gartmore House, 1740-1745 and a mausoleum for the first Duke of Montrose at Aberuthven, 1741-1742. William Adam's most famous son, Robert (1728-1792), also built houses in Perthshire. These include Glencarse House, 1790, destroyed by late 19th-century alterations and Pitfour Castle *c.* 1775, enlarged by William Burn in 1825 without serious damage to the original house.

The other significant neo-classical architect to work in Perthshire in the second half of the 18th century was James Playfair (1755-1794). He designed the Temple of Virtue and Honour, Dupplin Castle in 1789, now demolished; Lynedoch Lodge in 1789 and the dairy at Balboughty on the Scone Palace estate in 1790. His most significant building shows the influence of Sir John Soane and Claude Ledoux in the remarkable mausoleum in the churchyard of Methven Church. The mausoleum takes the form of a Greek temple embedded in elaborately rusticated masonry. It is remarkable both in terms of scale and massing.

Pitfour Castle, St Madoes, heralded the Castle style in mansion houses. The house is symmetrical with detailing derived from Roman fortresses and the medieval castles of Italy and the Adriatic. John Patterson became the principal exponent of the style in Scotland after the Adams' deaths in 1794. His best work in the style was Monzie, c. 1795-1800 but this was reconstructed in 1908-1912 by Sir Robert Lorimer after a fire in the original house. Abercairney Abbey by another Adams'-trained architect, Richard Crichton, was built in 1805 and demolished in 1960. The neo-Gothic style developed from the Castle style and a number of important Perthshire houses were built by architects from Edinburgh and the south. Archibald and James Elliot designed Taymouth Castle, Kenmore, 1806-1810. It was enlarged from 1818-1821 and 1827-1828 by William Atkinson and again in 1836-1839 by James Gillespie Graham. The Elliots normally produced classical interiors for their houses but at Taymouth elaborate Gothic rooms were provided. They also designed castellated stables and a gateway at Dunkeld House in 1809, restored the lower wing after a fire in 1814 and provided lodges c. 1815.

The symmetry of these early Georgian Gothic buildings imposed obvious limitations on the design but the Picturesque movement, first seen in painting, then in landscape design and architecture, resulted in experiments in irregular composition. This new freedom was linked to a widening of stylistic horizons, the neo-Gothic vocabulary being enlarged by the introduction of Jacobean, Scots Baronial, Tudor and other themes. William Atkinson designed Scone Palace as an asymmetrical neo-Gothic house, 1803-1812 and Rossie Priory in 1810, now much reduced by the demolition of the principal rooms. Sir Robert Smirke of London built Kinfauns Castle, 1820-1824, in the castellated style and Coltoquhey House c. 1820 in a Tudor style. Kinfauns is typical of the best of house designs and is described in detail later.

William Burn (1789-1870), who had been a pupil of Smirke, set up practice in Edinburgh in 1811- 1812 and by 1830 had the largest architectural practice in Scotland. He took David Bryce (1803-1876) as a partner in 1841, leaving him to run the Scottish practice. Between them they designed all the most influential mansion houses in Perthshire over the next sixty years. Burn was responsible for Murray Royal Hospital, 1822-1827; Snaigow House, 1824-1826, Tudor Gothic; Dupplin Castle, 1828-1832, Jacobean (demolished in 1967); Faskally, 1829, Scots

Vernacular; Finnart House, 1838, Jacobean and Bridge of Earn village, 1832, only partly executed. Bryce continued with the Home Farm steading, Keir Estate, 1832; Leny House, 1845, Scots Jacobean; Stronvar House, 1850, Scots Jacobean; Blair Castle, 1867-1872, (alterations, additions and remodelling); Culdees Castle, 1867, Scots Baronial additions and Meikleour, 1869, Classical French Chateau. These were among the last of the great mansion houses and the next generation of architects were more involved with villas and building remodelling.

The term 'mansion house' is in fact misleading as it infers a single dwelling. In reality a mansion house was a multi-functional structure forming the focal point of a self-contained rural community normally referred to as an 'estate'. Kinfauns Castle, an excellent example and possibly the most complete mansion house in Perthshire, provides the following typical accommodation. The house comprised a family residence for the owner's family, including nurseries, playrooms and schoolroom. The principal apartments included a reception, functions and recreation suite linked to guest accommodation not only for friends and acquaintances of the family and travellers with letter of introduction but also for their entourage, including body servants. Additionally, there were the owner's business premises, a suite of service rooms accommodating not only all the normal domestic functions but also the supportive trades and service industries that might be found in a medium-sized town, storage facilities, accommodation for all classes of domestic servant, a chapel and a recreation garden. This in turn was supported by an agricultural facility, a horticultural facility, a transport facility incuding housing for horses, vehicles, grooms, drivers and stable lads, a game-sports facility, forestry, access facilities and a security system.

The functioning of the household, the purchasing of provisions and the servicing of the entire establishment came under the control of the butler while the maintenance of the buildings, control of tenants, game-sports, forestry and other estate functions were under the estate manager.

The family apartments were somewhat anonymous in architectural expression as they lacked the scale and splendour of the principal apartments. They were situated to one side of the main frontage, well away from the public entrance and from the gardens associated with the principal apartments, allowing the owner's family seclusion and privacy. They overlooked a private flower garden and had an independent entrance. These apartments were not totally divorced from the principal apartments as the owner, his wife and grown up family would all use some of the principal apartments for entertaining, both during the day and in the evening. The family apartments were also serviced from the main service wing by servants' stairs and corridors as distinct from the main corridors and family corridors.

The accommodation provided in the family apartments comprised a gentleman's room or business room with strong room, deed room and lavatory, a lady's sitting room or boudoir, linked to the garden by a conservatory and the master bed-chamber suite with dressing rooms, closets and lavatories. There were also bed-chambers for the family, a nursery and schoolroom and a waiting room, associated with the business room.

It was important that the family could utilise the facilities provided in the principal apartments and there was always a physical link between the family accommodation and the principal corridors.

The principal apartments comprised a breakfast room served from the same service room as the dining room, the dining room which also served, in the morning, as a waiting room for male visitors, the drawing room which was the lady's reception room, the morning room which relieved pressure on the drawing room, the ante-drawing room for family use, the library which related to the drawing room or to the gentleman's business room or to a study, a music room, the picture gallery which may have doubled as the principal corridor, the billiard room which may have doubled as a smoking room, the smoking room which was divided from the principal rooms and corridors in a situation where ventilation would carry away the smoke and the odd room where younger members of the family could indulge in hobbies. These rooms were linked to the principal staircase leading to the guest bedrooms. The most usual kind of bedroom was one for a married couple with a dressing room attached for the gentleman. Standard furniture included a small writing table, a washstand, mirror, wardrobe, couch, chairs, easy chairs, a chest of drawers, a chiffonier or cabinet and a double bed. Bachelors' bedrooms were often provided with an alcove dressing-place. The dressing-room would, like the bedroom, have its own fireplace. It acted as a space for a toilet and could vary considerably in size as ladies always required additional space. The furniture consisted of a dressing table, washstand, wardrobe, or drawers for a gentleman with a writing table and chairs. The lady required similar furnishings but on a more extensive scale and with the addition of a centre table. The dressing room for a lady must have always interconnected with the bedroom but should also have had its own outer door. The gentleman's dressing room had a single outer door, opening near the door to the bedroom and within a private lobby. Arrangements of this type allowed the housekeeper flexibility in providing accommodation. Single persons were normally allocated a bedroom without dressing room. Lesser guests might have been allocated a similar bedroom but important guests would either have had a bedroom used by the lady with the gentleman taking his private toilet in the dressing-room or two dressing rooms where one was used by the lady as a retiring room for washing.

In overall planning there were various classes of bedroom accommodation. The family were in a private suite. Bachelors' rooms may have constituted a special class as did young ladies' rooms. Nurseries were always separate. Occasionally an invalid suite was provided. Subordinates' rooms for the accommodation of a tutor, governess, lady's companion, secretary or the like constituted another class. Technically there was little difference in the accommodation provided but each social and sexual group was kept separate, with the owner's immediate friends and family in the most convenient and salubrious situations and the subordinates and nurseries furthest from the principal rooms.

When dealing with the more prestigious bedrooms discreet access for the lady's maid was essential and in many instances the lady's maid slept in a small room adjoining the wardrobe room. The room, occupied by the lady of the house, was frequently provided with a private staircase usually commencing beside the doors to the gentleman's room and boudoir on the floor below and would often be disguised to prevent its being mistaken for any other stair.

Guest suites and individual bedchambers were graded according to their proximity to the main staircase and corridors and all the important suites had individual water closets in each of the dressing rooms.

Bachelors' rooms were sited away from the main guest rooms with some form of separate access. Young ladies' rooms, on the other hand, were closer to the guest rooms but often related to the governess's room. Invalids' rooms were normally provided on the ground floor and comprised a suite consisting of a bedroom, sitting room, attendant's room, private lobby and appurtenances. Married children who stayed in the family home were provided with similar self-contained suites.

The nurseries and schoolrooms were linked under the charge of a nurse. Older children were withdrawn from this arrangement and put under the control of a governess. The normal arrangement was to have three children and a nurse in a sleeping room and as large a day room as circumstances allowed, as this was used not only for play but also as a dormitory for guests' children. Each night nursery had its own water closet and bathroom. Wardrobes were placed in the day nursery or in a lobby or closet. A scullery was provided with fireplace, sink, closets and shelving for the use of the nurse. Nurseries were positioned at the point where the family sleeping rooms and servants' rooms linked, that is at the back staircase on the first floor. This provided good access from either side of the house. When there were no children in the house, the nursery suite was converted into a superior guest suite. When this occurred, a strangers' nursery was often provided in a more remote location.

The schoolroom for older children served not only as a classroom but as a day room for the children and a sitting room for the governess. The complete schoolroom suite comprised a schoolroom, a governess's room, private entrance lobby, book closet, washing closet and water closet. It was located to be within easy reach of the lady of the house, preferably on the ground floor. It was linked to the odd room, as has previously been mentioned.

The supplementaries comprised male and female cloakrooms, the female linked to the family part of the house and the male to the principal rooms, male and female lavatories and water closets linked to the cloak-rooms with others en-suite with the bedchambers, bathrooms and occasionally a plunge bath.

The thoroughfares comprised porch, entrance hall, garden entrance and other, secondary entrances, such as the gallery, central hall, saloon, ante-rooms, vestibules with other passages and staircases. Passages of between 6 ft (1.8 m) and 12 ft (3.6 m) wide were considered corridors and those from 14 ft (4.2 m) to 20 ft ((6 m) wide were galleries.

The chapel formed a pivotal point between the family, reception and servants' rooms. It was divided into two areas, one with pews for the servants and a gallery with a fireplace and space for armchairs for the family and important guests.

The offices formed the remainder of the house and comprised kitchen offices, upper servants' offices, lower servants' offices, laundry offices, bakery and brewery offices, cellars, storage and outhouses, servants' private rooms, supplementaries and thoroughfares.

There was a strict moral code applied to the planning and organisation of the offices to discourage or prevent any form of meeting by male and female servants outwith the supervision in the servants' hall. Working rooms for males and females were segregated as were the private apart-ments and even the passageways. Males came under the direct supervision of the butler and females under the housekeeper.

The rule applied to servants' comfort demanded that all work rooms be in every way wholesome and all private rooms be equal to those of a similar class of persons in their own homes – perhaps a little better but not too much so. The organisation of the offices was normally left to the architect, with the instruction that every apartment should be placed in its proper relation to those others with whose business its own is more or less connected, that the supervision of all should be efficiently provided for, that each in itself be complete for its own purposes, that every servant, every operation, every utensil, every fixture should have a right place and no right place but one. Not an easy task, considering the range of activities occurring on a daily basis.

The kitchen offices were perhaps the most complicated group as they comprised all forms of food storage and preparation, rear door deliveries, cleansing of crockery, cutlery and implements and a communication route to the room serving the dining and breakfast rooms, the servants' halls, stewards' room, housekeeper's room and still room.

Cooking on solid fuel appliances produced considerably less heat. Kitchens therefore had to have high ceilings and good ventilation to prevent the heat tainting sensitive foods. Few kitchens today could match the range and versatility achieved in the mansion house kitchen of the mid-19th century. It had to be capable of producing not only the highest quality food for the owner's family and house guests but also serve as a works canteen for all the household and guest servants on the premises.

The kitchens were directly linked to the scullery. The door was close to the kitchen fireplace and fuel was brought through the scullery to the kitchen. The scullery was used for the preparation of fish, game and vegetables as well as for cleaning dishes, implements and containers. The scullery communicated with storerooms such as the dairy, larders or pantries through well-ventilated passageways to prevent the heat and steam from creating problems elsewhere.

The cook's pantry close to the kitchen was for the storage of partly used cold meats, bread, pastry, milk and butter. In the larger establishments there was a dry larder for cooked meats, a wet larder for raw meats, a pastry larder, a bread larder, a dairy for milk, butter and cheese, a game larder and a fish larder. These had to be on the north side of the building and capable of being well ventilated whilst excluding insects and vermin. Care had to be taken at the planning stage to prevent contamination from middens, ash-steads, drain traps, beer cellar vents, scullery, wash-house, laundry, stable or even by heat from a flue passing through the walls.

The meat larder often had an adjoining butcher's shop. Bacon was kept apart in a separate bacon larder. This was associated with a salting room and smoking- house but these were at a distance from the house to prevent nuisance from smells and smoke. The smoking-house was fitted with louvre-frames in the roof.

The upper servants' offices provided the control points for the whole household. The butler had to overlook the main approach to ensure that he was on hand to welcome guests. He had to be close to a rear entrance to allow him to meet with provision merchants to order and pay for materials for the household. He controlled access to the male servants' quarters, had to be accessible to the steward, housekeeper and the gentleman's room and was directly responsible for the household silver, which was stored in a strong room and cleaned in a room forming a link between the strong room and his office. He would then check out each item that was required and check it back after use. His room can always be distinguished as it was the only room with barred windows, visible from the entrance drive. He also controlled the beer and wine cellars and was occasionally assisted by an under butler.

The housekeeper fulfilled a similar role in controlling the kitchens and the female side of the household. She had a still room for the preparation of cold drinks, tea, coffee, preserves, cakes and biscuits. There was also a china closet and a scullery and she and her immediate assistants shared the upper servants' hall with the butler and steward as a dining space and common room.

The lower servants' offices comprised a lower servants' hall, again used for dining and as a common room, housemaids' closets, repeated in various parts of the house and containing cleaning equipment, candlesticks and coal to service the bedrooms. There were cleaning rooms for knives, shoes, lamps and so on.

The laundry offices comprised a soiled linen closet, laundry, wash-house, hot room, drying room, hot closet and linen room. The bakery and brewery were usually linked and could be detached from the main building, as could the lumber rooms and luggage rooms.

The gardens contained walled gardens, glass houses for various types of fruit such as grapes, nectarines, peaches, pineapples, a mushroom house, ice house, fruit stores, cisterns, flower gardens, herb gardens, ornamental gardens, cold frames, compost heaps and dung heaps. There were ornamental rides for the horses as well as servants' accommodation.

The game rooms comprised a keeper's house, kennels and kennel house, game larders, the gun room and racks for fishing rods. There were also boathouses, fishing stations and piers. The other accommodation related to the house included a farmhouse, farmyard, poultry house and poultry yard, a sawmill, joiner's shop, carpenter's shop, smithy, mills for flour, oatmeal, barley and snuff, a coal yard, wood yard and charcoal burners.

Security for the estate was provided by an enclosing wall, pierced at intervals where the access drives entered from the public road or from the pier. These points were protected by decoratively designed lodge houses whose aim was to impress visitors or those passing by but not necessarily to give comfort to the occupants. Bedrooms, for example, could be cramped into inadequate spaces in attics with little or no headroom or could be on the other side of the drive from the living quarters.

FOURTEEN

VERNACULAR BUILDINGS

Vernacular buildings are those structures erected by or for the use of the common people, including all that might be considered working or middle class.

The vernacular buildings of Perthshire are extremely rich not only in the building types to be found but also in the variety of materials used. This accepted, it must be recognised that there is a vast gap in our knowledge of the early development of these building types, that is, between the prehistoric period and the 18th century. The gap is the result of former generations of archaeologists concentrating on prehistoric and Roman remains almost to the exclusion of medieval and post-medieval archaeology. Information from the 18th century to the present day can be found both in archival sources and in published reports. The problem created by the neglect of this period of archaeology is now being addressed by both government bodies and by academic institutions. The Royal Commission on the Ancient and Historic Monuments of Scotland has been carrying out aerial, archival and terrestrial surveys of deserted settlements in specific areas of Highland Perthshire and this work is being supplemented by various academic institutions under the auspices of the Historic Scotland-led Medieval and Later Rural Settlements Group. These surveys are mainly non-intrusive and can do little more than record the physical features of each site, the relationship between building remains and the field systems, geographical features and soil conditions. They also record obvious features such as cut and fill to create platforms as building stances or for other purposes. The significance of these features will only gradually emerge as medieval and post-medieval vernacular sites are excavated and the findings published.

An archaeological excavation that illustrated the potential of medieval sites was made in the late 1960s prior to the construction of the Marks and Spencer store in High Street, Perth. This uncovered the remains of over fifty buildings in two former tenements of ground stratified from the 12th to the 15th century. Reconstruction drawings prepared at the time indicated small, bivouac-type structures from the 12th century through various types of timber-framed buildings including a small example of stave construction until the evidence was obliterated by the foundations of a 16th-century parliament hall. This site was particularly rewarding owing to the high water table setting up conditions similar to those in a peat bog. Unfortunately the report of this excavation has never been published. Similar conditions must exist in the rural areas of Perthshire and many parts of the original pattern of building will remain lost until archaeological excavation is undertaken and published.

The surviving vernacular buildings of the county present similar problems, particularly those dating from the 18th century or earlier. These survivals represent only a part of the pattern of development but still indicate several phases of development even on a single site or on a single building. Care must be taken with the interpretation of surviving evidence to avoid obvious mistakes. One example of misinterpretation is the thatching of the reconstructed crannog on Loch Tay using reeds, a material known to have been introduced into the Tay estuary in the 18th century as a means of preventing erosion and not used for thatching until almost the end of the 19th century. Another area where particular care must be taken is in relation to large, prosperous farms where rebuilding, to meet the expectations of a rich farmer's family, may have wiped out building types that conceivably existed on these farms but would not have occurred elsewhere.

The documentary evidence from the late 17th and early 18th centuries indicates that many farmhouses and cottages were, at that time, crude timber-framed structures with walls of wattle and daub, tempered earth, turf or alternating layers of stone and turf with roofs of cabers and wattle, covered with turf, occasionally left as the only covering but more commonly finished with thatch. Thatching materials included straw, heather, broom, bracken, rushes and so on, the eventual choice of material depending largely on availability and value to the house owner. This means that although a farmer had straw available and that straw would make the best thatch, he would often thatch in an alternative material as the straw was more valuable for some other purpose such as making dung or as cattle feed. All the materials used, perhaps with the exception of the main timber frame, were easy to work using implements commonly found on the farm. As a result, many buildings of this type were erected by the tenantry or owner rather than by the building industry.

A number of former fermtouns survive on the Braes of Carse, the local name for the southern foothills of the Sidlaw Hills in Perthshire. These fermtouns reflect the types of layout and construction described in the documentary evidence. Abernyte, Kinnaird and Rait all retain elements of their earlier layouts. Abernyte appears as two separate fermtouns in 18th-century plans – Abernyte and Balfron. Abernyte farm was 'improved' in the 19th century and may have taken over Balfron's field system as

Balfron remained 'unimproved' and was renamed Abernyte as distinct from Abernyte farm. Kinnaird is interesting in the relationship between the laird's towerhouse and the fermtoun, although recent development has blurred many of the original features. Of the three fermtouns, Rait is the most interesting as the west end retains much of the early layout. This is more linear than that of the other two fermtouns and can be compared with an early illustration of the nearby Kirkton of Scone. The Kirkton of Scone is illustrated by Captain Slezer in his 1693 publication *Theatrum Scotae*. He shows a linear layout of buildings placed between a burn and a roadway, all curving on plan to follow the line of the burn. The buildings are low, with shoulder height eaves and doorways, similar to the heights still found in blackhouses in the Western Isles. The walls are built to running levels, that is, a staff is used to determine the wall height at any point along the front or back of the building rather than adopting a datum before using a water or spirit level to maintain a level eaves course. The doorways are the full height of the walls and the windows are small apertures, tucked under the eaves and unlikely to have been glazed. They may have had closing boards or shutters to close the opening in inclement weather but even this was not common at that time. The gables are also low and are gently curved at the top to follow the line of the ridgeless thatch. Examination of the buildings in the west end of Rait provides superficial similarities: a similar layout, a similar relationship between burn, buildings and roadway, low eaves' heights closer to head height than to shoulder height but also built to running levels, higher and more angular gables and larger window openings with a range of window types and glazing patterns. Alteration works carried out in the 1970s resulted in part of the roof being removed. This exposed a series of features very similar to those illustrated at Scone. The Rait buildings had been increased in width by the thickness of the front wall. The internal gable clearly indicated the original width of the house and the original profile, similar to the gables at Scone. The gable profile had been changed from a gentle curve to an angular form using alternating layers of stone and turf. The gable had then been heightened to accommodate the extra width of the front wall, using turf laid in parallel to the skew. When the 19th or 20th-century brick chimney breasts were removed, large balks of timber were left projecting from the gable. These had supported a cat and clay chimneyhood and the shadow of the smoke ladder was clearly visible on the gable wall above the balks. The rounded gables and the rear wall are constructed of claywall – a form of shuttered tempered earth having stones placed against the face of the shutter as the earth is consolidated round them. Small cruck slots were also found in the back wall but not in the more recent front wall. There was some doubt as to the purpose of these slots as the dimensions were small but a cruck-framed building at Laidhay, Caithness has similar-sized crucks spanning the same width as the original Rait house. Recent work in Rait has identified other cruck remains, one set located at the east end of this once continuous terrace. The front wall is of masonry construction bound with clay mortar. The line of the original front wall was clearly defined by corner stones weighing in excess of half a ton each, indicating that the house may have had turf walls prior to the claywall that survives today.

Rait was also a kirk-toun, although the original parish is now incorporated within Kilspindie parish. The ruins of the church still survive, as do a number of mills and the outline of the original fort, from which the settlement derives its name. Rait's importance diminished on the completion of the Perth-Dundee turnpike road in the late 18th century and shortly afterwards it is described as a sleepy backwater, a description that still applies today. Scone, on the other hand, was completely demolished and moved to a new site as part of the creation of a private park round Scone Palace.

Larger, more imposing farmhouses must have existed on the prosperous farms of the Carse of Gowrie and in other areas where a large farm had easy access to either water transport or to a substantial market. This is illustrated in the works of the Scottish genre painters of the late 18th and early 19th centuries who painted the interiors of many Scottish farmhouses as timber-framed aisled structures similar to some of those surviving in the Low Countries of Northern Europe. It is uncertain whether these buildings were originally constructed for the use of farmers or whether they were inherited from landowners after they constructed a new mansion house but either way they should exist as archaeological evidence. None of the paintings can be directly linked to Perthshire but, as the Carse of Gowrie was long considered the granary of Scotland, the thesis is likely to be sound. Constructional hangovers from a timber building tradition are to be found in the county. There are a large number of butt-purlin roofs in late 18th-century buildings. These originate in half-timber construction. The 1784 pisé-walled barn at Flatfield has timber joists carried through the wall and pegged against plates on the wall face in the same manner as timber buildings are pegged together in Northern Europe. The building known as Kinnoul's lodging which formerly stood in the Watergate, Perth, was the last known timber-fronted townhouse in Scotland. It was demolished in the late 1960s.

Other large farmhouses and small mansion houses are constructed with masonry walls. The house at Old Mains of Rattray falls into this category. It survives as the ruin of a two-storey, three-window symmetrical house dated '16 David Crichton 94' over the central entrance and 'DC 1694' on the kitchen fireplace lintel. A single-storey peind roof extension to the west is dated '17 DC IR 20' on the entrance lintel. There is no internal communication between the extension and the house and the presence of a large kitchen-type fireplace suggests that this may have been the brew-house, a common feature on Perthshire estates and large farms until the mid-19th century. The building was accepted at face value as a two-phase development until it lost its roof. Water damage resulting from this removed sections of plaster and harl, exposing an earlier window pattern consistent with a four-window facade with central doorway, although it may conceivably have been a five-window design. Unaltered gable windows covered by the 1720 extensions show that the original window opening had roll mouldings. These had been cut to a chamfer on the south facade at a later date, possibly when the new fenestration pattern was introduced. Glazing grooves in the underside of the lintels and the upper sections of the window jambs indicate the use of leaded lights over timber shutters. There is also evidence for barred ground floor window openings. Other exposed evidence shows that the roof had a steeper pitch than that surviving. A reconstruction drawing was prepared in 1983, after a prolonged study of the structure by Brian Paul, then a student at the School of Architecture, Dundee and shows the most probable reconstruction. The elevation shows the building when first visited by the authors in the late 1970s.

The Carse of Gowrie provides one of the richest sources of early surviv- ing vernacular buildings in Scotland. A rich area of this type with a long and prosperous agricultural base was obviously capable of producing superior buildings that would stand the test of time. One such building is the former school and schoolhouse at Cottown, St Madoes. The school was originally built in 1745 and the schoolmaster is recorded as having had to flee from the rebel Jacobites in 1746. The building was destroyed by fire in 1766 and permission was sought and granted to 'rebuild in clay', that is, with mudwall. The west section of the present building is constructed partly of poor quality red sandstone from a small quarry on the property and partly of mudwall. The sandstone is limited to part of the south wall and may be the remnants of the 1745 structure. The remainder of the structure is mudwall on a low sandstone rubble base. This 1766 structure was extended to the east (also in mudwall) but to a greater eaves height. The 1766 building was then heightened to create a level eaves line round the entire structure. The 1766 roof is close coupled using pit sawn timbers partly dressed with a side axe. The east extension roof is also close coupled but using circular sawn timbers partly dressed with an adze. The sprockets forming a bellcast to accommodate the increased eaves height to the 1766 work are also circular sawn and adze-dressed, suggesting that they may have been done at the same time as the extension. This is contradicted by the evidence of the mudwall, since the 1766 walls and extension walls are both built in a pink/brown clay, whereas the heightening of the 1766 walls is in a distinctive brown clay. The fenestration of the building has changed considerably over the years. At least two gable windows have been blocked as has a squint in the north west corner designed to overlook anyone approaching from the road. The fenestration of the south elevation has changed completely with the insertion of large windows into the principal rooms. The existing building has stud and mud flues supporting clay brick chimneyheads. The west gable flue partly covers a blocked window in that gable. The 1766 east gable is now internal and has a flue built against each principal face. The flue against the west face is dated 1818 in the stud and mud work. The building has recently been purchased and conserved by the National Trust for Scotland in collaboration with the National Heritage Fund, Historic Scotland and the Perth and Kinross Heritage Fund and will soon be open to the public. Interpretation of the various features is being linked to the known history, to give the visitor some idea of the changes that have occurred over the last 250 years.

Informally planned buildings similar in form and plan types to those found in Abernyte, Cottown, Kinnaird and Rait continued to be construct-ed in the highland areas of the country well into the 19th century. This reflects the cultural time lag between the richer and poorer parts of the county or between the large farms on good agricultural land and small farms and crofts on marginal land. These structures replaced earlier turf-walled buildings constructed on stake and rice armatures, as described at Rannoch in the *Old Statistical Account* of the 1790s. One such structure is Lower Chamberbane, Strathtummel, surveyed in the 1970s and inter-preted through at least four phases using the fragments of evidence left in the surviving structure. Another multiple-phase structure is the byre dwelling at Morlannich, Killin. This building has recently been purchased and conserved by the National Trust for Scotland with assistance from Historic Scotland. The crucks and roof timbers in this building may sur-vive from an earlier turf-walled structure. The thatch is currently covered with corrugated iron and has not been scientifically examined but it may also date from the turf-walled period, although it would have been regularly top-dressed throughout the building's history until it was eventually clad in corrugated iron. The walls are likely to date from the mid-19th century and are of unusual construction. They comprise two drystone skins connected across the thickness of the wall by through stones form-ing bonders across the small scale hardcore core. The drystone skins are not pinned in the normal way but are held in place by clay mortar at the tails of the inner faces of the external skins. The external finish is a lime slurry pointing finished with limewash. The internal finish is clay or lime plaster, limewash and multiple layers of wallpaper. The concrete floors, corrugated iron porch and roof sheeting are likely to be late-19th or 20th century as there are photographs of the house before these additions. The sapling-framed wallpaper-constructed canopy chimneyhood in the kitchen may also date from this period but may replace an earlier cat and clay chimneyhood.

All the buildings discussed above are multiple-phased structures illustrating that changes were taking place from the end of the 17th century to the present day. Whether this general pattern of change can be projected back into the 17th century or earlier cannot be confirmed until archaeologists have examined and excavated a number of differing types of site and have linked these to the available documentary evidence. Archaeological investigation of existing thatches may help in this process as it is hoped to establish archaeological signatures for various types of thatch that may be read in future excavations, thereby assisting in the interpretation.

The 'improved' farmhouses of the 18th and 19th centuries developed in similar ways to the larger mansion houses. They were built to the same principles and in the same style but to a smaller scale and normally to simpler designs, often taken from pattern books rather than being individually designed.

The 18th-century Perthshire farmhouse is usually Palladian in concept with a symmetrical house set in the centre of the south range of the farm square. The farmhouses built in the first quarter of the 19th century are still symmetrical but are narrower in frontage and deeper in plan and are set to the east of the steading, usually within their own garden. The second quarter of the 19th century sees the Romanticism of the design of the farmhouse. The house is still symmetrically planned but the elevations are forced into a somewhat asymmetrical design with false gables and dormers combined with changing eaves levels. One of the principal exponents of this style was W Mackenzie, the City Architect for Perth, who designed and published farm building designs in the 1830s. His design for Elcho farmhouse and steading appears in J C Loudon's *Encyclopaedia of Cottage, Farm and Villa Architecture*. The asymmetrical Romantic farmhouse continued to develop throughout the remainder of the century, progressing through Baronial styles to the neo-vernacular of the Arts and Crafts movement. The most impressive designer in this category was James Marjoriebanks Maclaren, who used the vernacular tradition round his home area of Doune (formerly Perthshire) in the charming group of neo-vernacular cottages, farmhouses and steadings on the Glenlyon estate, Fortingall. Maclaren had a short life as a practising architect but his designs influenced Sir Robert Lorimer, Charles Rennie Mackintosh and Charles Voysey.

There are some unexpected characteristics in the early improved farm buildings. The earliest masonry-built improved farmhouses are normally wide, two-storey single-pile structures built using accurately cut, occasionally polished, ashlar blocks of similar quality to the mansion houses in the area. This is the result of using the same firms of masons for both mansion house and farm buildings. This only occurred with the earliest improvements and by the beginning of the 19th century the demand for new masonry-built farm steadings was such that many 'cowboy' firms sprang up, leading to some very poor quality stonework. This has resulted in many of the farms built at that time gaining an unwarranted appearance of antiquity which confuses researchers when they first work in the area. The quality of mason work improved steadily throughout the remainder of the century until a highly sophisticated square-snecked rubble evolved that is characteristic of the best of Scottish masonry.

Contrary to popular opinion, many of the vernacular buildings erected by architects, surveyors and from pattern books were constructed of materials other than masonry. Perthshire, particularly the Carse of Gowrie, has many fine improved farmhouses and steadings constructed of brick, claywall, half-timbering, mudwall, pisé and timber. Fine brick farmhouses survive at Flatfield and Kingdom, Errol. Although many other examples are known, the rest have all been harled since the 1950s, probably in a mistaken effort to make them appear more Scottish. Flatfield and Kingdom were obviously experimental structures at the time of building as the external walls are 24 in (60 mm) and 22 in (55 mm) thick solid brickwork on the ground and first floors respectively. The brickwork is built off a rubble base using hand-made clamp-kiln clay bricks. At Flatfield, the openings have masonry surrounds and brick relieving arches over the ground floor windows. Kingdom is of similar construction but with brick jambs to the openings and brick flat-arches rather than lintels. Both of these farmhouses were originally thatched but this had been replaced with Welsh slate before the end of the 19th century. Flatfield was built in 1785 and Kingdom a few years later. Claywall is much more difficult to recognise unless slappings are being formed in the walls but the two-storey school and schoolhouse at Glendoick, erected in the 1830s, is constructed of this material. This building is now harled.

Half-timbered farms and farmhouses were designed for the Rossie Priory estate. Only minor sections of half-timbering survive, mainly around Knapp, although the Episcopal Church at Glencarse is reminiscent of the style of half-timbering as is shown in the line drawings. Mudwall is more common in pre-improvement farms and in villages such as Errol. Probably the most impressive example of a mudwall farmhouse is Horn, an early structure remodelled by the neo-classical Dundee architect David Neave in the 1820s. Pisé is again difficult to recognise but the 1784 court of farm offices at Flatfield is probably a pisé structure; tests will have to be carried out to verify this. Timber-framed, weatherboarded farmhouses and steadings are found on Lord Kinnaird's estates at Rossie Priory and Lord Mansfield's estates at Scone Palace.

Many interesting innovative constructional techniques were introduced to Perthshire in the 19th century. Robert Smirke used mass concrete foundations in the construction of Kinfauns Castle in 1820. Vernacular builders in the Carse of Gowrie and local architects conversant with the use of shuttering for claywall, mudwall and pisé immediately adopted the new material and used it in the construction of chapels, cottages, houses and steadings. Lord Kinnaird erected a stone crusher to provide aggregate for the new material in the 1850s and by the time that text books were being produced in the 1870s, Perthshire was providing many of the quoted examples. Many of the buildings appear to be built of no-fines concrete even as early as the 1870s, many decades before its supposed invention. Corrugated iron is another 19th-century innovation utilised by Perthshire builders. The material was invented and patented in 1828 and became an instant success. In the lowland areas corrugated iron was used for industrial buildings and to roof cattle courts on large farms. The range of structures built using the material is endless and includes ballrooms, churches, church halls, cinemas, garages, hospitals, hangars, libraries, schools, shops, village halls and workshops. In Highland Perthshire the use of the material is extended to include dwellings, game larders, shooting lodges and smoke houses. Corrugated iron is extremely versatile and in many instances it was re-used, either in sheet form or by moving the complete building. William Atkinson, architect and designer of Scone Palace and Rossie Priory, also produced pattern books. He advocated the use of brick cavity walls in Perthshire in the 1810s but this was not adopted as standard until after the Second World War.

Perthshire, having some of the richest agricultural land in Scotland and also some of the most remote marginal land, has a unique spread of vernacular building remains. It is important that this is fully recognised and that some of the more unorthodox constructions receive the protection they deserve.

FIFTEEN
INDUSTRY AND COMMERCE

INTRODUCTION

Although Perth and Kinross is often thought of as a largely agricultural area, it has had a long history of industrial and commercial activity, particularly Perth. As early as 1209, King William's charter to Perth stated that the burghers were to have their guild merchant excluding fullers and weavers. Both the evidence of Perth street names (Skinnergate, Ropemakers' Close, Baxters' Vennel, Shuttle Row, Fleshers' Vennel etc) and archaeological excavations from the 1970s onwards which have revealed some evidence of industrial activity' on every site excavated suggest almost unbroken industrial and commercial activity in Perth from the 13th century onwards.

By the time of Rutherford's map of Perth in 1774 (see Chapter 12, page 156) a wide variety of industrial activities was being carried on in Perth. The map shows the Mills and Bakers' Granary, the New Row Factory (for linen sheetings, then cotton), a printed cotton manufactory, the mill-wynd factory, a tanned leather manufactory, a snuff mill and an oil mill. Macfarlane's Map of 1792 shows a snuff mill, a barley mill, a saw mill, two cotton mills, two breweries and Perth Mills and Granary. Stobie's Map of Perthshire dated 1783 shows numerous water-powered sites across the county, many concerned with the milling or threshing of grain, others with the manufacture of linen with a concentration of bleachfields around Perth.

Linen was the dominant textile in Perth and its surrounding area and a ring of bleachfields was established from the 1750s onwards at Luncarty, Huntingtower and Stormontfield. In the 1780s a boom in cotton took place, resulting in the establishment of spinning mills at Cromwellpark and Stanley. An economic crash in 1810 wiped out about 60 textile firms in the Perth area but Stanley, Huntingtower and Stormontfield carried on into the 1970s and 1980s and the oldest bleachfield, Luncarty, founded in 1753, is still operating today.

In the 19th century, whisky emerged from a Highland cottage industry operating on the edge of the law to a large scale industry with a strong emphasis on marketing and looking to markets outside Scotland for its growth. The Perth-based firms of Bell's, Gloags and particularly Dewars played a prominent part in these developments. Perth's position on the edge of the Highlands and its importance as a railway centre gave it particular advantages as a blending and bottling centre for whisky.

Towards the end of the 19th century, in 1885, Francis Norie-Miller founded General Accident, a response to the Employers' Liability Act of 1880 which made employers liable for accidents to their employees. From small beginnings employing four staff, it grew to a multi-million pound com-pany with world-wide interests, employing just over 1000 people at its Perth headquarters in 1995.

CURRENT EMPLOYMENT PATTERNS IN PERTH AND KINROSS

Perth and Kinross is a relatively prosperous and dynamic area of Scotland. The total population in 1991 was 120,607 compared with 113,790 in 1981, an increase of 6% compared with a decrease of 9.4% in the population of Dundee in the same period. Unemployment levels in Perth and Kinross are relatively low - 7.2% for men and 4.9% for women in 1991 compared with 15.6% for men and 10.4% for women in Dundee in the same year. In May 1995, 3516 of the Perthshire workforce (8.3%) were unemployed and claiming benefit.

Nowadays, as in the rest of Britain, most people in Perth and Kinross are employed by the service industries. A 10% sample of economic and employment status in Perth and Kinross in 1991 showed that out of a total sample of 5484, 1662 (30%) were employed in Other Services and 1325 (24%) in Distribution and Catering. Manufacturing accounted for 11% of the sample (616), Banking and Finance for 9.6% (527) and Agriculture for only 6.9% (381) compared with 17% in 1961. (See Table 1 and Figure 16).

Table 1
Economic and Employment Status
Perth and Kinross 1991 (10% sample)

	Number (10% sample)	Percentage (%)
Total	5484	100.0
Agriculture, Forestry and Fisheries	381	6.9
Energy and Water	115	2.0
Mining	68	-
Manufacturing	616	11.0
Contruction	425	7.7
Distribution and Catering	1325	24.0
Transport	327	5.9
Banking and Finance	527	9.6
Other Services	1662	30.0
Unclassified	38	-

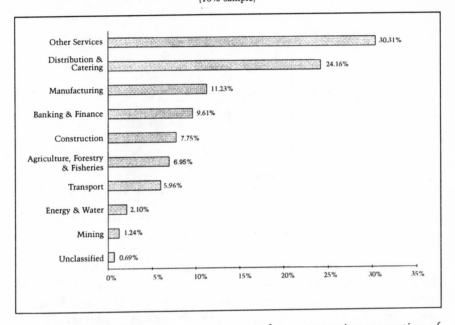

Figure 16

Economic and Employment Status – Perth and Kinross 1991

(10% sample)

As in the rest of the country, women make up a growing proportion of the workforce in Perth and Kinross. In 1991, out of an economically active population of 60,882, women made up 44% (26,595) compared with 32% in 1961. The number of economically active men had actually declined from 39,310 in 1961 to 34,287 in 1991. The rise in the number and proportion of economically active women from 1961 to 1991 is explained by the rise in the number of married women in the workforce from 6790 in 1961 to 16,797 in 1991. (see Table 2 and Figure 17).

Table 2

Economically Active Population

Perth and Kinross 1961 and 1991

	Total over 16 in 1991	Economically active in 1991	Economically active in 1961
Total	100,054	60,882	57,780
Male	46,943	34,287	39,310
Female	53,111	26,595	18,470
		[44%]	[32%]

Figure 17

Economically Active Population – Perth and Kinross 1961 and 1991

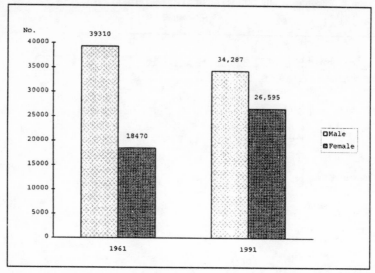

Women dominate the growing service sector of employment making up 55% of those employed in Distribution and Catering (739 out of 1325) and 66% of those employed in Other Services (1108 out of 1662). A higher proportion of women between 16 and 59 were in employment in Perth and Kinross (67%) compared with Scotland as a whole (61.6%).

Perth and Kinross also reflected the growing mobility of the UK workforce. In 1991, out of a 10% sample of 5484, 14% (793) of Perth and Kinross residents worked outside the district. Men were more mobile than women – 553 men travelled outside the district to work compared with 215 women. High status workers tended to be more mobile – 215 of the total were employers or managers and the overwhelming majority travelled by private car – 596 or 75%.

TEXTILES

Little remains today of the once important Perthshire textile industry. It had been founded on abundant supplies of water power and a substantial local flax-growing industry, later diversifying into cotton and jute. As late as 1966, Stanley Mills were still producing cotton belting, Deanston Mills had just closed, Blairgowrie and Perth still had jute mills, there was still a substantial bleaching and dyeing industry around Perth and Todd and Duncan were spinning cashmere in Kinross. Today, Todd and Duncan are still manufacturing cashmeres at Lochleven Mills in Kinross and bleaching is still carried on at Luncarty outside Perth by Burt Marshall Lumsden Ltd but these are the last relics of a once thriving industry.

WHISKY

The whisky industry has had a long connection with Perthshire. Today there are distilleries at Aberfeldy, Blackford (Tullibardine), Crieff (Glenturret) and Pitlochry (Blair Atholl and Edradour). Two of these (Aberfeldy and Blair Atholl) are owned by United Distillers, the others by Glenturret Distillery Ltd, Tullibardine Distillery Ltd and Edradour by Campbell Distillers Ltd. In addition, United Distillers has a substantial administrative headquarters at Cherrybank in Perth (the old headquarters of Bells).

The industry has seen major changes in the last twenty years. Although Dewars became part of Distillers as early as 1925 it retained a degree of autonomy and Bells remained independent until taken over by the giant drinks company, Guinness PLC in 1985. The following year, Guinness took over Distillers so that control of the industry had now firmly moved away from Perth. Similarly, other parts of the industry are now owned by French interests such as Edradour which is operated by Campbell Distillers Ltd, who are in turn owned by Pernod Ricard.

The oldest distillery in Perthshire appears to be Glenturret outside Crieff, established in 1775. Today it combines whisky manufacture with operating as a major tourist attraction. Blair Atholl Distillery at Pitlochry was founded in 1798. It has a workforce of 40 and an annual output of 1.5 M litres of alcohol. It produces a single malt (Blair Atholl) and its blend association is Bell's.

Legal restraints on distilling were eased from the 1820s onwards. Edradour, above Pitlochry, was established in 1825 and is a fine example of a relatively little altered early 19th-century distillery in a magnificent setting under Ben Vrackie. It is almost domestic in scale with a workforce of three and an output of 100,000 litres a year, which is the equivalent of a week's production in most distilleries. It produces a 10-year single malt (the Edradour) and is also an integral part of the two company blends – House of Lords and Clan Campbell.

Aberfeldy, which was a Dewar's distillery, is a larger scale operation, typical of the distilleries of the late 19th century which were producing for the wider market beyond Scotland. It was founded in 1898 and currently has 20 employees producing Aberfeldy Single Malt and Dewar's Blend. Alfred Barnard's book on the distilleries of Great Britain, published in 1887, lists seven distilleries operating in Perthshire at that time, including the Isla Distillery, Perth; Blair Atholl and Edradour Distilleries, Pitlochry;

Auchnagie and Ballechin Distilleries, Ballinluig; Grandtully Distillery, Aberfeldy and Glenturret Distillery by Crieff.

Bell's was founded in 1825 by T R Sandeman and taken over by James Roy in 1837. Arthur Bell did not enter the firm until 1851. It became a limited company in 1922. In 1973, it moved to headquarters at Cherrybank on the outskirts of Perth. In the same year, Raymond Miquel became chairman and the company entered into a phase of rapid expansion. Pre-tax profits rose from £3M in 1974 to £35M in 1984 when Bell's had 21% of the domestic market. Exports had also risen from £6.7 M in 1974 to £38.6M in 1984. This kind of success made Bell's a prime target for takeover bids, particularly as its market share was slipping and it was seen as weak in the key North American market. Ernest Saunders, Chairman of Guinness, targeted Bell's with the slogan 'Bell's has lost its way' and, after an acrimonious takeover battle, the company was taken over by Guinness in 1985.

Dewars had lost its independence earlier than Bell's. John Dewar, who came from a cottar family in the Highland Perthshire parish of Dull, near Aberfeldy, had opened a wine and spirit shop on Perth High Street in 1846. His sons, Thomas and John, expanded the business greatly. Thomas, who became Lord Dewar, was the marketing man who established himself in London in the 1880s and made Dewar's a leading brand in the English market and from the 1900s in overseas markets such as Australia, India and South Africa. His brother, John, who became Lord Forteviot, managed production back in Perth. The firm moved to the Glasgow Road, Perth in 1893 and four years later became a limited company. In 1911, the company built a large brick bond storage centre on Glasgow Road, Perth, with access to national markets via Perth's excellent railway connections. By this time, the firm owned seven distilleries and the Glasgow Road blending and bottling plants. In 1925, Dewar's became part of the giant Distillers Company, an amalgam of major whisky companies such as Haig, Johnny Walker and Dewar's and two gin firms – Booth's and Tanqueray (Gordon's). Although there was sharing of grain buying and of some production and bottling facilities, marketing and selling remained separate and this continued for sixty years, by which time the company was called United Distillers.

In 1962, Dewar's built a major new bottling plant at Inveralmond on the Dunkeld Road, Perth, which was well placed for access to the national road network via the A9. The plant cost £1.5M to build and at its height employed 900 people largely producing for the export market. The 1970s saw whisky coming under increasing competition from other spirits such as vodka and gin and United Distillers' market share in the UK fell from 54% in 1974 to 20% in 1984. This made Distillers a target for corporate predators in the takeover culture of the 1980s. In 1985, James Gulliver of the Argyll Group made a bid for Distillers which was repulsed but the company succumbed to a bid by Guinness in the following year. The methods used in the Guinness takeover resulted in the eventual resignation of the Guinness chairman, Ernest Saunders and the imprisonment of a number of major players. In January 1993, Distillers announced the closure of the Inveralmond bottling plant, with a loss of 300 jobs by the summer of 1994.

GLASS MANUFACTURING

Moncrieff Glassworks were founded in 1865 by John Moncrieff on South Street in Perth. In the 1880s they moved to St Catherine's Road near Perth harbour, becoming a limited company in 1905. The principal product was gauge glasses for laboratories and for steam boilers. The company diversified into the production of decorative coloured glassware under the trademark Monart when the production of chemical glass came under fierce competition from foreign imports in the 1920s. The Ysart family from Barcelona played a prominent part in the design and production of this decorative glass. Monart was the result of a design partnership between Mrs Isobel Moncrieff and Salvador Ysart and was produced from 1924 to 1961. It was sold through Watsons of Perth and Liberty's of London and also through outlets in Glasgow, North America and Australia. The principal production was vases, bowls, lamps and ashtrays.

In 1946, Salvador Ysart and his sons Augustine and Vincent left Moncrieff to set up a rival company (Ysart Brothers Glass) on Shore Road, Perth, producing decorative glass under the trade name Vasart. By 1956, both Salvador and Augustine had died and George Dunlop of Pirelli Glass, Potters Bar, joined the firm. In 1964, Teacher's, the whisky firm, took over the company and built a new and larger glass factory at Muthil Road, Crieff, renaming the company Strathearn Glass. Vincent Ysart was appointed the works manager of the new firm but lasted less than a year, being replaced by Stuart Drysdale. Drysdale in turn left the firm to set up Perthshire Paperweights in 1968. In 1980, Strathearn Glass was taken over by Stuart of Stourbridge and renamed Stuart Strathearn. It is now part of the Waterford Wedgewood Group.

Paul Ysart stayed with the Moncrieff Company, producing Monart Glass from 1947 to 1961. In 1963, he moved to the newly opened Caithness Glass factory in Wick as Technical Adviser and Training Officer and collaborated with Colin Terris on the manufacture of paperweights. Moncrieff had passed out of family control in 1952 and saw its workforce steadily reduced from 200 in 1980 to 40 in 1988, by which time it was manufacturing heat resistant glass under the trade name Monax and was owned by the Caradon Group of Walsall. Glass-making ceased at Monax Glass in December 1995.

The tradition of glass manufacture continues today in Perthshire, with Caithness Glass Ltd on the northern edge of Perth, which opened in 1979 and produces artware and paperweights, Perthshire Paperweights in Crieff and Stuart Strathearn in Crieff, which concentrates on the engraving of crystal blanks.

GENERAL ACCIDENT

General Accident was founded by Francis Norie-Miller in 1885 in response to the Employers' Liability Act of 1880, which made employers liable for accidents to workers. The number employed by the company in 1885 was 4 and the premium income was £2600. In 1925 General Accident acquired General Life Assurance Company and by 1929, the company had a workforce of 2000 with 40,000 agents on commission, a premium income of £8M and assets of £12M.

Today, General Accident is one of Britain's largest insurance companies, employing over 1000 people at its headquarters at Pithleavis, outside Perth. It is represented in more than 40 countries and around two-thirds of its premium income comes from outside the UK. Its business is wide-ranging, from private home owners and motorists to companies. Its subsidiary, GA Life, based in York, provides life assurance, savings plans and pensions. General Accident also has one of the largest networks of estate agents in Britain.

In 1994, General Accident had a premium income of £4253M of which £1520M came from the UK and £1249M from the US. Pre-tax profits were a record £428M. The company retains strong Scottish connections on the Board. Its chairman is the Earl of Airlie and the deputy chairmen are Lord Nickson, chairman of the Clydesdale Bank and Sir Alick Rankin, chairman of Scottish and Newcastle. Directors include City figures such as Sir Nicholas Goodison but also those with strong Scottish connections such as Mr L Bolton of the Alliance Trust, Lord Macfarlane of Bearsden and the Earl of Mansfield.

STAGECOACH LIMITED

Perth has always functioned as a transport centre. It was traditionally the lowest spot for crossing the River Tay and became a road network as a result. When the railways were developed in the 19th century, Perth became an important railway network and out of this came an important trade in the blending and bottling of whisky. It is therefore an appropriate place for the headquarters of a major national transport company.

From small beginnings in 1976, Stagecoach has grown into a major national and international player on the transport scene, greatly helped by the 1980 Transport Act which deregulated bus services in Britain. It was founded by a husband and wife team, Robin and Ann Gloag, as a self-drive motor caravan and minibus firm known as Gloagtrotter. Ann Gloag's brother, Brian Souter, an accountant, joined in 1980 and the firm moved into private hire minibuses.

The 1980 Act allowed operators to run express services over 48 km (30 miles) without authorisation from the Traffic Commissioners. In Ocober 1980, Gloagtrotter began overnight services from Dundee to London via Perth, Stirling, Cumbernauld and Glasgow for £9.50 single, under-cutting the Scottish Bus Group by £2.00. In January 1991, the service was extended to Aberdeen and the name Stagecoach was adopted.

In the spring of 1982, Brian Souter and Ann Gloag's uncle, Fraser McColl, the Scots-born president of a Canadian oil services company, took a £25,000 stake in the business and acted as guarantor for two new coach-es. The rail strike of July 1982 proved a shot in the arm for the company, which by now held licences for 14 vehicles. In March 1983, Robin Gloag left the company following the break-up of his marriage to start a locally operating company - Highwayman Coaches of Perth.

In 1985, McLennan of Spitalfield was acquired, adding Perthshire rural bus services to existing Perth routes. The following year, in September 1986, Stagecoach (Holdings) Ltd was formed to act as a holding company for existing interests and future acquisitions. A period of rapid expansion followed in the climate of deregulation and takeover fever that charac-terised the late 1980s. Hampshire Bus was acquired for £2.2M in April 1987, Cumberland Motor Services for £2.8M in July 1987 and United Counties Omnibus Company Ltd for £4M in November 1987. By July 1987, the company had 560 vehicles, 1400 staff and an annual turnover of £24M. The acquisition of United Counties increased the total fleet to 914.

The rapid expansion continued in the late 1980s. In April 1989, Stagecoach bought Ribble Motor Services Ltd of Lancashire for £6.3M and East Midlands Motor Services Ltd for £4.5M. By 1989, the share capital of Stagecoach was 2M ordinary shares, of which Brian Souter and Ann Gloag owned 1,997,600 and 5M partly convertible preference shares owned by financial institutions. This extraordinary expansion had been financed partly by lease finance and hire purchase for acquiring new buses. Funds had also been generated internally by the sale of property and other assets surplus to requirements from the companies acquired.

The Monopolies Commission estimated that Stagecoach had generated £4M from the sale of fixed assets in 1987, generating profits of £1.5M and £7M in 1988, generating profits of £3.4M. The Commission commented

'Stagecoach has a reputation for "seeing off the competition"...This is consistent with its own stated philosophy of strong oligopolists and niche operators. It moreover needs to service its capital and make a profit.'

Stagecoach's expansion has continued and, if anything, accelerated. At the end of the financial year ending April 1995, its turnover had risen by 77% from the previous year to £338M, largely due to eight new acquisitions. Pre-tax profit had risen by 72% to £32.6M. The company had expanded overseas to Malawi, Kenya and New Zealand, beginning with the acquisition of United Transport Malawi Ltd in 1990. It had, however, been required to divest itself of 20% holdings in Mainline Partnership (Sheffield) and SB Holdings (Strathclyde) by the Monopolies and Mergers Commission. Despite these problems, Stagecoach was beginning to move into acquiring railway companies with the beginnings of the railway privatisation programme in late 1995.

TOURISM

Tourism is a major employer in Perthshire. In 1994, expenditure by tourists in Perthshire was estimated at £167M, 6% of the Scottish total. Income generated by tourism was estimated at £221M, some 25% of Perthshire GDP and some 70% of tourist income in Tayside. Tourist expenditure in Perthshire supports an estimated 7680 full time equivalent jobs – approximately 20% of total employment in the area. There is wide seasonal variation in tourism employment from an estimated 5812 full time equivalent jobs in February at the lowest point of the season to 10,454 at the August peak.

The main tourist centres are Perth, Pitlochry,Crieff, Aberfeldy and Blairgowrie. There is a large winter ski facility at Glenshee, north of Blairgowrie. Field sports contribute significantly to Perthshire's tourist economy, from grouse shooting and deer stalking in Highland Perthshire to salmon fishing in the Tay or trout fishing on Loch Leven.

CONCLUSION

Perth and Kinross has suffered less than many other parts of Scotland from the often painful readjustment to new patterns of industry and employment. It had fewer of the old traditional industries such as heavy engineering, shipbuilding and textiles than Dundee or the west of Scotland. It had a broader pattern of employment, including significant growth industries such as financial services and tourism. Perthshire's central position in Scotland and excellent communication links with the rest of Scotland and the UK via roads, motorways and rail has stood it in good stead. Finally, Perth and Perthshire have consistently come towards the top end of national polls to establish 'quality of life', a significant factor nowadays in influencing firms' decisions to relocate or to stay in an area.

SIXTEEN
PLACE-NAMES

It is always difficult to present a balanced picture of the place-names of a Scottish county the size of Perthshire. The range of topographical conditions, linguistic history and agricultural development together form complex patterns that provide us with great variety. The Highland parishes in the north and west contrast sharply with the low-lying carse lands and straths of the south in terms of the pattern of nomenclature.

As one might expect, Perthshire contains a high percentage of Gaelic names. Indeed, when one looks at the westernmost parishes, such as Fortingall, Kenmore and Killin as well as Blair Atholl in the north, the Gaelic element predominates, almost to the exclusion of non-Gaelic names. In contrast, parishes in the Carse of Gowrie, such as Inchture, Errol and St Madoes contain large numbers of Scots place-names and this is also true of parishes like Auchterarder, Madderty and Trinity Gask in Strath Earn. P-Celtic names of Pictish origin, many containing the well-known *pett* 'portion' may be found mostly in the south-east but examples are well established inland, as far north as Atholl and there are certainly instances of other generics, such as *dul* 'haugh', *aber* 'confluence', *rath* 'fortress' and *tref* 'farmstead' in various parts of the county. Indeed, a closer inspection of many of these earlier Celtic names suggests a good deal of inter-borrowing between Gaelic and Pictish, reminding us not only of the considerable linguistic overlap that took place here but also of the complex historical relationship between these two peoples.

Preceding even these are the names of the major rivers of Perthshire. The entire county is physically dominated by the great rivers of *Tay*, *Earn*, *Isla*, *Tummel* and several others. These uncompounded names originate in Early Celtic or pre-Celtic Indo-European languages. *Tay*, for example, is recorded by Claudius Ptolemy as *Tava* and by Tacitus as *Taus*. It probably has as its root an Indo-European *ta-* 'to melt, dissolve or flow' (Nicolaisen, 1968, 145). Parallel forms occur in various parts of Britain, in the names *Thames*, *Tame*, *Tamar*, etc and *Zenn*, *Tanaro*, *Taverone* on the continent of Europe. The *Earn*, for which our documentary evidence is much later (*Eirenn* 1100, *Erne* c. 1190 and *Eryn* c. 1195) is likewise a good candidate for a pre-Celtic name, probably containing a word for 'water' or 'stream' which appears in the English river-names Aire and *Ure* as well as the French *Isere*.

The *Almond* and the *Isla* both have parallels in Scotland, in Lothian and Banffshire respectively. *Almond* may originate in an Indo-European *embh-* 'moist', 'water' and the *Isla* 'to abound in moisture'. Others in this category of major river names include *Alan, Teith, Devon* and *Ardle*.

These are all pre-Roman names and their powers of survival are directly related to the fact that major rivers are a most important landscape feature. They act as routeways, as boundaries between one people and another; they provide food and drink, yet are capricious in mood and capable of enormous destruction. It is no wonder that our early forebears treated them with respect, even veneration.

Perthshire of old was divided up into four major districts, with names that have survived up to the present day. *Atholl*, which covers the north and west, *Gowrie*, running from the Aberdeenshire and Angus marches in the east to include the lower Tay and the Carse, *Strathearn*, which forms the catchment area of the Earn and its tributaries and *Menteith* in the south-west, lying north of Forth and west of the Ochils. *Atholl* was included in one of the ancient Pictish provinces, Fotla, which also contained *Gowrie*. There is currently doubt about its derivation.

Earlier scholars, such as WJ Watson, believed it to be 'new Ireland' basing their conclusions on the recorded early forms of the name – *Athfhotla* in the *Annals of Tigernach* (c.739), *Athotla* in the *Book of Deer* (11th century) and others. The current Gaelic form is *Athall*. Watson suggested that *ath* represented the repetitive element and *Fotla* the poetic word for Ireland. *Gowrie*, which has early forms *Gouerin* and *Goverine* (1306) may well be from an early Pictish personal name, perhaps similar to that of Gabran, King of Dal Riata who died c.560. *Strathearn's* derivation is clearly 'strath or valley of the Earn and, with *Menteith*, was an old part of the Pictish province of Fortriu. The old forms of the name are *Meneted, Manethat* (1264), *Meneteth* (1286). The initial part is clearly from *mon* 'hilly ground', 'high ground' which is now the Gaelic *monadh* 'hill', Welsh *mynydd* being of similar origin. The specific is *Teith*, the river-name, giving 'high ground of the Teith'. A Menteith man in Gaelic, was always referred to as *Teadhach* and the district itself was called *Teadhaich*.

There are several other district names which deserve mention. *Breadalbane*, which occupies much of central western Perthshire west of the watershed with Argyll, has been equated with an earlier form *Brunalban* (c. 970), for old Gaelic *brun* 'bank', 'slope' but the more recent version contains *braghad* 'upper part'. It effectively describes the situation of newly conquered Gaelic settlements in the western and upland parts of

Perthshire during the latter part of the first millenium when Pictish power was on the wane.

Pictish names in Perthshire are themselves important indicators of settlement. If we examine their distribution, we find that the most frequent are names in *pett-/pitt* 'portion', 'share'. The problem with these names is that the second element (specific) is usually Gaelic, so we are probably dealing with a farm-name which may have been coined by Gaelic speakers in a Pictish administrative unit. It is likely that these date from about AD 800 and must represent a period when Gaelic was widely spoken but in which the Pictish language had not yet died out. The majority of names in *pit-* are located in light soils, in well-sheltered locations, mostly away from the heavy clays of the flood-plains. Their derivations speak of a mixed farming economy – cattle rearing, grazing and cereal production, if not in Perthshire at least in neighbouring counties such as Fife and Angus.

Pitcairn, Dunning (NT 1995) is the 'portion of the cairn'. There are two *Pitcastles* both in Logierait, (NO 9053 and NO 9755) 'the portion of the castle', *Pitfour* (NO 1920) 'portion of the pasture' contains the Gaelic *por*, a borrowing from a p-Celtic word which is paralleled in the Old Welsh *pawr*. *Pitkellony* (NN 8616) in Muthill, *Pitkeathly* (NO 1116) near Bridge of Earn, *Pitlochry* (NN 9358) 'stony portion' (called *Baile-chloichridh* by modern Gaelic speakers) and *Pitroddie* (NO 2224) 'fight portion' in Errol are some of the other Perthshire examples.

The element *aber-* 'confluence, river-mouth' is also p-Celtic and is found in several Perthshire examples. Although it is scarce in Scotland south of the Forth, it is common in Wales in such names as Abergavenny, Aberfan, Abertillery, etc. Normally, the second element comprises the name of the stream to which the confluence applies. Although some of these are quite obvious as to their derivation, such as *Aberargie* (NO 1615) on the Farg and *Aberuthven* (NN 9715) on the confluence of the Ruthven Water and the Earn, others preserve earlier stream-names which have been replaced by modern ones. This is the case with *Abernethy* (NO1816) where a *Nethy* must have been the predecessor of the present Ballo Burn, *Aberdalgie* (NO 0720) on the Cotton Burn, *Aberbothrie* (NO 2446) on a burn that must once have been called Borthrie, a tributary of the Isla and *Abercairney* (NN 9122) which today lies on the Muckle Burn. There are exceptions to this rule however. *Aberfoyle*, (NN 5201) is simply 'confluence of the sluggish stream' (G poll) and *Aberfeldy* (NN 8549) is fairly rare because it contains a personal name, *peallaidh*, that of a Celtic water-spirit or *uruisg*, widely known (and feared) in local Gaelic tradition as late as the 19th century and who has left a number of names such as *Eas Pheallaidh* 'Peallaidh's waterfall' in Glen Lyon.

The equivalent of *aber* in Gaelic is the term *inbhir*, which becomes *inver* in anglicised form. It is possible for both to be found in Perthshire, applied to confluence situations on the same stream. *Abernethy* and *Innernethy*, only a mile apart and *Abernyte* (NO 2531) and *Innernytie* (NO 1235) are in similar close proximity.

Other settlement names from the pre-Gaelic period are sometimes difficult to trace, but there are some significant and important examples. *Carpow* (NO 2017) near Abernethy is *caerpwll*, 'fort on the pool or pow' and is probably the name 'Ceirfuill' that appears in the Pictish Chronicle. It is a highly strategic location, guarding the eastern approaches to the mouths of the Earn and Tay. A number of names containing Gaelic *monadh* 'hill ground', 'hill country' are almost certainly from an earlier p-Celtic word similar to the Welsh *mynydd*, Old Welsh *minit*, 'mountain', a term widely found in Pictland. *Moncrieffe* (NO 1121) 'moor of the trees' for example, is probably the scene of the battle of *MonadCroib* AD 28 between two Pictish armies, and *Stormont* (NO 0847) in the eastern part of Perthshire, lying between Tay, Isla and Ericht may mean 'stepping-stones moor' from an old Gaelic word *stair*, *stoir*, 'stepping stones over a bog or river'.

The name *Perth* itself is p-Celtic, deriving from a Pictish word similar to the Welsh *perth* 'bush, copse'. The earliest documented is from *c.*1128 where it is written as *Pert*. The city was also known as St Johnstone, from the 13th century, when its church was dedicated to St John the Baptist and the local football team preserves this old name.

Rattray (NO 1845) in Blairgowrie contains the p-Celtic generic *treabh* 'dwelling', 'village', similar to Welsh *tref* 'homestead', 'hamlet', which is the approximate equivalent of *baile* in Gaelic. Early forms Rotrefe 1291, Rottref 1296 and Rothtref 1305 confirm this element, the first part being G *rath* 'fortress'.

Gaelic names form the majority of the corpus of Perthshire settlement-names. Although Gaelic was spoken in the north-west until the 1970s, the language died out in the Carse of Gowrie and in Strathearn in the medieval period. It is fair to say that downriver and east of Perth, Gaelic was spoken as a majority language only for some 200 years, perhaps from *c.* 950 to *c.* 1150. It is all the more surprising, therefore, that it forms a very significant percentage of the names. Minor names in this zone, of course, are largely Scots but when one looks at Fortingall or Blair Atholl, we find a very high percentage of the total which are of Gaelic origin – in some areas over 90%. This is partly due to the lack of Scots penetration of the upland zones and to the fact that agricultural activity here was of a markedly different nature compared to the lowlands. The extensive grazing lands of north and east Perthshire were subjected to the processes of the shieling system, involving seasonal settlement and this is reflected in a variety of Gaelic terms associated with transhumance activity.

When we examine all the habitative names of Gaelic origin, we find that *baile* 'farmstead' and *achadh* 'field' are the most common elements. *Baile* is prolific, one might almost say the standard Gaelic generic in the Perthshire straths, providing us with a range of derivations, both descriptive and commemorative. Densities in the Carse and Strathearn are fairly low but when one moves into Strath Tay and Strath Tummel, we find large numbers of *baile*- names. These on the whole remain as farm settlements and it is perhaps significant that of the 71 parish names in the county, not a single one contains *baile* – (*Balquhidder* is from *both* 'hut'.) Most are located on or near rivers, in reasonably favourable sites agriculturally.

Personal names, alluding to ownership, are commonly compounded with *baile*-. *Balmacneil* (NN 9850) in Little Dunkeld, *Baledmund* (NN 9459) in Logierait, *Balmalcolm* (NO 3108) in Collace, *Balhomais* (NN 8249) 'Thomas's stead' in the Appin of Dull and *Balchalum* (NO 2325) 'Calum's stead' in the Carse, are examples of these but it is much more common for *baile* to be compounded with an occupational name, such as we find in *Ballanucater* (NN 6302) 'the fuller's stead' near Thornhill, *Balnaguard* (NN 9451) ' the craftsmen's stead' in Little Dunkeld, *Balgowan* (NN 9755) 'the smith's stead' in Logierait, with another west of Methven, *Ballindean* (NO 3622) 'the dean's stead' in the Braes of the Carse and *Balvarran* (NO 3622) 'the baron's stead' in Strathardle. Most, however, are descriptive, either of the topography or of the speciality of the agriculture involved. *Ballinluig* 'stead in the hollow' from *baile an luig* is found in several places - in *Strathardle* (NO 0957) and twice on the *Tummel* (NN 9457) and (NN 9752); *Balnamoan* (NN 9952) 'peat-stead', *Ballachraggan* (NN 6706) 'stead of the little rock' are in Logierait, *Ballinlick* (NN 9740) 'flagstone-stead' and *Ballinloan* (NN 9740) 'pool-stead' are in Strathbraan; *Balnacraig* (NN 7447) 'stead of the rock' is near Fortingall and *Balvoulin* (NN 8761) 'mill stead' in Glen Fincastle.

Balgray (NO 01730) a few miles north of Scone is *baile greagh* 'horse-stud farm' (there are two similar in Angus) and *Balgower* (NN 8607) near Dunning is 'goat-stead'. *Balgonie* (NO 1917) near Abernethy is probably 'dog-stead'.

The place-name generic which is closely associated with *baile* is *achadh* 'field', a term which in Perthshire is usually found as *auch*-. Compared with *baile*, it is much less common in the county, being found in the most remote areas and often in upland situations at the upper limits of arable cultivation (*see* Nicolaisen map, *SPN*, 140). *Auchessan* (NN 4427) 'field of the little waterfall', between Crianlarich and Lix, *Auchreoch* (NN 3330) 'brindled field' in Strath Fillan, *Auchgobhal* (NN 8870) 'field of the fork' in

Glen Tilt, from *gobhal*, 'crutch', 'forked place', *Auchnacloich* (NN 8439) 'stone field' in Glen Quaich, *Auchleeks* (NN 7464) 'flagstone-field' in Glen Errochty, *Acharn* (NN 5631) 'cairn field' in Glen Dochart, *Auchnafree* (NN 8133) 'field of the deer forest' in Glen Almond and *Auchnaguie* (NO 0052) 'field of the wind' in the Braes of Tulliemet are typical of these. They are certainly scarcer on the lower ground and we must conclude that the element bore little relevance, at least in terms of naming, to Gaelic speakers in the Lower Tay, the Carse and Strathearn.

There are several Gaelic elements that indicate settlement in riverside situations and on dry sites in otherwise marshy topography. When Gaelic names were being coined at the height of Gaelic expansion, much of the lower valley land was impossible to cultivate, due to seasonal flooding, forest and scrub. The alluvial soils of these areas remained largely undrained and it was not until after AD 1100 that much improvement and reclamation took place.

Two significant Gaelic elements, *dail* 'water-meadow' and *innis* 'island', 'dry site in marshy ground' tell us a good deal about the nature of settlement in this period.

Dail which today is used in the west as a term for 'park' or 'haugh' by Gaelic speakers, applies in virtually every case to sites beside a major river, mostly in the straths. The further inland one goes, the more restricted these sites become. They occur sometimes at altitudes of over 1000ft (300 m) in the uppermost recesses of the glens. Typical are *Daldhu* (NO 0270) 'black haugh' in Glen Feamach, *Dalnacarn* (NO 0063) 'cairn haugh' in Glen Brerachan, *Dalmunzie* (NO 0871) 2 miles (3.22 km) north-west of Spittal of Glenshee, *Dalreoch* (NN 0662) 'brindled haugh' in Kirkmichael, *Dalnacardoch* (NN 7270) 'smithy-haugh', *Dalnaspidal* (NN 6472) 'hospice-haugh' in Glen Garry and *Dalcroy* (NN 7759) 'hard haugh' at the west end of Loch Tummel. All of these are descriptive of haugh situations. The name *Dull* (NN 8049) between Aberfeldy and the mouth of Glen Lyon, is an example of the uncompounded form, but probably originating from pre-Gaelic times. The present *dail* is a case of a pre-Celtic term being adopted into Gaelic, from an earlier *dol*, which we still find in Wales, Cornwall and Brittany, applied to a 'meadow, valley or dale'. Significantly, below Dull, beside the Tay, is *Dalrawer* (NN 8148) 'fat haugh' presumably alluding to the width of the plain at this point, in the centre of a four-mile (6.44 km) swathe of haughland between Aberfeldy and the confluence of the Tay and the Lyon. It is fairly rare to find *dail* in a final position but just a few miles up Glen Lyon is *Chesthill* (NN 6947) found in a document of 1502 as *Sestill*, in Gaelic *Seasdul*, giving, perhaps, the derivation of 'haugh by a terrace or bench'.

The term *innis* has, like *dail*, a pre-Gaelic history, since it has origins in both Wales (*ynys*, as in *Ynys Mon* for Anglesey) and Ireland (*Inishmaan*, Galway, *Inish Kenny*, Cork). We find islands such as *Inchcolm* in the Forth, *Inchmarnock*, Bute and *Inchmurrin* in Loch Lomond but the Perthshire examples are all sites originally in marshy riverine locations or, occasionally, major river-meadows. The term *innis* has been well described as 'an island of cultivation' in otherwise difficult terrain. Most of the *innis*-sites are now in extensive agricultural landscapes, however, having formed the core of an early settlement on a raised, dry site in the Dark Age period. In the Gaelic-speaking areas, however, the term was used until the modern period, meaning both an island and a clear space suitable for grazing live-stock, in perhaps wooded country (Fraser, 1993, 258-9).

The Scotticised form is *inch* or *insh* and the element is found largely along the major rivers of Scotland north of the Forth-Clyde line, although examples do also occur in Strathclyde and Lothian. It is likely to be com-parable in date to the *dail*-names, perhaps AD *c.* 900-1000. Some of the most significant Perthshire examples occur in the Carse of Gowrie. *Inchmichael* (NO 2425) 'Michael's inch' and *Inchmartin* (NO 2628) 'Martin's inch' are both sites with saints' names as the specific. *Inchture* (NO 2828) occurs as Inchethore in 1183 and has an obscure derivation. *Inchaffray* (NN 9422) near Crieff in the parish of Madderty, has a ruined abbey on slightly raised ground beside the Pow Water. A charter of c. 1199 describes it as *Incheafferen quod Latine dicitur Insula missarum*, trans-lated as 'which in Latin is named the island of the masses'. This is from the Gaelic *aifreann* 'the mass' indicating that some of these early *inch*-sites were associated with the establishment of churches. The lands along the Tay have a number of them, including *Inchtuthil* (NO 1239) 'Tuathail's meadow', an early Gaelic personal-name, applied to a flat meadow situa-tion close to an important Roman fort. *Inchewan* (NO 0240) 'Ewan's inch' is near Birnam and *Inchmagranachan* (NO 0044), *innis magh ranachan* 'the haugh of the plain of the place of bracken' is located on the east bank of the Tay just south of Dalguise. *Morenish* (NN 5935) on Loch Tay-side is *mor-innis* 'great inch'. The *North* and *South Inch* in Perth are well known, as are the *Bloody Inches* (NO 1438) and *The Inch* (NO 1440) just upstream from the confluence of the Tay and the Isla.

One of the best indicators of early Gaelic settlement is the term *cill* 'church', found in numerous sites throughout north and west Scotland, although there are few examples in Perthshire. *Killin* (NN 5732) is *Cill Fhinn* in Gaelic, thought to be from *fionn* 'white, but it could equally apply to an unrecorded saint, Fionn. *Kilmadock* (NN 7100) near Callander is 1275 Kylmadoc, 'my Doc's church', from Docus, itself a form of a name Cadog, an important 6th-century Welsh saint. Nearby *Kilmahog* (NN 6008) is from an Irish saint, Cucaca. *Kilmaveonaig* (NN 8765) in Blair

Atholl, first recorded in 1275, is in Gaelic *Cill Mo-Bheonaig*, after Beoghna, second abbot of Bangor (d. 606) and *Killiechassie* (NN 8650) near Aberfeldy is Kelcassin (1200), from St Cass's church. All of these certainly belong to a very early stratum of ecclesiastical names.

There are various terms for 'portion' in Gaelic, indicating the parcelling out of land to various tenants, or to individuals in society who had hereditary offices. The word *earann* 'portion', 'share', is most commonly found on the shores of the Lake of Menteith, in such names as *Arnprior* (NS 6194) 'the prior's share', *Arnvicar* (NS 5898) 'the vicar's share' and *Arnclerich* (NS 6099) 'the clerk's share', all of which were associated with the Priory of Inchmahome. Further east, *Arngask* (NO 1310) 'portion of the promontory', *Airntully* (NO 0935) 'portion of the hillock' and *Arnbathie* (NO 1725) 'drowned portion' are good examples of this early Gaelic generic.

Enclosures of one kind or another were common features of Dark-Age settlement. There was frequently a need to protect a farm or hamlet from the depredations of wild animals and many settlements were surrounded by a palisade of timber, a thick hawthorn hedge or, more commonly, a stone dyke. Such enclosures, in Gaelic, were called *gart*, originally *gort*, perhaps derived from a p-Celtic *garth* (Welsh). It is interesting to note that Old Norse *gardr* occurs in Cumbria and Galloway as *garth* and has the same meaning (in examples like *Applegarth* in Dumfries-shire). *Garth*-names in Perthshire include several in Menteith, including *Gartrenich* (NS 5698) 'bracken enclosure', *Gartur* (NS 7692) 'new enclosure', *Gartmore* (NS 5297) 'big enclosure' (from *crion* 'small) and *Gart*, east of Callander. A later development of *Gart* is its diminutive *goirtean* 'little field', Scotticised to -*gorten* or -*gorton*. *Redgorton* NO 0298) 'red field', is one of the few Perthshire occurrences.

A number of habitative names include the word for 'house', which in Gaelic is *tigh* but which is often anglicised to *Ty*-. *Tighmore* (NN 7460) 'big house' in Bohespic, *Tighanloan* 'house on the water-meadow' in Kenmore parish, *Tyndrum* (NN 7244) *tigh an druim* 'house of the ridge' and *Tynreoch* (NN 7123) 'brindled house', west of Comrie are typical of these. Of more historical significance is *Tynayere* in Fortingall (NN 7346), a highly corrupted form of the 16th-century spellings Tunere, Tynnaif, Tennaiffis and Tennaffis (1640). This is from *tigh-neimh*. The -s ending implies two farms, the nearby Duneaves and 'Tigh-neimh Ghearr', meaning 'little or short Duneaves'. The name means 'house of the nemed', an allusion to the historic ecclesiastical site or *nemed* located nearby.

The term *dun* 'fort' is a common element in Perthshire, signifying an early defensive site or a later medieval fortalice in the west of the county. *Dunacree* (NN 8348), *Duntaylor* (NN 8448), *Dunskiag* (NN 8348) in Dull, *Dundavie* (NN 8761) and *Duntanlich* (NO 0424) in Blair Atholl, *Dunard*

(NN 8953) in Logierait, *Duntaggart* (NN 8748) in Aberfeldy, are typical. *Duncrub* (NO 0114) near Dunning may contain the p-Celtic *crup* 'haunch, hump' and was cited by one early writer, Skene, as being close to the battle-site of Mons Graupius.

The medieval period saw the development of small parcels of land in the form of *crofts* (G croit) being a feature of settlement in certain parts of Perthshire, notably the north-west. Names such as *Croftintygan* 'the pine-marten's croft' in Kenmore, *Croftgarbh* (NN 7246) 'rough croft' in Fortingall, *Croftchose* (NN 5330) 'croft of the nook' in Killin, *Croftspardan* (NN 8950) 'rafter croft' in Logierait and *Croftness* (NN 8548) 'croft of the waterfall' in Dull are typical of many such names in the area.

Marq 'merkland' is a fiscal term, describing land ostensibly valued at one merk Scots. These are fairly rare, but *Margbeg* (NN 6736) 'little merk-land' in Kenmore, *Margmore* (NN 8547) 'big merkland' and *Maragdugh* (NN 6959) 'black merkland' in Fortingall are established names, the last-named presumably alluding to the darkness of the soil.

We may now turn to consider settlement names which are formed from terms that relate to the topography. There are many of these, mostly farms and hamlets, although a few have acquired more importance because of some natural feature, such as a ford, becoming a focus for settlement. Typical of these topographic names are those which apply to settlements at the end of a loch. Gaelic *ceann locha* 'head of the loch' is a very com-mon combination, being found in names like *Kinlochrannoch, Kinlochard* and *Kinloch* (NN 8737) at the head of Loch Freuchie in Glen Quaich. The name *Lochearnhead* is simply a translation from Gaelic *Ceann Locha*.

Gaelic contains many terms which denote hills and knolls of various kinds and configurations: basic terms like *tom* 'hillock' in Loch Tay-side, *Tomban* (NN 8265) 'fair hillock' on the Garry near Calvine, *Tomchulan* (NO 0264) 'the whelp's hillock' in Glen Brerachan and *Tonnagrew* (NN 9439) in Strathbraan 'the tree hillock'. The term *tulach* 'hill', 'knoll' occurs frequently as a generic. It is often found in a simplex form as *Tulloch* but can be anglicised to *Tilly-* and *Tully-* and there are many such examples in Perthshire. This term has a wider range than *tom*, being found in Strathearn and the Perth area as well as in the glens. *Tulloch* (NO 0925 and NN 7763) are examples of the simplex form. Others include *Tullichglass* (NN 7238) 'grey knoll' above Ardtalnaig on Loch Tay-side, *Tullichuil* (NT 8047) 'back knoll' near Kenmore, *Tullypowrie* (NN 9154) 'knoll of the pasture-place' in Strathtay, *Tullybelton* (NO 0333), 'the beltane knoll' in Auchtergaven parish and *Tullymurdoch* (NO 1952) 'Murdoch's Knoll', north-west of Alyth. It is also possible for a *tulach* to form the specific, as in *Airntully* (NO 0935) 'the share of the knowe', and *Kintillo* (NO 1317) 'head of the knowe' near Bridge of Earn.

The word for 'ridge' in Gaelic is normally that for 'back' – *druim*, often anglicised to *Drum-*. Again, this can be found in settlement names in a simplex form, such as in *Drum of Cowgask* (NN 9620) in Trinity Gask and *Drum of Garvock* (NO 0316) near Forteviot. Most, however, are compounded and range from simple, topographic descriptions to more complex derivations. *Drumbauchly* (NO 0126) near Methven means 'ridge of the crozier', on land originally occupied by Culdees, as was the nearby *Bachilton* (NO 0023), 'crozier-toun'. *Drumlaken* (NN 8517) 'flagstone ridge' is west of Muthill; *Drumchork* (NN 7719) is 'corn ridge', south of Comrie; *Drumfad* (NN 9109) 'long ridge' is just east of Blackford and *Drumour* (NN 9739) 'dun ridge' is in Strathbraan. Druim is one of the Gaelic terms borrowed into Scots, so its range tends to coincide with the maximum extent of Gaelic spech, since the term is found south of the Forth as far as Midlothian.

The other 'ridge' term, much less common than *druim* is *uachdar*. This is usually anglicised as *Auchter-* and is found in Perthshire, as well as in neighbouring Angus and Fife. *Auchterarder* (NO 9312), is *uachdar ard-thir*, 'ridge of the high land', an unusual combination. *Ochtertyre* (NN 8323), is *uachdar-tir* 'top of the land', west of Crieff.

Other hill terms include *carn* 'cairn', *cnoc* 'hill' (giving Scots knock) *creag* 'rock', which becomes the Scots *craig* and *aird* 'height', 'high place'. These have generated scores of minor place-names in the county. *Gasg* describes a tail of land running out from a plateau and is usually found as *gask*. *Arngask* (NO 1410) is well-named 'portion of the tail', *Findo Gask* (NN 0020) 'Findoca's tail' commemorates St Findoca, described in early sources as 'a virgin who has a church in the diocese of the Dunblane'.

Terms denoting slope and slope quality are common. Gaelic *blar* 'plain' is found in names like *Blair Atholl* 'the plain of Atholl', *Blairgowrie* 'the plain of Gowrie' and scores of others. *Leathad* 'hill-slope' is the generic in *Laidnaskea* (NN 8951) in Logierait and *leac* 'flagstone', 'stone slab' is found in its secondary form *leacann* 'stony slope'. This has produced the unusual *Lix* (NN 5430), actually a pluralised form of *Licks*, originally a compounded version of the three farms, Wester, Mid and Easter, which were written as 'the three Licks' in the 17th century. Antiquarians of the Victorian era erroneously ascribed this name to a lost Roman legion, the 59th, although no such legion ever existed!

With such an extensive coverage of woodland, it is not surprising that the Gaelic terms denoting various kinds of forest are common in the county. *Coille* 'wood' is found usually in the form *Killie-* (not to be confused with *kil-* names for *cille* 'church'.) *Killichonan* (NN 5458) is, in fact, one of these, meaning St Conan's church'. So careful perusal of early forms of the name is essential. *Drumnakyle* (NN 7857) 'ridge of the wood' in Blair

Atholl parish and *Faskally* (NN 9160), 'wood-stance', are typical of instances where the word occurs as a specific. The other term *doire* 'oak-thicket' is found in *Dericambus* (NN 6747) 'thicket of the meander' in Glen Lyon and *Derculich* (NN 8952) in Strathtay.

The great rivers of Perthshire have long attracted settlement on their banks, sometimes beside haughlands formed by alluvial deposits, through which rivers like the Lyon, the Tay and the Isla flow in great meanders. The term *camas*, Scots *camus* or *cambus* is used to describe such situations. *Cambusmichael* (NO 1132) opposite Stanley on the Tay is 'St Michael's meander', *Cambusurich* (NN 5056) is on a bend of the River Ericht and *Camusvrachan* (NN 6147) is on the Lyon, at the confluence of Allt Bhrachain.

One further feature of Gaelic names in Perthshire which deserves attention is the use of endings which mean 'place of' or 'abounding in'. This usually takes the form of *-ach* or *-ich* at the end of a name, the first element of which normally contains a descriptive term. Hence *Grenich* (NN 8060) on Loch Tummel is *grian-ach* 'sunny place', *Frenich* (NN 8258) across the loch is *freumh-aich* 'place of roots'; *Slatich* (NN 6347) in Glen Lyon is *slat-aich* 'place of withies' and nearby *Ruskich* (NN 6447) is from *rusg* 'fleece' or 'skin', giving 'place of fleeces'. Similarly the Gaelic ending *-aidh* has a roughly equivalent role, so that *Clunie* (NO 1044) means 'place of meadows', *Kipney* (NN 9630) in Logie Almond is 'place of tillage-plots', *Campsie* (NO 1233) on the Tay near Stanley is 'place of meanders' and *Tarvie* (NO 0164) in Glen Brerachan is 'place of bulls', from Gaelic *tarbh*. The many *Logies* are simply from *lag* 'hollow', plus this locative ending.

In south and east Perthshire, Gaelic was beginning to decline by about 1250. Although, as we have seen, a number of Gaelic terms were absorbed by Scots, the medieval period saw a rapid expansion of the Germanic language at the expense of the Gaelic. It is not surprising, then, that many of the farms established after 1200, in the Carse, Strathearn, as well as in that part of the county south of Dunkeld and east of the Tay, use Scots onomastic terms. Most of these names are transparent in meaning.

An example of farm-names in Cargill parish gives us a flavour of the material – *Newbigging, Gallowhill, Whitefield, Woodhead, Knowhead, Stobhall, Burnside, Broadgreen, Milestone, Springfield, Nethermill, Newmill, Hatton, Wolfhill*. Almost all of these can be easily understood, as to derivation, to this day. Some people may not be completely certain what a *knowe* looks like and the term *bigging* 'house', 'building' is now obsolete. Similary, *Milestone* may conceal the derivation Miles' ferm-toun from the personal name, rather than from any connection with the more obvious modern meaning. *Hatton* is 'ha toun', indicating the presence of a substantial house or 'hall'. The exception to these Scots names is the name

Strelitz (NO 1837), a settlement established for ex-soldiers who fought in a long forgotten continental war.

This is not to say that Scots terms are absent in the place-names of that part of Perthshire which retained Gaelic as a spoken tongue until the present century. The many *Miltons* and *Newtons* are scattered all over the county and *Kirkton* is a common name for a hamlet which contains the parish kirk, for example on *Loch Tummel* (NN 7958). The coming of new roads and bridges in the 18th century saw new names like *Bridge of Gaur* (NN 5056) at the head of Loch Rannoch, *Bridge of Garry* (NN 9161) and *Gatehouse* (NN 8747) on the Military Road south of Aberfeldy.

With such a variety of terrain and a complex history, Perthshire's place-names can only be treated in a very general way in a short survey of this kind. There is always the temptation to read too much into the derivation of a particular name, or indeed into the mapped distribution of a single element. One has to view these in a much wider context, taking not only the linguistic evidence into account but also the testimony provided by manuscripts and charters, geological and geomorphological evidence and, in particular, the archaeological record. It is only when we have a broad view of all these historical sources that the place-name evidence can be fitted neatly (or roughly, as the case may be) into the whole picture of the past.

We must also remember that place-names are in a continuous process of evolution. With the death of Gaelic in Perthshire, many of the topographic names which appear on current Ordnance Survey maps are no longer being used and serve only as records of a people who used topographic names in great detail when they lived and worked in the land. The thousands of topographic names in the county which form such an important body of historical and linguistic evidence deserve a chapter in their own right, since this survey has dealt only with settlement names. It is also the case that recent urban developments in centres like Perth, Auchterarder, Blairgowrie, Bridge of Earn and many other towns and villages have produced new nomenclature in the form of street-names, many of which reflect the culture of the area rather than names of established historical provenance. Another large body of evidence is present in the form of field-names. These often preserve earlier names and are also important sources of information on the agricultural history.

SEVENTEEN

THE TRAVELLING PEOPLE

Many people know of the existence of the Scottish travelling people only through reports in the press or on television. They are being moved on from often quite ugly and useless pieces of land on which they have been forced to stop but where the very sight of them seems enough to inflame the prejudices of local people. They have recently become confused in the public mind with the so-called New Age Travellers, with whom they have no connection whatsoever. The latter are a new phenomenon and are composed of people who have never been used to living a nomadic life and have no idea how to do so. They are also not the same people as the gypsies who spread across Europe and are to be found south of the Border, although they have mingled with them and in some cases inter-married. Our travelling people did not come from somewhere else but have been here since ancient times.

In Perthshire, the travellers go back a long way and local farmers and landowners make a distinction between those who come from elsewhere and 'oor traivellers' – the Stewarts, Willliamsons, Macphees, Townsleys, Macgregors and Reids, to name but a few of the traveller clans who have traditionally camped and pursued their trades around our glens and straths. To this day there is a more tolerant attitude towards them amongst country folk than amongst town folk.

On our local council, when there was a discussion about setting up a travellers' caravan site in accordance with government guidelines and policy of non-harrassment, very widely differing views were put forward. Some councillors obviously saw travellers as local inhabitants with human rights; others saw them as a problem, a menace and people for whom there was no place in modern society. Many are now settled in towns and some can be hard to distinguish from other town dwellers. Others have more problems settling down, especially as local councils tend to house them in problem areas where they pick up the least desirable connections. Some occupy the travellers' sites at Inveralmond, Carsie, Abernethy, Kinross and Marlee and retain their lifestyle and make their living by turning their hands to almost anything. It is possible to distinguish them by their weatherbeaten look when they come into town to shop for groceries.

When I was teaching in Perth, there were traveller children in many of my classes. This is also true of Blairgowrie, where Belle Stewart went to school and where in her day there was some persecution of travellers by both pupils and teachers. But in my experience there was little of this, at least in the school where I worked and what there was arose from misunderstanding and lack of knowledge about them. On a recent visit to a secondary school in Blairgowrie I was heartened to hear the head English teacher say, 'They're all Blairgowrie bairns to us.'

Those of the older generation still value their traveller heritage but most of those who have been to school and watched TV now do not want to hear about it. Until recently, travellers have tended not to pursue higher education but that is changing too and those who continue at school and go to college do well for themselves. I know of three at college, one doing law, one doing pharmacy and another doing hotel management. At one time that would have been unheard of for a traveller.

You can see travellers on the streets of our towns, hear their quick tongues as they stop for news with friends, see their scrap lorries standing at traffic lights or even come upon them huddled in some neuk of a vennel ceilidhing round a few cans of beer on the day their giro is paid. In a village like the one where I live, there are times of year when there is a succession of knocks on the door from people collecting rags or scrap, offering to sharpen knives, selling paper flowers, mending mats or offering to tarmac the path with material they say is 'left over' from a big job up the road, looking for old jewellery, selling bags of 'fertiliser'or otherwise looking for a living.

But who are these people with Scottish names and what makes them different from the rest of the population? All kinds of romantic legends have been told about their origins and history, most of which are untrue. Even today romantic modern legends have been created that falsify their image and treat them as separate from the rest of the population. Like the legendary progenitors of the clans, the ancestors of the travellers, who were metal workers, have a shadowy past vouched for only in oral tradition. In recording and researching oral tradition, I have learned not to say 'only' in this pejorative fashion, because I have found that it is not as unreliable a means of passing on history as we have been taught to believe. Some of our Perthshire travellers, like the Stewarts of Blairgowrie and Betsy Whyte have become famous for singing and storytelling and Betsy's book *The Yellow on the Broom* has been a bestseller and was adapted for the stage by Ann Downie. The Stewarts have toured the world and been the subject of folklore study since the 1950s.

They do not all have the same ideas about their ancestry, of course. Some of them claim to come from the remnants of the scattered clans after

Culloden but their metal-working skills are older than that. They would hardly have acquired these overnight and certainly not at a time when Highland dress and the weapons and ornaments that went with it were being proscribed. Ross Noble, the Highland Museum curator, believes they were the metal workers of ancient Celtic society. Duncan Campbell of Glenlyon, a writer and journalist who published his memoirs in 1910, said his grandfather remembered the *luchd siubhail* (Gaelic for travelling people) as skilled silversmiths, who made swords and dirks, as well as rings, armlets, brooches and clasps for plaids.

After the Act of Proscription of 1746, they turned more to tinsmithing and making useful articles like flagons, bowls, jugs and kettles as well as horn spoons, baskets and heather besoms, for the 'country hantle' as they called the settled people. Duncan Campbell himself had childhood memories of watching the tinkers at work mending and fashioning such things with their skilful hands in his father's kiln. There are farmers alive today who speak appreciatively of the way the travellers have kept them supplied with tattie creels and reenges (brushes) and how they have shawed their neeps and lifted their tatties and cleared their fields of stones. As far as they are concerned, the travellers have always been part of the landscape.

This brings us to some of the other theories about the travellers' origins. It is very easy to see them as a gypsy poeple, part of the huge horde that migrated across Asia and Europe. A treaty was made by James V (1512–1542) with the 'Lord of Little Egypt', which was how gypsies were regarded in the Middle Ages. Gypsies certainly came to England and crossed the Border but did not spread as far north as Perthshire, perhaps because they found nomadic craftsmen already practising the same trades. I cannot look at the Pictish carved stones, of which there are so many in Perthshire, with their wonderful horses and dogs and monsters, without thinking of the stories told by Perthshire travellers about their own ancestors' lifestyle that was all bound up with the same animals and whose traditional tales featured such creatures (Figure 18). The forebears of travellers who now deal in second-hand cars used to deal in horses, which were a vital necessity to them and, even today, travellers like to have a good dog that can catch rabbits and hares. The stories I recorded from the Stewart family are full of talking animals such as horses, dogs, cats, stags, birds and even frogs. These stories are centuries old and are part of the oral culture on which the majority of the population has turned its back, with its materialism and technology. The oral culture of the travellers is another proof of their ancient lineage.

Hamish Henderson, our greatest living authority on folk tradition, born in Blairgowrie in 1917, has pointed out that the shape of the travelers' bow tent, made by stretching covers over bent hazel wands and securing them

Figure 18

**Perthshire and Kinross Travellers' Sites and some
Pictish Standing Stones**

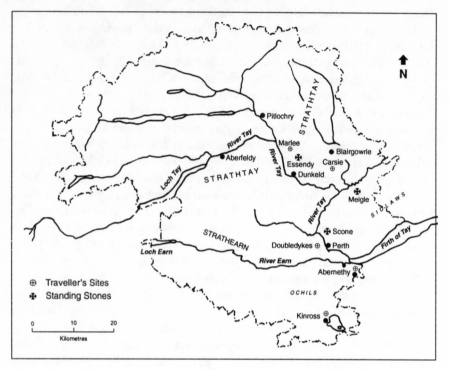

at the base with heavy stones, is typical of the modular structures created in the paleolithic age, when men were hunter gatherers. It seems that the travellers' skills, their way of life and traditions and the design of their dwellings tell us more about their origins than any historical document. It is true that there have been times when the number of people living a nomadic life in Scotland has been swelled by the addition of others forced landless and nameless onto the road by upheavals such as the Jacobite Risings, the Clearances and the Industrial Revolution and, most recently, by unemployment and poverty. Many of these have been solitary wanderers, unlike the traveller family groups, who refer to them as 'blue bucks'. Some of these have married into traveller clans and learned their way of life, while others have struggled and often perished without the wisdom of the travellers to guide them.

Our Perthshire travellers are clearly a Highland people, who still preserve the old clan values of kinship and hospitality. They respect even their farthest removed cousins and attach a very high value to family life, social life and ties of home and community. They really know the meaning of the word *ceilidh* and many of them are gifted pipers, fiddlers, singers and storytellers and have used these skills in making their living. This was why the travelling people played such an important role in the Folk Revival of the 1960s and 70s and won a respected place in Scottish culture. Two of them, Jeannie Robertson and Belle Stewart, were honoured by the Queen for their services to folk music. This began in the family circle, as with Gaelic tradition. The singing style of Perthshire travellers, whole-hearted and full-throated, is undoubtedly a Highland one and their story repertoire is also rooted in their Highland heritage.

When they settle, the travellers may no longer live in extended families but they do tend to live within travelling distance of one another and frequently visit and keep in touch. There is an old saying that 'Travellers are aa sib' meaning they are all related to one another. There have been times when I felt this to be true and any attempt to put down on paper the family tree of any of my traveller friends has run into tremendous difficulties. Even a whole wall cannot encompass it and I think a computer database would be required to take it all in. The generations before the older generation of travellers now living in Perthshire had families of fifteen and sixteen or more, once again echoing the realities of previous times.

There is a great deal of misunderstanding among settled people of what travellers are really like. Like any group of people, you have to get to know them as individuals, mix with them and share their experiences, before you can get a true picture. I have been privileged to learn about them in this way and their friendship is something I treasure and respect. People talk about travellers as dirty, illiterate, lazy and anti-social. As with any group of people, it is impossible to generalise and there are always good and bad people in any commnity. But often what people mistake for dirt is the look people have when they live out of doors and a shabbiness that comes from wearing whatever comes to hand for everyday purposes. When travellers want to 'dress up' they can do it to stunning effect but they don't always choose to do so. People are apt to equate dirt with wickedness and those who see the travellers as 'dirty' usually think of them as wicked too. Jimmy Macgregor, a local retired policeman who has served in several rural stations in Perthshire declares that, in his experience, the travellers are no more or less law-abiding than any other section of the public.

Unlike English gypsies, few Scottish travellers are entirely illiterate, even among the older generation, though many, because of the circumstances of their life, have had minimal schooling. In Perthshire the law has taken an enlightened view of the tinker folk and allowed them to travel from April till October, as long as they put in 200 school attendances between these months. Many people confuse lack of schooling with lack of brain power but I have not found this to be so. Countless generations of travellers have depended on their ability to talk to people to earn their living and most of them are articulate, expressive and extremely quick-witted. I thoroughly enjoy the company of travellers when they are in a mood for swapping news and yarns and repartee; their oral skills are enviable. They also have clever hands. They make or improvise almost anything and they are adept at trading and dealing.

As for being lazy, this conclusion has been reached by people who have seen traveller men apparently just hanging about, unaware that they are actually discussing deals, arranging work and making plans to go to where they can earn a bob or two. A visiting anthropologist once pointed out that when travellers are working, for example lifting tatties in a field or labouring on a road, they are indistinguishable from other workers. On the berryfields or amongst the tatties and neeps, they would work in family groups. Traveller women are usually the ones who go from door to door hawking or gathering 'fichles' (rags). Children become part of the family work team at an early age and spend more time with their parents than most settled children. They are not disciplined by their parents but are quick to catch on to adult ways.

Travellers, as Highland people, are extremely sociable among themselves and will show the same friendliness and kindness to anyone they trust. Living in extended family groups in the past, like the clans, when everything was shared, has led to their not having a highly developed sense of property. The same traveller who will generously give to you, will also take from you if you happen to have something he or she needs. Complaints about anti-social behaviour come from people who see them, forced out of traditional camping places into laybys and derelict areas 'making a mess'. How they themselves would cope in similar conditions, without water or waste facilities, is never considered. Travellers, if they are on the road, have to do in public what settled people have the privilege of doing in private - washing themselves and their clothes, disposing of their rubbish, cooking and cleaning. They would much rather be able to camp or stop where there are trees and bushes, not at a roadside or on a rubbish tip, in places where there is running water and where they are at a distance from other people but near enough the village or town to get to the shops. They like their privacy as well as anyone else.

The site at Inveralmond on the outskirts of Perth is a good situation and, despite the fears and objections expressed by local people (many of whom did not realise that Doubledykes has been a traditional stopping place for travellers for centuries), there have not been problems. At Carsie, the site founded by John Stewart after years of struggling to get permission and funding now excites little comment from its neighbours. It sees families come and go, as well as the core of semi-permanent residents, who send their children to school in Blairgowrie. Sometimes there can be problems when people from families liable to be on bad terms with each other arrive at the same time, although having the site run by travellers has the advantage that such situations can be foreseen and either avoided or controlled. Other Perthshire traveller sites or sites where travellers are welcomed are found at Abernethy, Kinross and Marlee, between Blairgowrie and Dunkeld.

There have been periodic surveys to assess how many travelling people are still on the road in Scotland but such exercises seldom achieve a reliable result. According to their findings there were fewer travellers in Perthshire than my friends knew to be the case and certainly fewer than I would have expected, as compared with other areas. To begin with, travellers, by definition are liable to be on the move, so they could be picked up twice or not picked up at all, in different areas. There are those who travel for part of the year, then settle for the winter. Travellers, many of whom, quite understandably, have a deep distrust of officialdom, are very unlikely to give information to those conducting the survey about members of the family who may not wish to be identified.

But even when it has built a site, a local authority does not always then regard the travellers who stay there as their responsibility, even though they pay rent for their stances to the local housing department. When seven caravans, which had been towed into the field beside Doubledykes to allow for refurbishment of toilet blocks were destroyed by the floods of January 1993, there had to be some serious agitation before the local council felt obliged to compensate the owners. These people, native to our country, who have been compelled by historical change and social upheaval to struggle for survival, and who have survived by their own practical abilities and talents, who have preserved our oral traditions and a Celtic spirituality that transcends modern materialism, deserve some respect and some justice as fellow human beings, as we approach a new millennium.

EIGHTEEN

PERTHSHIRE SCOTS

We hear a great deal about the dialects of Scots and their distinctiveness and up to a point it is true they can easily be told apart. A Buchan speaker is not likely to be confused with a Glaswegian, or a Borderer with an Orcadian. At the same time, although there has not been a standard Scots as the language of public life for three centuries, there does exist a core of Scots that underpins most of the dialects and is understood by most of the indigenous population. Life in the present day with its media influences and a population that moves and mingles freely, is very different from that of the past when people tended to live and work in their own localities and speak their own dialects and regard the way people spoke ten miles away as different. But we have inherited this way of looking at dialects, seeing their differences rather than their similarities. One thing that has struck me in researching the dialect of Perthshire is that, while there are always local words and local turns of phrase, the main dialectal differences lie in pronunciation.

Perthshire at one time would have been Gaelic-speaking and Gaelic is still spoken there. Atholl Gaelic is reputed to be the earliest form of Scots Gaelic. From the 18th century, Gaelic gradually disappeared and, while it is encouraged in the present day and is taught in Perthshire schools, it remains very much a minority language and a second language for those who learn it. According to the late Professor Jack Aitken of the Scottish National Dictionary Association, the form of Scots spoken in Perthshire is also one of the oldest. It has been as vigorous as any other of our dialects and appeared quite as distinctive to my south-west-attuned ear when I came to Perth in 1959. The first points I noticed were the way Perth people would say 'Ir ye riddy?' 'Dinna pu - ye'll brak it' and an idiosyncratic pronunciation of the letter 'h' as 'itch'. In the 1990s it is not so easy as in the 1890s to isolate the characteristics and vocabulary of Perthshire Scots from those of surrounding areas, such as Angus and Fife. The best I can do is to recognise those forms which have survived from the past, when they were looked on as belonging distinctively to Perthshire.

In order to build up a picture of Perthshire Scots I have used four main sources: the work of poets whose work appears in *The Harp of Perthshire*, an anthology edited by Robert Ford in 1893, the books of Sir James Wilson in the early part of this century - particularly the one specifically on Perthshire Scots, the poetry of William Soutar (1898-1943) and the evidence of present day Perthshire Scots speakers whom I have recorded.

The community in which any language or dialect is spoken has social characteristics which influence its use. Since the 18th century the city of Perth itself has been a place in which class distinction has existed. You have only to read George Penny's fascinating book The *Traditions of Perth* to see this. He himself was a weaver when weaving was a respected trade and more on the side of working people than the gentry or the prosperous middle class but, at the same time, he shows enough social pretension to eschew the extreme radicalism of his day (prudent, of course, if you were going into print, as we see from the life of Burns) and writes his book in English, with no concessions whatever to Scots. But he describes 'The Beautiful Order' which was the nickname for the oligarchy of well-to-do families who ruled Perth at the time, as that 'abominable system' by which he thought the city had been ruled for too long.

The surrounding country districts have always been more democratic in outlook and even the Perthshire gentry have had more of the common touch, as exemplified by the different attitude that exists in rural areas to the travelling people or tinkers, who have been around since time immemorial. In my experience, the best Perthshire Scots is found among people who live or grew up in country places and it is in Perth itself that you find a bourgeoisie with the desire to speak English rather than Scots. This is encouraged, for example, by one or two personnel managers of local firms, often themselves non-Scots, who complain because people seeking work use Scots words when they are being interviewed (and presumably do not get appointed). One wonders what the European Court of Human Rights would have to say about that. At least it proves that people, even young people, still speak Scots.

Sir James Wilson (1853-1926), who was educated at Perth Academy and Edinburgh University before going on to Balliol College, Oxford and serving in the Colonial Service in the Punjab, produced several books on Scots dialects, including *Lowland Scotch as spoken in Lower Strathearn*, published in 1950 by Oxford University Press. He uses a form of phonetic transcription that is very useful in conveying the exact pronunciation of the words. Here is an example of it with its equivalent in present day Scots spelling with glossing:

> *Hoo ur yee dhe-day?* Hoo are ye the day?
> *Aa'm brawlay; hoo's yersel?* I'm brawly; (fine) hoo's yersel?
> *Aa cannay cumplen. Aa'v haed a sair hoast. Just a bit glusk ee cauld. Bit noo Aa'm quaaat oa'd.* I canny complain. I've had a sair hoast (cough). Jist a bit glisk (touch of) the cauld. But noo i'mquit o't.

Yee'r az hweit's a dush-clot. Ye've goatun a fell bit shaak.. Ye're as white as a dish cloot. Ye've gotten a fell bit shak (severe shake).

Ach, Aa'm warslin oan. Ach, I'm warslin (struggling) on.

Weel, Aa howp yee'l sin be in yur oardnur. Weel, I hope ye'll sune be in your oardnur (in your usual health).

Being of an earlier generation who were taught language through the medium of grammar, he gives a very full and systematic picture of its parts of speech and their functions. For example, he notes as a preposition the use of 'ee' for 'in the' or 'on the' and as a conjunction 'bunnay' for 'except', which seem to be distinctly Perthshire usages.

Obviously in this book there are many words which have fallen into disuse through historical and social change. We do not have much use nowadays for a *thaak biggin* (thatched cottage) or a *swey* (swinging rod) over a fire for hanging pots. We do not eat *braaxay* (mutton of diseased sheep) or *bair bannuk* (coarse barley cake). You will seldom see anyone wearing a *lum hat* or *huggurz* (stockings without feet) although the latter sound rather like the leg-warmers that were so fashionable a few years ago. *Toadday* is still popular for combating the `flu but I have not managed to get anyone to give me a glass of *cuddul-ma-deeree* (raspberry wine). The latter expression is one of those, of which I have heard several, which have come into Scots from Gaelic and could be related to *cadail* (sleep) and *mo dileas* (my darling). *Cuddle-ma-dearie* was a spiced fruit wine given to children at Hogmanay when the grown-ups were having their drams. I am sure it was designed to make them sleep.

The main differences in pronunciation among dialects involve vowel sounds and Perthshire is no exception. Long 'a' and 'o' vowels as in *baanuk, braaxay, paarish, waatur, toadday, oaven, oarnamints, roabin* are found in other forms of Scots and not just in Perthshire. But the short 'i' sound as in *iggs, riddy, itch* (for letter 'h' and a short 'e' as in *renn* (rain), *gren* (grain) and *chen* (chain) are typical of Perthshire. Robert Ford identified the Perthshire pronunciation of *ui* as *i* in words like *spin* (spoon) and *lim* (loom). Another vowel sound that comes into much Perthshire speech is the indeterminate 'u' sound as in *mulk, churry, hwun* (when), *seelun* (ceiling). I even heard an old cattleman from Perthshire talking about *hulls and dulls* for hills and dales. This 'u' sound also inserts itself between consonants in words like *ingul* (ingle), *castul* and *cuppul*.

The 'ai' sound is common in Scots in words like stane and hame but in Perthshire you'll hear it as well where other dialects have an 'ee' sound, as in *shaif* (sheaf), *baid* (bead), *laid* (lead) and *mail* (meal).

Other vowel sounds were shared with other forms of Scots like the 'oa' of *shoap, boacht* and *coarn;* the 'ai' sound of *hame, gae* and *stane;* the 'ei' sound of *jyne, ile* and *byle;* the 'ow' sound of *fower, growe* and the 'oo' sound of *coo, toon* and *doon.*

As regards consonants, the Perthshire dialect in Sir James Wilson's day shared many of the characteristics of other Scots dialects, like the guttural sounds of 'ch' as in *loch*, the 'g' as in *brig* and the 'k' as in *kirk*. There was also the dropping of the final 'g' in *singin*, the consonant after 'm' or 'n' in *thunner, wunner, rummle* and *brammle*, the final 'l' in *baw, caw, waw* and the 'v' in *loe, deil* and *siller*. This is common to many Scots dialects but Perthshire speakers kept the final 'd' that was usually dropped in words like *haund, laund, warld*. There were also curious usages, like *kwinty* (twenty) and *akween* (atween), which seems to suggest a kind of glottal stop and which I have heard, although the speakers in question were not aware of using it. I am not so sure about one that looks very unfamiliar when it is written down, which is *tnee* (knee) and *tnowe* (knowe). I suspect that this was also an attempt to render something like a glottal stop or semi-glottal stop before the 'n' sound. There are also words in which sounds are transposed, such as *brunt, girss, scart, kittle* and *girsle* but these are not confined to Perthshire.

As regards vocabulary, James Wilson's lists contain many out of date words. Men no longer wear the *bred blue bannut, gravut* or *rauchun* (shepherd's plaid) and one does not see many *brats* (rough aprons) these days. Women have given up wearing *mutches* (linen caps), *huggurs* (stockings without feet) or *gertuns* (garters) and *steys* are largely replaced by girdles and corselettes. There are garments, however, whose style and cut may have changed but for which the names remain the same, such as *sark, breeks, troosers, galluses, goon, peeny, jaiket, pooch*.

Modern kitchens do not feature *dressurs, kirns, girnels* or *saut backuts*. There is no kichen fire over which to see a *cruk* (hook) or a *swey*. The word *hammuk* is recorded as an old kind of dresser. If there is a *beilur* it is of a different kind than the old water boiler for the clothes. *Creepees* and *boax beds* are also things of the past.

But animals and birds, fish, trees and flowers do not change and local names for them are found everywhere in Perthshire. Some of these are mainstream Scots but some are local or have local pronunciation. The poetry of William Soutar gives us a whole list of names for living creatures and growing things. His parents had a country background in the farming community, from where these words undoubtedly came but they lived in a fine new semi-detached house in a residential area of the town, kept a servant lass and considered themselves of good social standing. John Soutar was a partner in a craftsman joiners' business, liked poetry and song and, with his wife, was a devout churchgoer. William was educated at Perth Academy and Edinburgh University which resulted in his feeling that his right nostril was Scots and his left nostril English. He gave a good deal of thought to this dilemma and an example of his poetry on the subject also illustrates his use of Perthshire Scots:

THE MAKAR

Nae man wha loves the lawland tongue
but warsles wi' the thocht
there are mair sangs that bide unsung
nor a' that hae been wrocht.

Ablow the wastrey o the years,
the thorter o' himsel
deep buried in his bluid he hears
a music that is leal.

And wi' this lealness gangs his ain
an there's nae ither gait
though a' his feres were fremmit men
wha cry: *Owre late, owre late.*

Among the words Soutar uses in his poetry are many which would be used locally, in the country if not in the town, including *bawkie bird* (bat), *clocker* (beetle), *flech* (flea), *fuggie-todler* (small yellow bee), *gollacher* (earwig), *gowk* (cuckoo), *grumphie* (pig), *happer* (grasshopper), *hurchin* (hedgehog), *kay* (jackdaw), *lowrie-tod* (fox), *mauch* (maggot), *mavie* (song thrush), *merle* (backbird), *mowdie* (mole), *nowt* (oxen, cattle), *paitrick* (partridge), *peesie* (plover), *puddle-doo, puddock* (frog), *roden tree* (rowan, mountain ash), *rottan* (rat), *sauch* (willow), *segg* (rush), *speugie* (sparrow), *stirrie* (starling), *taed* (toad), *whutterick* (willow), *yorlin* (yellow-hammer).

The sounds animals make include *bowf* (bark), *chark* (grate), *chirm* (chirp), *chunner* (murmur), *clapper* (rattle), *croodle* (coo), *drool* (trill), *frunsh* (whine), *ganch* (snarl), *glowk* (caw – of crows over carrion), *jabber* (gabble), *nicher* (neigh), *pleep* (chirp), *rowt* (roar), *runch* (crunch, grind teeth), *skelloch* (screech), *wheep* (whistle, squeak), *wheeple* (whistle), *yalloch* (shout), *yowp* (cry), *yowt* (howl, bellow).

There are other expressive words for sounds and movements of the weather such as *blowf, blowther* and *bluffert* for gusts and blasts of wind and rain. Robert Nicoll (1814-1837) uses the words *blad* and *bladdin* when writing about a wind sharp enough to strip the leaves off the trees. The Alyth poet John Smith describes the wind in 'The Windygowl' as:

Sabbin an skirlin
Twinin an twirlin
Dingin doon a'thing to get free.

Ae mament o hush
Syne on wi a rush
Daddin, bladdin windock an door.
The sough or the yell
O breeze or o gale
Blaws owre Windygowl evermore.

Soutar uses *birl* and *birze* for spin or hurry and push or press, as well as *breeshle* and *breenge* for come on in a hurry and rush impetuously. He would *chap* at a door or *chitter* with the cold, *ding* down an adversary or *dunch* him with his head or his fist. He would *fluther* or *fudder* if he was in a hurry and *gallivant* here and there through the country. As a boy he must have *grammelt* up trees, or *heezed* up a friend to reach the top of a wall. If he fell he might *birse* his knee and that would make him *hirple* or *hochle* or even *shauchle*. Walking with a friend they might *link owre the lea* (walk arm in arm over the field) but on his own he might *lamp* along with big strides. Many Perth people still use *jamp* for jumped, otherwise they would say *lowped*. Leaves on a birken tree would *reemle* and *reeshle* in a gentle breeze while a dog would *rug* and *runch* at a stick held in its owner's hand. You would *shog* a branch to shake an apple down, then *smool* away before anyone saw you. An old woman would *stech* and *stotter* up a steep hill but a young lad would *speel* up easily and *sprauchle* on the grass when he got to the top. If you *traiked* through a tattie field you could *thraw* your ankle on the *haulms*. I once saw a bairn *wamble* across a bank and *whummle owre* into the water, where he *wamphled* until his brother pulled him out with a scarf *wuppit* round a stick.

In wet or *dreepin* weather, you would get *drookit* (soaked) and your feet might be in the *dubs* (puddles). Snow might come in *floichans* or *flauchts* (flakes) that *flichter* and *flowff* (flutter) in the air. If the summer is good, you might *beik forenent the sin* (dry in the sun) like the bones of Bessie Bell and Mary Gray in the Perthshire ballad:

> Bessie Bell and Mary Gray
> They were twa bonnie lasses.
> They biggit a bour on yon burn brae
> An theekit it owre wi rashes.

The water in a burn in spate *fraiths owre a linn* (froths over a waterfall), while that on a quiet lochan *lippers and lappers* (ripples). You can send a *chuckie-stane skimmerin owre* (pebble skimming over) its surface.

When it comes to idioms and phrases, Perthshire is as rich as any other part of Scotland, although in this, too, it shares in a common heritage and sometimes it is only the pronunciation that differs from other parts of Scotland. I have identified a few that present day speakers still use. '*Wha's aucht thae buits?*' could still mean 'Who do these boots belong to?' Tinkers are still '*gaun-aboot bodies*' or '*gaun aboot fowk*'. Someone receiving a dram might still say to his host '*Caw canny wi the waater.*' It could be said of someone whose nickname or shortened name was always used '*He aye goat Jimmy*'. At four o'clock in the afternoon when the children run out of the playground you still hear, '*The schuil's skellin*'. If someone is ill and does not manage to visit a friend as promised, they still say,

'I couldnae git – the flu garred me gae tae ma bed.' Those delayed on the road on the way to a concert might say, *'We're owre late. We'll no can git in.'* Trying unsuccessfully to speak to someone surrounded by a large number of people, you might say later, *'I couldnae git spoken til him.'* A local lad once said to a teacher, *'Dinna be dour wi ma girl-friend,'* meaning that she should be nicer to her in class. The answer he got was *'If she's no dour wi me I'll no be dour wi her.'* An example of new usage of old words can be overheard in the supermarket, from someone searching for a particular commodity, *'I doot it's doon the neist dreel.'* A dreel is a row or drill in a field of tatties or neeps. Other expressions that are current today include *'tuim's a whustle'* (empty), *'smilin like a biled tottie'* (smiling broadly), *'A ken yer meanin by yer mumpin'* (I understand you are annoyed), *'A rowin stane gaithers nae fugg'* (a rolling stone gathers no moss), *'aa hechts an howes'* (all ups and downs), *'he stappit it aneth his oxter'* (he puts it under his armpit), *'a gangan fit's aye gittin'* (a going foot is always gaining), *'The pruif o the pudden' the preein o't'* (the proof of the pudding is in the eating), *'Aw thing hiz an end an a pudden haes twa'* (everything has an end and a pudding has two), *'The keeng may come i the cadger's gait'* (fortunes can change), *'guid gair's little bookit'* (quality can be found in small size), *'She hadnae a sark tull her back'* (she had not a shirt to her back).

Among the Perthshire speakers I have recorded is the late Jock Lundie, a ploughman all his working life, expert in handling horses and a tireless worker for better conditions for farmworkers, who retired and lived in Auchtermuchty. A fine traditional singer, he also had a good Perthshire tongue in his head. Here is a sample of his speech in an anecdote taken from a tape of his life story that appeared in *The Sang's the Thing*:

> A wanted awa tae the market, Blairgowrie market, the feein market. The farmer's wife cam oot an she said tae me, 'He says if ye get the trochs filled by dennertime, ye can get awa tae the market.' So the market day came an the pit we were on was finished an A went hame for ma denner an come back. A carried aw thae trochs masel tae feed the sheep. A struck the earth an aa thing aff the pit an gied him a haund wi the cutter. An A says, 'Noo Donald ye can dae onything ye like. A'm gaun awa tae the market.' A wis gettin three shillins a day, an when A got ma pey on the Setterday, there was one an six for aw the time A wis off at the market - taken off! Yes!

The late Willie Barclay was a cattleman whose story I recorded near the end of his life in Catmoor House in Scone. He was nearly blind, very deaf and in a wheelchair, but just sparking with life and fun:

> Aa've been aroon Perth aa ma days. Aa wis brocht up wi a step-auntie. Ma faither wis kilt in the First World War and the auld wife gane aff her heid and Aa'd nobody. But the Auntie *made* me. She had a dairy, ye see. Mony a nicht Aa gret for ma mither.

When Aa was up in Dunkeld there and auld Mrs Roberts was livin, there wus pipes an aathing, ye ken. Aa the sheep men wud be there and there was tummlers o whusky sittin at ivery coarner o the place. It wus only nine boab a boattle at that time! Aa've seen us at five o'cloack in the moarnin, an some richt sangs tae – an the pipe boy wi his pipes.

Another Perthshire speaker I have recorded is the late Belle Stewart of Blairgowrie, the world famous folk singer, who might modify her Scots when speaking to people from elsewhere but spoke with her Perthshire voice to me. Many of the words she thought were travellers' cant were in fact old Scots words, like *lerroch tree* for larch and *arn tree* for alder:

I wus born at a place, a stretch caaed Stenton, on the river Tay at Caputh on 18th July 1906. I wus born in a wee, wee, bow tent, the auldest-fashioned thing a tinker kin build. Ma father wus pearl-fishin at the time. I wus registered at aboot eleven o'clock in the mornin, same day I wus born. Ma father walkit fae Caputh an he went an registered me an he come back tae the camp an ma mither got up when I wus aboot fower or five oors auld; she got up an walkit wi him tae the minister. I wus baptised in that kirk because long ago, ye got a guid piece at the minister's or a hauf-croon.

NINETEEN
TALES AND LEGENDS

To get a true perspective on the tales and legends told in Perthshire, one has first to understand an important fact about story tradition. This is that it is a universal feature of human culture, not just a local phenomenon. There are many books of tales in existence that contain only local legends, historical tales and ghost stories attached to places or people in a particular area. It is true that every locality has these stories, but these are only three of the categories of folk tale that exist. There are also, for example, myths and wonder tales, which are universal and international but which crop up in different countries or different regions that reflect the life and culture in whose context they are found. This is particularly true of Perthshire, which is rich in both Highland and Lowland tradition and where stories and storytellers of a quality second to none have come to light.

Nowadays, storytelling is thought of as something to amuse children but in the past, before there were schools, churches, books, theatre, television and all the other modern sources of wisdom, culture and entertainment, there was storytelling, which fulfilled the functions of recording, teaching, artistic creation, counselling, guidance, entertainment and therapy. Storytellers had an honoured place in society and told stories for the whole community, old and young, who normally listened in mixed groups, not divided up according to age, as happens nowadays, if it happens at all.

The travelling people, pre-eminent among which are the Perthshire ones, who have done so much to preserve our oral traditions of song and story, place enormous value on stories not just because they are enjoyable to listen to but because they pass on wisdom. They say, 'These stories were our education.' In other words, they went to school for basic skills in reading, writing and counting but they turned to their story heritage for insight into how to cope with life's problems, how to live in harmony with nature and how to handle their own hopes and fears, emotions and dreams. These were the functions of storytelling that helped to strengthen ties of kinship and community, reinforce traditional values and attitudes and guide people along the path of life. Some of the great religious teachers of the world, like Jesus or Mohammed, have used stories to enlighten people about spiritual truths that are difficult to grasp in abstract terms. Any good teacher or entertainer, anyone trying to pass on a worthwhile message knows that if they do it through the medium of a story, people will listen to it.

That does not mean that storytelling is just a form of preaching. Obviously people want to enjoy stories, have a good laugh or a good greet, experience fear in a safe situation, solve mysteries or work out tricky answers. The repertoire of the Perthshire storytellers I have recorded affords all of these opportunities. They have excellent versions of international wonder tales that are very ancient, a great number of supernatural tales, some of types common in Celtic tradition, some international, some local, concerning ghosts, witches, haunted places, changelings and brownies and other tale types, such as parables, animal fables and body-snatcher stories. Historical legends are found in the ballads they sing. From other storytellers, you will hear stories attached to castles and other places that have stood for centuries and seen all kinds of events and tales of clan history, hero tales and accounts of feuds, massacres and great feats of strength and courage.

Stories and legends can also be found in books like *The Fair Lands of Gowrie* by Lawrence Melville, (Culross Press) and *Perthshire in History and Legend* by Archie McKerracher, (John Donald). In the work of Rennie McOwan much can be gleaned of the lore and legend of Perthshire, such as the Beltane Rites on Ben Ledi. George Penny's *Traditions of Perth* (Culross Press) is a wonderful source of anecdote that illuminates life in the past, while *The King o the Black Art* (Aberdeen University Press) is my collection of the story repertoire of the Stewart family, recorded in the course of a project to study its historical, psychological and aesthetic context. This collection was considered by Professor Stuart Sanderson to be 'one of the two most important made in Britain this century'. Other versions of their stories will also be found in *Till Doomsday in the Afternoon* by Ewan MacColl and Peggy Seeger (Manchester University Press). Betsy Whyte's *Yellow on the Broom* (Chambers) is primarily an account of her childhood in Perthshire but it is also threaded through with tale and legend. For example, Cameron Cameron, the eccentric Perthshire laird who figures in the book was, according to Betsy herself, 'based on a character in stories my mother used to tell'.

Stories can change and migrate and be adapted to new times, as has been the case with a story which I heard from Belle Stewart as *The Shearer of Glenshee*. This is how I tell it:

> Long, long ago, one bitter winter's night, the snow was falling in Glenshee –
> the Glen of the Fairies – and a poor tramp man was struggling upwards through
> what the climbers and skiers of today would call 'white out conditions'. The folk
> of the glen would have called it 'blin drift'. He couldn't see an inch in front of

him. He knew if he didn't get shelter he'd die of the cold. Then he caught just a glimpse of a wee peep of light ahead of him and he made for it as hard as he could. To his great relief he found himself at the door of a farmhouse and he knocked on it.

At last the door opened and a face looked out upon him, a face full of shock and surprise that anyone should be on the road on such a night. 'Let me in,' the tramp begged, 'or I'll dee.'

'Come awa ben,' said the farmer, helping him to the ingle neuk. 'My God, what are ye daein oot on a nicht like this?'

'I'm a man o the road,' the tramp told him. 'I'm used wi aa weathers, but this is the warst I've seen.'

'Weel, ye'd better stay here till the storm lifts,' said the farmer. He gave the man a blanket to cover himself while his clothes dried and offered him a bowl of brose. He was quite glad to have some company for he lived alone and when he found that the tramp was a decent man, though dressed in rags, he sat and cracked with him for an hour or so. But then he said, 'Noo, I hae tae get my sleep, for I'm an early riser. You can bed by the fire. Dae ye smoke?'

'Na, na,' said the tramp man.

'That's guid, because I wadna want ye tae set the place alicht pittin a spunk tae your pipe.'

'I'll no dae that,' said the tramp man.

Next morning both the farmer and the tramp were up early but when they looked out the window, the snow was still falling as thick as ever. 'Ye'll no get awa yet,' said the farmer. He had his beasts safely in the byre, so he asked the tramp to help him milk them and give them their feed. Then the tramp man kindled the fire while the farmer made some brose and they sat down by the fireside to eat it. It was another two days before the storm lifted and by that time, the farmer and the tramp man were just about friends.

'Weel, I'll be gaun noo,' said the tramp. 'Thank ye for aa your kindness tae me. I dinna aye meet fowk like you.'

'I'll tell ye what,' said the farmer. 'We've had guid crack thegither these three days. Will ye no stay on for bit? I could dae wi some help here aboot the place. I'm no as young as I used tae be.'

The tramp man was tempted. Farm work was something he was used to and it was in the open air. The farmer was a good man.

'There's a wee bothy oot the back, whaur a shepherd used tae bide. I could sort it for you,' the farmer said.

'Aa richt,' said the tramp. 'I'll maybe bide a season wi ye.'

So he became the farmer's right hand man and he turned out to be a really good worker. Every morning he was up early to help with the milking and he'd see to the sheep and the hens as well. The farmer was very glad he'd asked the man to stay, even though he'd said it was just for a while. But the man enjoyed his work and he liked having his wee bothy to himself.

Then it came to the time of the year when they sheared the sheep. What would happen was that the men from Glenisla would come over and help the Glenshee men shear their sheep, then the Glenshee men would go over to Glenisla and do the same. But that was one job the man of the road had never done before. 'I'll dae ma best,' he told the farmer, 'but I ken it's a skilled job and I'll maybe no be ony guid at it.'

'Jist watch the ither men,' the farmer told him, 'and then try yersel.'

So the man did just that and at first he wasn't very good but after a while, he seemed to pick it up and he just got better and better. In fact, he became so good that the others stopped to watch him. He could shear three sheep in the time it took them to do one. So he became known as the Shearer of Glenshee. He was famous in the two glens for his skill with the shears. This went on for a number of years and the Shearer just seemed to get more and more skilful. The men of the two glens really admired him and he lived well on the farm with the old farmer.

Then one day the farmer rose and didn't see the Shearer about as usual. He went to look for him and found him lying on his bed with a raging fever and a cough that tore at his chest. 'I seem tae have caught a wee cold,' was all he said. But the farmer got his horse out and rode all the way down to Blairgowrie to get the doctor, so worried was he about his old friend.

When the doctor came, he looked at the man, sounded his chest and felt his pulse but he shook his head. In those days, they didn't have the medicines they have today and the Shearer had double pneumonia. 'All you can do is keep him warm and feed him a little broth,' said the doctor. 'I'm afraid there's nothing I can do.' The farmer was inconsolable. He nursed the Shearer as well as he could but after three days, he died.

Word went round the two glens like lightning, for news always travels fast in country places. The men of Glenisla came over to join the men of Glenshee, to wake the corpse for three days and nights as was the custom. During that time, there was a lot of eating and drinking and piping and storytelling and at the end of it, there was the burial. The Shearer's coffin was to be carried over the rough hillside to the auld kirk yard. Now, by this time, they'd all had a fair few drams of whisky and as everyone knows, that's when folk can get very argumentative.

What happened then was that a big disagreement got up about where the Shearer should be buried. The Glenshee men said, 'He was the Shearer of Glenshee, so of course he'll be buried in Glenshee.' The Glenisla men said, 'He sheared in Glenisla as much as he sheared in Glenshee, so we want to bury him in Glenisla.' Well, of course, that kind of argument can only lead to one thing: first they shouted at each other, then one man hit another, who hit him back and, in no time at all, they were all hammering the living daylights out of one another, while the coffin stood forgotten among the bracken.

Then there was one almighty roll of thunder and everything went black. The men of the two glens fell to their knees in terror. Fighting at a funeral! No wonder God was angry with them. They all started saying their prayers as hard as they could. Then gradually the darkness melted away and the daylight returned. They stood up and looked around them shamefacedly. And there in the bracken sat not one coffin but two! So the men of Glenisla took one and buried it in Glenisla and the men of Glenshee took the other and buried it in Glenshee. To this day, no one really knows where the Shearer of Glenshee is buried.

Belle got this story from her mother, who heard it from the people of the glen on her hawking trips but I found a reference to an older version of the story in *Historic Scenes of Perthshire* by Thomas Marshall, in which the same account is given of the burial of St Fillan.

There are many legends of William Wallace which have a Perthshire connection, notably the one about his sojourn with his uncle Archie Crawford at Kilspindie, when he slew the son of the English Governor who insulted him in the street in Dundee and hid in a house disguised as a spinning woman, till he could make his escape up the Carse after dark. He also tricked his way through the gates of Perth by giving his name as Will Malcolmson (not a lie) to spy on the garrison and returned to visit a girl, who was forced into betraying him, though once again he got away in female attire, killing several guards as he did so. He also had a terrifying experience at old Gascon Hall, forerunner of the House of Gask, when the headless ghost of a traitor he had slain came to haunt him. There is another legend, that gave rise to the ballad Gude Wallace, which recounts how in the guise of an old man, Wallace discovered the whereabouts of the English soldiers who were hunting him. He got into the house and slew several of them before making his getaway. All these stories and others can be read in Blin Hary's *Wallas* of which there are several modern translations.

The Fair Lands of Gowrie harks back to the old legend of the Roman legionaries first seeing the Tay and exclaiming 'Behold the Tiber!' with Sir Walter Scott's riposte that no Scot would ever 'hail the puny Tiber for the Tay.' It also has the story of the witch of Collace, who gave her mutch to her giant son to use as a sling to cast stones to stop the building of pre-Reformation St John's Kirk in Perth. The cap strings broke when he was firing the missiles, which fell to the ground at Boglebee near Dunsinane Hill, where they lie to this day. Lawrence Melville also tells how a husbandman called Hay was given land and the title of the Earl of Errol by Kenneth Macalpine for helping him against the Danes. Later on there was the legend of the Earl of Errol's childless marriage to Kate Carnegie for which she scorned him. He retaliated by begetting a child by a milkmaid, who was kept under surveillance until she had given birth. The story survives in a ballad.

Archie McKerracher's book is a treasure house of tales of every kind from the legend of Pontius Pilate being born in Fortingall to the account of the massacre of the Macneishes by the Macnabs in the 16th century, the Curse of the Breadalbanes, stories of Rob Roy Macgregor, legends of fairy hills and healing wells, the minister at Balquhidder who disappeared to fairyland and the prophecies of the Lady of Lawers.

One of the most entertaining stories in the book is that of the ghost of Meggernie Castle, who appears in a haunted tower bedroom and tries to kiss whoever is sleeping in the bed. The strangest detail of this ghost is that she is just the top half of the corpse of a lady of the castle who was savagely murdered and cut in two by her husband and hidden in a chest buried in a wall of the tower. He went abroad for a while then returned to bury her but had only buried one half of her when he was discovered and slain.

This is only one of the countless ghost stories told about every historic building or locality in Perthshire, where the Celtic belief in the supernatural is not yet dead. Even today I have met people who have a story to tell about an uncanny experience they have had or an apparition they have seen, in a haunted house or even on the streets of Perth itself. One man told me he had met the ghost of his dead sister in South Street in Perth. I was also told of a haunted bakery, a haunted schoolhouse and an old granary, now a restaurant, where a black-robed monk has been seen.

This leads appropriately to consideration of another aspect of our local tradition: its Gaelic roots. 'The Three Dogs', found in Iain Og an Ile's *Popular Tales of the West Highlands* as 'Tri Coin nan Srang Uaine', concerns three magical hounds called Swift, Knowall and Able, got one by one in exchange from a stranger for three cows, which a poor boy is sent to market to sell by either his sister or his mother. He is punished for what they see as his foolishness but in fact the dogs are worth more than money to their owner because they catch game for the pot and eventually save his life. When he goes out to push his fortune, he marries a rich woman and moves into a big house, which causes him to neglect his dogs who almost die but he realises his folly and seeks for them and finds them again. In one of the versions of the story I found the dogs turn out to be the boy's long-lost brothers. The meaning of the story is clearly seen, when you consider that speed, knowledge and strength are the very qualities needed to survive in the natural world. This story is found in European tradition as the first part of a story called ' The Dragonslayer' and is also related to one called 'The Faithless Sister.' Its relevance to the living conditions of the past is indisputable, while its meaning for us today reinforces the 'green' initiatives that argue the importance of living in harmony with the natural world.

Other stories, told by the Stewarts, which are rooted in Gaelic tradition, include 'The Shepherd and the Wee Woman' in which a young herd has an encounter with a supernatural being related to the *bean nighe* or little washerwoman. If the washerwoman is seen by men going into battle at a ford, washing blood-stained shirts, that is an omen of defeat and death. In the story, the wee woman steals the herd's muffler, which causes him to fade and dwine and when he returns to recover it, he tries to hit the wee woman with his stick. As a result of this he has to fight her every night for a year and a day, the snag being that, every time, she turns into a man of towering strength who beats him black and blue. That is to teach him 'not to hit everything you meet on the road', which is a good lesson for travellers.

The Stewarts also tell a story they call 'Me Masel' or *Mise Mo Fhein*. This is about a brownie at the mill at Fincastle, who plays nasty tricks on the family, who seek revenge and when asked by his mother who has injured him,says Me Masel, which is the name he has been told by his assailant. As well as existing in Gaelic tradition, it is also linked to the tale of blind Polyphemus in Greek legend, when Ulysses calls himself Noman and the giant cries 'Noman hath hurt me'. This is a good illustration of a folk tale motif that can be found in many different times and places. How this comes about is a fascinating mystery but it is a clear indicator of the immense power and resilience of oral tradition.

A popular type of story which is very widespread is the kind in which someone has to answer riddles or answer what seems to be impossible questions. The story called 'The King and the Miller', a version of 'The King's Questions' is an example of this. The miller has to tell the king how many stars are in the sky, what is the weight of the moon and what he is thinking at that moment. The questions are answered by what we now call lateral thinking. 'The Lord's Prayer' is an anti-clerical tale of how a tramp tricked a minister into buying him a new pair of boots and the minister tricked the soutar into paying half the cost of the boots, the reason being on both occasions that the opening words of the Lord's Prayer mean all men are brothers, therefore bound to help one another. The basis of the joke lies in the way it plays on the Highland sense of kinship.

Changeling stories are a feature of European tradition and are found in both Gaelic and Scots tradition. 'Johnny in the Cradle' is the version I recorded in Perthshire:

> A travelling tailor finds a couple who have a baby who never stops crying. He offers to watch the child while they go to church. While they are away, the baby gets out of the cradle, plays the bagpipes and pours whisky for the tailor and himself. When the parents return, the tailor tells them out of earshot of the cradle how to get rid of the changeling and get their own baby back again, by lighting a big fire and putting the baby on a shovelful of dung on top of the fire. It flies up the chimney shrieking curses and their own son knocks on the door.

Bodysnatcher stories were once widely told when, after the Burke and Hare case in 1828, graves all over Scotland were watched for weeks after a burial and heavy iron mortsafes were put on to keep them from being raided. Sometimes quicklime was put in the coffin to rot the corpse quickly before it could be raised. Duncan Campbell of Glenlyon, born in 1830, who became a celebrated writer, remembers in his childhood how a man with a gun would sit every night for three weeks after a funeral in the grave-watcher's house whose key was kept by his father. He said he heard 'resurrectionist stories that frightened me a good deal more than the usual run of ghost stories'. The travellers felt particularly vulnerable to the Burkers, as they called them and still make a ritual of telling these stories, as an expression of their fear of outsiders. Burker stories among the travellers usually follow a pattern. First, a situation is created in which people are encamped in a lonely spot, or are given shelter on a farm where the farmer is in league with 'the doctors' or 'noddies' as the Burkers are identified. Then they are attacked and escape only by the skin of their teeth. This allows the storyteller to help his listeners to bring out and face and live through their inner fears and thus overcome them. This shows one of the therapeutic uses of storytelling and the acute psychological insight which the travellers have preserved in an intuitive way. Burker stories are also found in George Penny's *Traditions of Perth* but are told rather for their horrific, or sometimes humorous effect:

> The resurrectionists having placed it [the corpse] as they imagined beyond danger, left it doubled up on a barrow, under a covering at the side of the wall of Gowrie House and adjourned to a notorious house at the foot of South Street. Their motions however had been observed by some boatmen who had just come up with the tide. They removed the body and one of their number assumed its place. The violators of the grave having screwed up their courage by a hearty refreshment were proceeding with the barrow when one inquired if they would take up the South Street. The boatman, beginning not altogether to relish his new position, at once got rid both of them and the difficulty, by roaring out, 'No, by God! You'd better take the Watergate!'

In *The Story of Glenisla*, by David Grewar, published in 1926, there is an ancient legend of a clan chief called John Grant, nicknamed the *Cam Ruadh*, who conforms to an archetypal figure in Celtic folklore, of a small, deformed and incredibly ugly man who nevertheless is extremely attractive to women, who can travel over the ground at superhuman speed and who performs great feats of courage and bravery. This kind of story has a background in Celtic mythology and lore of its gods, but what also strikes me is its affinities with the exploits of Rob Roy Macgregor, which are well documented. There was also a forebear of Rob Roy called Patrick Macgregor, nicknamed Gille Ruadh, who was hanged as a cattle thief in 1626 and who gave rise to the ballad 'Gilderoy', which is in the *Orpheus Caledonius*. Another historical story that has a ballad attached to it is that of the burning of Airlie Castle in the 17th century, by the Argyle Campbells.

Another potent local legend is that of the Stone of Destiny, on which the old Kings of Scots were crowned at Scone, which was reputed to have come over from Egypt through Spain and Ireland and which Edward I thought he had taken from Scone Abbey in 1296. The local belief is that Edward was fobbed off with a fake and the real stone is buried somewhere near Dunsinane Hill above the village. The original stone was supposed to have been black basalt with carvings on it and the one that was kept in Westminster Abbey was a lump of Perthshire sandstone. The Stone was meant to have been returned to Scotland by the Treaty of Northampton in 1328 but it wasn't. In 1950 three Scottish patriots recovered the Stone and the story is that the one that went back down to Westminster Abbey was not the same one that came up. So the legend goes on.

Undoubtedly the finest stories to be found in Perthshire are the versions of the international wonder tales I recorded from the Stewarts. These are stories which have a reference number in the international tale-type index built up by Antti Aarne, a Finnish folklorist and Stith Thompson, an American folklore professor. The title story of the book *The King o the Black Art*, (AT 325) versions of which exist in every country of Europe and is also found in Iain Og an Ile's collection as *Fichaire na Gobha* and *Gille na Bhuidhsear* and is even connected with traditions of Asia, will serve as a good example. There is only room for a summary of it here:

A foundling, washed ashore, is reared by a poor fisherman and his wife as their own son. When he is in his teens a ship appears with a king-like figure in it who comes ashore and offers to take the boy and make him into a great magician. The parents agree and the boy goes away with the king for a year and a day. When he returns, he can do magic. The king offers a second and third time and each time the boy goes away, he returns an even greater magician. The third time he does not return and the father sets out to find him.

The father journeys through three great forests and is guided by three wise old men, till he reaches the castle of the King o the Black Art. There he carries out the instructions given to him by the wise old men, which are to knock boldly at the door, demand his son back and when the king throws twelve pigeons into the air, pick out the worst looking one. Thus he gets his son back and they set out for home.

On the way they stop at villages where there are fairs and the boy turns himself into a fine horse or dog which his father sells at the fair to the highest bidder, who is the King in disguise but he holds onto the halter each time. The boy is able to escape twice but the third time the King makes the father drunk and tricks him into letting him have the halter so the boy is recaptured.

In the King's stable, the boy prevails upon the groom to let him drink from a stream behind the castle and he shakes his head free of the halter and swims downstream as a salmon. The King turns into an otter and pursues him, so the boy becomes a swallow high in the air. The King appears as a hawk, so the boy becomes a ring on the finger of a lady sitting in a garden. He warns her not to part with him but rather to cast him into the fire. The King comes as a dealer offering to buy the ring but she casts it into the fire, so the King becomes a pair of bellows and blows the fire to make it burn fast. The ring becomes a grain of corn in the henrun so the King becomes a cockerel pecking the corn. The boy turns into a fox and bites its head off. He then rejoins his father and they return home.

This story is clearly very ancient, going back to pre-Christian, Druidic days of magician-kings. It reinforces kinship ties but also the shape-shifting, transformation chase through the four elements and the forms of life found in them and emphasises the importance of adaptability in the struggle for survival. Above all, it shows that every human being has the potential to develop as an individual and overcome difficulties. I have been struck by the way in which the characters in the wonder tales correspond to Carl Jung's archetypes of the unconscious, which adds weight to the idea that these stories function at different levels, to entertain, educate and provide imaginative insight into human problems. Seen in this light it can be better understood why our ancestors valued story tradition so highly and how we can benefit from taking a deeper interest in it. It is a priceless part of our Perthshire heritage.

Bibliography

AIREY, G.B., 1873. 'The Topography of Lady of the Lake in Black's Guide Trossachs., A. & C. Black.

ANDERSON, J.G.C., 1984. *Field Geology in the British Isles*, Pergamon Press, Oxford.

APTED, M.R., 1966. *The Painted Ceilings of Scotland 1550–1650*, HMSO Edinburgh.

ARMSTRONG, M., PATERSON, I.B. and BROWNE, M.A.E., 1985. 'Geology of the Perth and Dundee District', *Memoir of the British Geological Survey*, HMSO, London.

ATKINSON, T., 1821. *Three Nights in Perthshire*, Creag Darach (1994).

BADDELEY, M.J.B., 1890–98. *Thorough Guides to Scotland*, T. Nelson & Sons, London.

BAINBRIDGE, J. 1980. 'Lord Breadalbane's mines', *The Scots Magazine*, 114, 38–45, Dundee.

BARNARD, A., 1887. *The Whisky Distilleries of the United Kingdom*, David and Charles reprint, Newton Abbot, Devon.

BARROW, G.W.S., 1973. *The Kingdom of the Scots*, London.

BARTY, A.B., 1994. *The History of Dunblane*, Stirling.

BEAUCHAMP, E., 1978. *The Braes of Balquhidder*, Heatherbank Press, Glasgow.

BEVERIDGE, E., 1923. *The Abers and Invers of Scotland*, Edinburgh.

BIL, A., 1922. 'Transhumance Place-Names in Perthshire', *PSAS*, 122.

BLACK, A.R. and ANDERSON, J.L., 1994. 'The great Tay flood of January 1993', *1993 Yearbook, Hydrological Data, UK Series*, Institute of Hydrology, 25–34.

BLACK'S GUIDES 1853–1920. *Trossachs*, A. & C. Black.

BLACK'S GUIDES 1861–1920. *Scotland*, A. & C. Black.

BLIN HARY. *The Wallas*, Scottish Text Society.

BOWLER, D., COX, A. and SMITH, C. (Eds.), 1995. *Four Excavations in Perth, 1979–84*, *PSAS*, 125.

BREEZE, D., 1996. *Roman Scotland*, Batsford.

BROWN, R.L., & ADAMSON, P., 1985. *Victorian and Edwardian Perthshire from Rare Photographs*, Alvie Publications.

CAMERON, I.B. and STEPHENSON, D., 1985. 'British Regional Geology. The Midland Valley of Scotland', *British Geological Survey*, HMSO, London.

CAMERON, K.J., 1988. 'The Schoolmaster Engineer Adam Anderson of Perth and St. Andrews, c. 1780–1846', *Abertay Historical Society* 27, 1–69.

CAMPBELL, A., 1802. *A Journey from Edinburgh to parts of North Britain*, London.

CAMPBELL, D., 1910. *Reminiscences and Reflections of an Octogenarian Highlander*, Inverness.

CAMPBELL, J.F., 1865. *Popular Tales of the West Highlands*, Edinburgh.

CAMPBELL, S.M., 1987. *Crieff*, Alvie Publications, St. Andrews.

CHAMBERS, R., 1859. *Domestic Annals of Scotland from the Reformation to the Revolution*, Vol. 1, 154, 157–9, Chambers, Edinburgh.

CHRISTIE, G., 1986. *Crieff Hydro 1868–1986*, Crieff Hydro Ltd.

COBBETT, W., 1833. *Tour in Scotland*, Aberdeen University Press (1984).

COCKER, A. and DIXON, W., 1951. *Loch Lomond, The Trossachs and Loch Katrine*, Blackie.

COOKE, A.J. (Ed.), 1975. *Stanley – Its History and Development*, University of Dundee.

COOKE, A.J., 1979. 'Robert Arkwright and the Scottish Cotton Industry', *Textile History*, Vol. 10, Pasold Research Fund Ltd.

COOKE, A.J., 1979 'Robert Owen and the Stanley Mills 1802–1811', *Business History*, Vol XXI No. 1 January, Frank Cass, London.

COOKE, A.J., (Ed.) 1984. *A History of Redgorton Parish*, University of Dundee.

CORBETT, L. etc., 1994. Ochil Hills: *Landscape, Wildlife, Heritage, Walks*, Forth Naturalist & Historian.

COWAN, I. and EASSON, 1976, *Medieval Religious Houses in Scotland*, (2nd Edition), Longman, London and New York.

CRAIG, G. Y. (Ed.), 1991. *Geology of Scotland* (3rd Edition), The Geological Society, London.

CREIGHTON, C., 1891. *A History of Epidemics in Britain*, unknown.

CRUDEN, S., 1981. *The Scottish Castle*, Edinburgh.

DAICHES, D., 1971. *Sir Walter Scott and His World*, Thames and Hudson.

DAVEY, C.J., 1991. *The last toot: The end of Salmon fishing in Broughty Ferry*. Centre for Tayside and Fife Studies, Occasional Paper No 2.

DAVIES, J. McG., 1993. *Social and Labour Relations at Pullars of Perth 1882–1924*. Centre for Tayside and Fife Studies, Dundee.

DEVINE, T.M. and MITCHISON, R., 1988. *People and Society in Scotland, 1760–1830*, John Donald, Edinburgh.

DIACK, F.C., 1920–1922. 'Place-names of Pictland', *Revue Celtique* 38, 109–132 and 39, 125–174.

DICKSON, A. and TREBLE, J.H. 1992. *People and Society in Scotland, 1914–1990*, John Donald, Edinburgh.

DODGSHON, R.A., 1981. *Land and Society in Early Scotland*, Oxford.

DOUGLAS, S., 1987. *The King o' The Black Art*, AUP.

DOUGLAS, S., 1992. *The Sang's the Thing*, Polygon.

DUCK, R.W. and McMANUS, J., 1985. 'Bathymetric charts of ten Scottish Lochs', *Tay Estuary Research Centre Report*, 9, University of Dundee.

DUFF, D., 1968. *Victoria in the Highlands*, Webb & Bower.

DUN, P., 1866. *A Summer at the Lake of Menteith*, Hedderwick, Glasgow.

DUNBAR, J.G., 1978. *The Historic Architecture of Scotland*, Batsford, London.

DUNCAN, A.A.M., 1974. 'Perth – The First Century of the Burgh', *Transactions of the Perthshire Society of Natural Science*, Special Issue (25th Anniversary of the Archaeological and Historical Section), Perth.

DUNCAN, A.A.M., 1975. *Scotland, The Making of the Kingdom*, Edinburgh.

DUNCAN, J., 1997. *Perth and Kinross: The Big Country*, J. Donald.

EAGLES, J.L.M., 1996. *The Chronicle of Perth*, Llanerch, Lampeter.

EYRE-TODD, G. and HASLEHURST, E.W., 1938. *Loch Lomond, Loch Tay and the Trossachs*, Blackie.

FAWCETT, R., 1985. *Scottish Medieval Churches*, Edinburgh.

FAWCETT, R., 1994. *Scottish Abbeys and Priories*, B.T. Batsford Ltd/Historic Scotland.

FENTON A. and WALKER, B., 1981. *The Rural Architecture of Scotland*, John Donald, Edinburgh.

FENTON, A., 1987. *Country Life in Scotland: Our Rural Past*, John Donald.

FINLAY, I., 1976. *The Central Highlands*, Batsford.

FLEMING, T., 1784. 'Account of a remarkable agitation of the waters of Loch Tay', *Transactions of the Royal Society of Edinburgh*, 1, 200–202.

FLINN, M. (Ed.), 1977. *Scottish Population History from the 17th Century to the 1930s*, 147, Cambridge University Press.

FORD, R. (Ed), 1893. *Harp of Perthshire*, Alexander Gardner, Paisley.

FOSTER, S., 1996. *Picts, Scots and Gaels*, B.T. Batsford, Ltd./Historic Scotland.

FOTHERGILL, R., n.d. *The Inches of Perth*, Perth.

FRASER, I.A., 1990–92. 'The Agricultural Element in Gaelic Place-Names', *Transactions of the Gaelic Society of Inverness*, LVII, 203–223.

FRASER, I.A., 1992–94. 'The Agricultural Element in Gaelic Place-Names', *Transactions of the Gaelic Society of Inverness*, LVIII, 223–246.

FRASER, W.H. and MORRIS, R.J., 1990. *People and Society in Scotland, 1830–1914*, John Donald, Edinburgh.

FRAZER, Sir W., 1880. *The Red Book of Menteith*.

FRERE, S., and ST JOSEPH, K., 1983. *Roman Britain from the Air*, Cambridge University Press.

FURGOL, E.M., 1990. *A Regimental History of the Covenanting Armies 1639–1651*, John Donald, Edinburgh.

GILBERT, J.M., 1979. *Hunting and Hunting Reserves in Medieval Scotland*, John Donald, Edinburgh.

GILLIES, W.A., 1938. *In Famed Breadalbane*, Munro Press, Perth.

GORDON, S., 1948. *Highways and Byways in the Central Highlands*, Birlinn.

GRAHAM, A., 1724. 'Description of Six Parishes in Perthshire', *MacFarlane's Geographical Collections*, SHS 1906.

GRAHAM-CAMPBELL, D., 1979. *Portrait of Perth, Angus and Fife*, Hale.

GRAHAM-CAMPBELL, D., 1994. *Perth: The Fair City*, John Donald, Edinburgh.

GRAHAM, N., 1747. 'An Inquiry into the Causes which facilitate the Rise and Progress of Rebellions and Insurrections in the Highlands of Scotland', *Doughty Deeds*, Heinemann.

GRAHAM, P., 1806. *Sketches Descriptive of the Picturesque Scenery on the Southern Confines of Perthshire*, Peter Hill, Edinburgh.

GRAHAM, P., 1812. *Sketches of Perthshire*, Peter Hill and J. Ballantyne, Edinburgh; and Longmans, London.

GRAHAM,R.B.C., 1895. *Notes on the District of Menteith*, A. & C. Black.

GRAHAM, R.B.C., 1914. *Scottish Stories*, Duckworth.

GRAHAM, R.B.C., 1925. *Doughty Deeds*, Heinemann.

GREWAR, D., 1926. *The Story of Glenisla*, Milne and Hutchison.

HALDANE, A.R.B., 1952. *The Drove Roads of Scotland*, David & Charles, Newton Abbot.

HALDANE, A.R.B., 1981. T*he Great Fishmonger of the Tay: John Richardson of Perth and Pitfour*, Abertay Historical Society Publication No 21, Dundee.

HANSON, W., 1987. *Agricola and the Conquest of the North*, Batsford.

HANSON, W. and MAXWELL, G., 1983. *Rome's North-West Frontier: The Antonine Wall*, Edinburgh University Press.

HANSON, W.S., and SLATER, E.A., (Eds.), 1991. *Scottish Archaeology: New Perceptions*, Aberdeen.

HARDING, A.W., 1991. *Pullars of Perth*, Perth and Kinross District Libraries, Perth.

HOGG, J., 1803. *A Tour of the Highlands*, Mercat Press, Edinburgh 1986.

HOLDSWORTH, P. (Ed.), 1987. *Excavations in the Medieval Burgh of Perth, 1979–81*, Society of Antiquaries of Scotland, Monograph Series No 5.

HOUSE, J., 1976. *Pride of Perth: The Story of Arthur Bell and Sons Ltd.*, Hutchinson, London.

HUTCHINSON, A.F., 1899. *The Lake of Mentieth*, Eneas Mackay, Stirling.

HUME BROWN, P. (Ed.), 1891. 'Report by Thomas Tucker upon the Settlement of the Revenues of Excise and Customs in Scotland', *Early Travellers in Scotland*, 171–2, James Thin.

HUME BROWN, P. (Ed.), 1891. 'A Short Account of Scotland...by Thomas Morer', *Early Travellers in Scotland*, 285–6.

HUME, J.R., 1977. *The Industrial Archaeology of Scotland*, Vol 2. The Highlands and Islands, London.

IRWIN, D. and F., 1975. *Scottish Painters*, Faber.

IRWIN F. and others, 1982. *Turner in Scotland*, Aberdeen Art Gallery.

JENKINSON, K.A., 1988. *Stagecoach and its Subsidiaries*, Autobus Review Publication, Bradford.

JENKINSON, K.A., 1991. 'Buses Mean Business?', *Stagecoach and its Subsidiaries*, Vol II, Autobus Review Publications, Bradford.

JOHNSTON, J.B., 1892. *Place Names of Scotland*, S.R. Publishers Ltd., (1970).

KEPPIE, L., 1986. *Scotland's Roman Remains*, John Donald, Edinburgh.

KERR, J., 1995. *Life in the Atholl Glens*, Perth & Kinross District Libraries.

KERR, J., 1987. 'Atholl shieling names', *NOMINA* 11, 131–141.

KING, E., (Ed.), 1998. *Blind Hary's 'Wallace'*, Luath Press.

KIRK, R., 1691. *The Secret Commonwealth*, reprint 1976. Cambridge for Folklore Society.

LANG, A., 1894. *Ban and Arriere Ban* (Poems), Longmans Green, London.

LENMAN, B., 1975. *From Esk to Tweed: harbours, ships and men of the east coast of Scotland*, Glasgow.

LENMAN, B., 1980. *The Jacobite Risings in Britain, 1689–1746*, Eyre Methuen (new edition, Scottish Cultural Press, 1995).

LIDDELL, C., 1993. *Pitlochry: Heritage of a Highland District*, Perth & Kinross District Libraries.

LYNCH, M., SPEARMAN, M. and STELL, G (Eds.), 1988. *The Scottish Medieval Town*, John Donald, Edinburgh.

LYNCH, M., 1991. *Scotland a New History*, Century, London.

MACCULLOCH, J., 1824. *The Highlands and Western Islands*, Vols 1–4, Longman Hurst.

MACKIE, E., 1975. *An Archaeological Guide to Scotland*, Faber & Faber, London.

MACGIBBON, D. and ROSS, T., 1887–92. *The Castellated and Domestic Architecture of Scotland*, Vols 1–5, Edinburgh.

MACGIBBON, D. and ROSS, T., 1896–97. *The Ecclesiastical Architecture of Scotland*, Vols 1–3, Edinburgh.

MACGREGOR, A.A., 1935. *Somewhere in Scotland*, Routledge.

MACGREGOR, A.A., 1965. *Land of the Mountain and the Flood*, Michael Joseph.

MACKENZIE, G.M., 1994–96. 'The Rarest Decision Recorded in History: The Battle of the Clans in 1396', in *Transactions of the Gaelic Society of Inverness LIX*, 420–487.

MARSHALL, W., 1880. *Historic Scenes in Perthshire*, Oliphant & Co.

MAXWELL, G., 1989. *The Romans in Scotland*, Mercat Press.

MAXWELL, G., 1990. *A Battle Lost: Romans and Caledonians at Mons Graupius*, Edinburgh University Press.

MCCOLL, E. and SEEGER, P., 1986. *Till Doomsday in the Afternoon*, Manchester University Press.

MCNAUGHTON, D.B., 1970. *Upper Strathearn*, Jamieson and Munro.

MCKEAN, C., 1985. *Stirling and the Trossachs*, Royal Incorporation of Architects in Scotland and Scottish Academic Press.

MCKEAN, C., 1994. *Stirling and the Trossachs: Illustrated Architectural Guide*, Rutland Press, Edinburgh.

MCKERRACHER, A., 1988. *Perthshire in History and Legend*, John Donald, Edinburgh.

MCMANUS, J., 1971. 'Estuarine development and sediment distribution with particular reference to the Tay', *Proceedings of the Royal Society of Edinburgh*, 71, 97–113.

MEIKLE, J., 1925. *Place and Place-Names Round Alyth*, Paisley.

MELVILLE, L., 1935. 2nd Ed 1985. *Errol: Its legends, lands and people*, Perth.

MELVILLE, L., 1981. *The Fair Lands of Gowrie*, Culross Press, John Donald (reprint), Edinburgh.

MIDDLETON, F. and WALKER, B., 1987. 'Fantasy at Fortingall', *The Scots Magazine*, New Series 127.3, June 245–252.

MITCHISON, R., 1970. *A History of Scotland*, Methuen.

MONOPOLIES AND MERGERS COMMISSION 1990. *Stagecoach (Holdings) Ltd. and Portsmouth Citybus Ltd.*, A Report on the acquisition by Stagecoach (Holdings) Ltd. of Portsmouth Citybus Ltd, London HMSO.

MORTON, H.V., 1929. *In Search of Scotland*, Methuen & Co. Ltd., London.

MORTON, H.V., 1933. *In Scotland Again*, Methuen & Co. Ltd., London.

MURRAY, N., 1978. *The Scottish Hand Loom Weavers, 1790–1850: A Social History*, John Donald.

MURRAY, S., 1803. *Guide to the Beauties of Scotland*, Byway Books (1982).

MURRAY, W.H., 1982. *Rob Roy MacGregor*, Richard Drew Publishers, Glasgow.

NAIRNE, C., 1961. *The Trossachs*, Oliver & Boyd, Edinburgh.

NATIONAL TRUST FOR SCOTLAND, 1972. *Ben Lawers and its Alpine Flowers*, NTS.

NEW STATISTICAL ACCOUNT, 1845.

NICHOLSON, R, 1974. 'Scotland: The Later Middle Ages', *The Edinburgh History of Scotland, Volume 2*, Oliver & Boyd, Edinburgh.

NICOLAISEN, W.F.H., 1976. *Scottish Place-Names*, London.

NICOLAISEN, W.F.H., 1968. 'Place-Names of the Dundee Region', *Dundee and District*, British Association for the Advancement of Science 145–152, Dundee.

PARRY, M.L., 1978. *Climatic Change, Agriculture and Settlement*,Folkstone Dawson.

PARSONS, C., 1964. *Witchcraft and Demonology in Scott's Fiction*, Oliver & Boyd., Edinburgh.

PEACOCK, D., 1849. *Perth, its Annals & Archives*, Perth.

PENNY, G., 1836. *Traditions of Perth*, reprinted Culross Press (1986).

PERTH BURGH RECORDS in the A.K. Bell Library.

PERTHSHIRE ADVERTISER (newspaper). Various issues from 1829 to the present.

PERTHSHIRE ADVERTISER, Centenary Volume 1929 (12 August 1929).

PERTHSHIRE CONSTITUTIONAL (newspaper). Various issues from 1835 to 1951.

PERTHSHIRE COURIER (newspaper). Various issues from 1809 to 1929.

PERTH FLOOD DEFENCES, 1995. *Proposed Plans for the Defence of Perth against flooding*, Water Services Department, Tayside Regional Council. *Perthshire Tourist Board, 1995. Business Plan 1996–7 to 1998–9*, Consultative Draft, Perth.

PRICE, R.J., 1976. *Highland Landforms*, Highlands and Islands Development Board, Inverness.

PRICE, R.J., 1983. *Scotland's Environment During the Last 30,000 Years*, Scottish Academic Press, Edinburgh.

PRIESTLEY, J., 1969. *Historical Account of the Navigable Rivers, Canals and Railways throughout Great Britain*, David & Charles, Newton Abbot.

PRINGLE, R.D., 1989. *Historic Scotland Guide*, HMSO.

PRYDE, G.S., 1965. *The Burghs of Scotland: a critical list*, London.

PUGH, P., 1987. 'Is Guinness Good for You?', *Financial Training*, London.

QUIGLEY, H., 1936. *The Highlands of Scotland*, B.T. Batsford, Ltd., London.

RCAHMS, 1990. *North-east Perth: an archaeological landscape*, HMSO.

RCAHMS, 1994. *South-east Perth: an archaeological landscape*, HMSO.

REID, A.G., 1899. *Annals of Auchterarder and Memorials of Strathearn*, Perth & Kinross District Libraries (1989).

RITCHIE, A., 1988. *Scotland BC*, Edinburgh.

RITCHIE, A., 1989. *Picts*, Edinburgh.

RITCHIE, G. and RITCHIE, A., 1981. *Scotland: Archaeology and Early History*, Thames and Hudson.

ROBB, W., 1929. *Twentieth Century Scots Verse*, Gowans and Grey.

ROBERTSON, J., 1799. *General View of the Agriculture in the County of Perth*, J. Morison, Perth.

ROBERTSON, R. MacD., 1961. *Selected Highland Folk Tales*, Oliver & Boyd, Edinburgh.

ROGERSON, R., MORRIS, A., PADDISON, R. and FINDLAY, A.M., 1990. *The Quality of Life In Britain's District Councils*, Department of Geography, University of Glasgow.

SALWAY, P., 1993. *Oxford Illustrated History of Roman Britain*, Oxford University Press.

SCOTT, REV. J., 1774. *Extracts from Perth Kirk Session Register 1555–1620*, MSS

SCOTT, REV. J., c. 1784. *A Register of Deaths at Perth*. MSS

SCOTT, REV. J., 1796. 'Parish of Perth', *Statistical Account of Scotland XVIII*, 489–539, Edinburgh: William Creech.

SCOTT, REV. J., 1814. 'Account of the Plague in Scotland', *Perth Museum and Art Gallery Archive*, No. 346. MSS.

SCOTT, Sir W., 1810. *Lady of the Lake*, J. & J. Ballantyne (Wordsworth 1995).

SCOTT, Sir W., 1814. *Waverley*, Constable (Penguin 1995).

SCOTT, Sir W., 1817. *Rob Roy*, Constable (Penguin 1995).

SCOTT, Sir W., 1828–30. *Tales of a Grandfather*, Adam Black.

SIMPSON, W.D., 1976. *The Highlands of Scotland*, Robert Hale Ltd.

SISSONS, J.B., 1967. *The Evolution of Scotland's Scenery*, Oliver & Boyd, Edinburgh.

SMALL, A. (Ed.) 1987. *The Picts – A New Look at Old problems*, Dundee.

SMELLIE, W.A., 1979. 'The City and Royal Burgh of Perth.' In Taylor, D.B. (ed.), The Counties of Perth and Kinross, *Third Statistical Account of Scotland XXVII*, 437–463, Coupar Angus: Culross The Printers, Scottish Academic Press.

SMITH, A., 1865. *A Summer in Skye*, Birlinn.

SMITH, S., 1988. *Horatio McCulloch*, Glasgow AGM.

SMITH, R., 1993. *The Great Flood*, Perth & Kinross District Council, Perth.

SMOUT, T.C. (Ed.), 1992. *Scotland and the Sea*. John Donald, Edinburgh.

SMYTH, A.P., 1984. *Warlords and Holy Men*, London.

SOUTAR, W., 1988. *Collected Poems*, Scottish Academic Press.

SPEARMAN, R.M., 1988. 'The Medieval Townscape of Perth.' In Lynch, M., Spearman, M. and Stell, G. (eds.), *The Scottish Medieval Town*, John Donald, Edinburgh.

STATISTICAL ACCOUNT 1791–99.

STAVERT, M.L., 1991. *Perth: A Short History*, (Second Edition), Perth & Kinross District Libraries.

STEPHENSON, D. and GOULD, D., 1995. *British Regional Geology, The Grampian Highlands*, British Geological Survey, HMSO, London.

STEVEN, C., 1994. *Enjoying Perthshire*, Perth & Kinross District Libraries.

STEWART, J., 1994. *Settlements of Western Perthshire*, Pentland Press.

STONES, J. (Ed.), 1989. *Three Scottish Carmelite Friaries*, Society of Antiquaries of Scotland, Monograph Series No. 6.

STOTT, L., 1992. *Enchantment of the Trossachs*, Creag Darach.

TABRAHAM, C., 1986. *Scottish Castles and Fortifications*, Edinburgh.

TAY DISTRICT SALMON FISHERIES BOARD ANNUAL REPORTS.

TAYLOR, D.B. (Ed.), 1979. *The Counties of Perth and Kinross*, Third Statistical Account of Scotland, Coupar Angus.

TAYSIDE REGIONAL COUNCIL, 1991. *Indicative Forestry Strategy*.

TAYSIDE REGIONAL COUNCIL, 1980 and 1993. *Tayside Structural Plan*.

TAYSIDE & FIFE Archaeological Journal, Vol. 1, 1995.

THE REGISTER OF THE PRIVY COUNCIL, 1884. 1st Series, Vol VI, 159–160.

THE SCOTTISH OFFICE, 1985, 1990, 1995. *Abstract of Statistics*.

THE SCOTTISH OFFICE, 1971, 1981, 1991. *Census Data*.

THIRD STATISTICAL ACCOUNT, 1964.

THOMAS, P.R., 1988. 'A9 Road Section – Blair Atholl to Newtonmore', in Allison, I., May F. and Strachan, R.A. (Eds.), *An Excursion Guide to the Moine Geology of the Scottish Highlands*, 39–50, Scottish Academic Press, Edinburgh.

THOMPSON, REV. W. *et al.*, 1845. 'Parish of Perth (March 1837)', *New Statistical Account of Scotland, X*, 1–142, Edinburgh, William Blackwood & Sons.

TOWNSHEND, C., 1840. *A Descriptive Tour of Scotland*, Chapman & Hall (1846).

TRANTER, N., 1957. *MacGregor's Gathering*, Coronet Books (1993).

TRANTER, N., 1965. *Outlaw of the Highlands: Rob Roy*, People from the Past Series No. 4, Dobson.

TRANTER, N., 1966. *The Fortified House in Scotland*, Oliver & Boyd.

TRANTER, N., 1971. *The Queen's Scotland: The Heartland*, Hodder & Stoughton.

TULLIBARDINE, Marchioness of, (Ed.), 1908. *A Military History of Perthshire, 1660–1902*, R.A. & J. Hay, Perth.

TURNER, I., CLARKE, A. and Andrews, F., 1990. *Ysart Glass*, London.

TURNER SIMPSON, A. and STEVENSON, S., 1982. *Historic Perth: the archaeological implications of redevelopment*, Scottish Burgh Survey, University of Glasgow.

TURNER, W.H.K., 1957. The Textile Industry of Perth and District, *Institute of British Geographers Transactions and Papers*, No. 23, p 123–140.

VICTORIA, QUEEN, 1868. *Leaves from the Journal of Our Life in the Highlands*, Smith, Elder & Co.

VICTORIA, QUEEN, 1883. *More Leaves from the Journal of Our Life in the Highlands*, Smith, Elder & Co.

WAINWRIGHT, F.T., 1963. *The Souterrains of Southern Pictland*, London.

WALKER, B., 1976. 'Some Regional Variations in Building Techniques in Angus, Fife and Perthshire', in Fenton, Walker and Stell (Eds.) *Building Construction in Scotland: Some Historical and Regional Aspects*, 52–64, Edinburgh and Dundee.

WALKER, B., 1977. *Clay Buildings in North-East Scotland*, Dundee and Edinburgh.

WALKER, B., 1979. 'Report on Cruck Framed Cottage, Drumdewan, Dull, Perthshire', *Vernacular Building* 5, 12–22.

WALKER, B., 1981. 'Rait, Perthshire, Scotland: An exploration in architectural archaeology', *Permanent European Conference for the Study of Rural Landscape: Collected Papers, Denmark*, Session 1979, 201–211, Copenhagen.

WALKER, B., 1983. *The Agricultural Buildings of Greater Strathmore 1770–1920* (2 vols.), (Ph.D. thesis, University of Dundee).

WALKER, B., 1985. 'Building Interpretation: The Cruck Framed House at Lower Chamberbane, Strathtummel, Perthshire', *Scottish Field Studies* 27–43.

WALKER, B. and Middleton, F., 1987. 'James Marjoribanks MacLaren'. *Charles Rennie Mackintosh Society Newsletter*, 47, 5–8.

WALKER, B., 1988. 'Lofted Open-Hall Farmhouses in Scotland', *Vernacular Buildings*, 12, 45–9.

WALKER, B., 1991. 'Brickwork is Beautiful'. *The Scots Magazine*, New Series 136.1, October 76–87.

WALKER, B. and MCGREGOR, C., 1995. 'The Mudwall School and Schoolhouse at Cottown, St. Madoes, Perthshire', *Out of Earth* II 204–207, Plymouth.

WALKER, B. and MCGREGOR, C. and STARK, G., 1996. *Thatch and Thatching Techniques: A Guide to Conserving Scottish Thatching Traditions*, Historic Scotland, Edinburgh.

WALKER, B. and MCGREGOR, C., 1996. *Earth Structures and Construction in Scotland*, Historic Scotland, Edinburgh.

WALKER, B. and GAULDIE, W.S., 1984. *Architects and Architecture on Tayside*, Dundee.

WALKER, B. and RITCHIE, J.N.G., 1996. *Exploring Scotland's Heritage: Fife, Perthshire and Angus*, HMSO, Edinburgh.

WALKER, B., 1990. 'The Buildings of Perth', *Discover Scotland 42: The Sunday Mail Guide to Scotland's Countryside*, 1160–1161.

WALKER, F., 1961. *Tayside Geology*, Dundee Museum and Art Gallery Publication, Dundee Museum.

WALKER, F., 1963. *The Geology and Scenery of Strathearn*, Dundee Museum and Art Gallery Publication, Dundee Museum.

WALKER, J., 1982. *The Scottish Sketches of R.B. Cunninghame Graham*, Scottish Academic Press.

WALKER, K. and WALKER B., 1989. 'Flatfield: An Independent Scottish Farm', *Vernacular Buildings*, 13, 10–14.

WATSON, A., 1995. *The Ochils: Placenames, Tradition, History*, Perth & Kinross District Libraries.

WATSON, W.J., 1926. *History of Celtic Place-Names of Scotland*, Birlinn.

WATSON, W.J., 1927–28. 'The place-names of Breadalbane', *Transactions of the Gaelic Society of Inverness*, XXIV, 248–279.

WATSON, W.J., 1929–30. 'The place-names of Perthshire: The Lyon Basin', *Transactions of the Gaelic Society of Inverness*, XXXV, 277–296.

WEIR, M., 1988. *Ferries in Scotland*, Edinburgh.

WHITTINGTON, G., 1985. 'The Little Ice Age and Scotland's Weather', *The Scottish Geographical Magazine*, 101.

WHITTOW, J.B., 1977. *Geology and Scenery in Scotland*, Pelican Books, Harmondsworth, Middlesex.

WHYTE, B., 1979. *The Yellow on the Broom*, Chambers, Edinburgh.

WHYTE, I.D., 1979. *Agriculture and Society in Seventeenth Century Scotland*, John Donald, Edinburgh.

WHYTE, I.D., 1983. 'Early Modern Scotland: Continuity and Change', in G. Whittington and I.D. Whyte (Eds.), *An Historical Geography of Scotland*, 126–7, Academic Press, London.

WHYTE, I. and K., 1991. *The Scottish Landscape 1500–1800*, Routledge, London.

WILKINSON, T., 1824. *Tours of the British Mountains*, Taylor & Hessey.

WILSON, Sir J., 1915. *Lowland Scotch as Spoken in Lower Strathearn*, OUP.

WILSON, W., 1908. *The Trossachs in Literature and Tradition*, Shearer, Stirling.

WITHERS, C.W.J., 1988. *Gaelic Scotland: the Transformation of a Culture Region*, Routledge.

WORDSWORTH, D., 1874. *Journal of a Tour in the Highlands* (Ed. J.C. Shairp).

WORDSWORTH, W., 1936. *Poetical Works*, Oxford.

YEOMAN, P., 1995. *Medieval Scotland*, B.T. Batsford Ltd./Historic Scotland.

1991 CENSUS REPORT FOR TAYSIDE REGION. Part 1, General Register Office for Scotland, Edinburgh, HMSO 1993.